RUSSIAN AND EAST EUROPEAN SERIES / VOL. 40

The

American Bibliography

of Russian and

East European Studies

for 1966

Editor: FRITZ T. EPSTEIN

Associate Editors: Penelope H. Carson
and Michael E. Shaw

Indiana University Press / Bloomington & London

for International Affairs Center

RUSSIAN AND EAST EUROPEAN SERIES
RUSSIAN AND EAST EUROPEAN INSTITUTE
INDIANA UNIVERSITY
Volume 40

Copyright © 1972 by Indiana University Press

All rights reserved

No part of this book may be reproduced or utilized
in any form or by any means, electronic or mechanical, including photocopying and recording, or by any
information storage and retrieval system, without
permission in writing from the publisher. The
Association of American University Presses' Reso-
lution on Permissions constitutes the only exception
to this prohibition.

Library of Congress catalog card number: 75-160125

ISBN 0-253-39040-0

Manufactured in the United States of America

PREFACE

This bibliography attempts to list books and articles about Russia and East
Europe which were published in the Western World in English during 1966.
The coverage of the present volume basically follows the pattern of the bibliography for 1965, as explained in its preface; but — in order to rectify a long-
felt need — items by British and American authors published in languages other
than English have been listed, if accompanied by an English summary.

One innovation in the foregoing bibliography has been extended: the listing
of reviews. In the 1965 bibliography an effort has been made, for the first time,
to include the reviews of books published in 1965 — a feature which has found
general approval. The bibliography for 1966 has profited from the regrettable
delay by systematic inclusion of reviews in Western European languages published between 1966 and 1968 about books with 1965 and 1966 imprints; also,
occasionally reviews in English of pertinent foreign-language books have been
included, when the review seemed of particular interest. Thus it can be assumed that all the more important reviews of 1965 and 1966 books in English
in the Russian and East European field can be found in the bibliographies for
1965 and 1966.

Because of the Editor's lengthy absences from Bloomington, the main bur-
den in compiling the bibliography has rested with Mrs. Penelope Hummer
Carson and with Mr. Michael E. Shaw. The Editor wishes to express his last-
ing gratitude to these assistants; their work has been facilitated by a small
group of unselfish and devoted contributors in various fields.

This is the last volume of the bibliography published under the auspices
and with the support of the Russian and East European Institute of Indiana University. The volumes of the bibliography (not consecutively numbered as a sub-
series) form part of the Russian and East European Institute's *Russian and East
European Series* (REES) which with vol. 37 became a publication of the International Affairs Center Publications department of the Indiana University Press.
Since 1957 the following volumes of the bibliography have been published:

  (I) for 1956 — REES Vol. 9, 1957; J. T. Shaw, ed.
 (II) for 1957 — REES Vol. 10, 1958; J. T Shaw, ed.
(III) for 1958 — REES Vol. 18, 1959; J. T. Shaw, ed.
(IV) for 1959 — REES Vol. 21, 1960; J. T. Shaw and D. Djaparidze, eds.
 (V) for 1960 — REES Vol. 26, 1962; J. T. Shaw, A. C. Todd, St. Viederman,
                             eds.
(VI) for 1961 — REES Vol. 27, 1963; A. C. Todd and St. Viederman, eds.
(VII) for 1962 — REES Vol. 29, 1964; A. C. Todd and St. Viederman, eds.
(VIII) for 1963 — REES Vol. 32, 1966; F. T. Epstein, A. C. Todd and St.
                          Viederman, eds.
(IX) for 1964 — REES Vol. 34, 1966; F. T. Epstein, ed.
 (X) for 1965 — REES Vol. 37, 1968; F. T. Epstein, ed.
(XI) for 1966 — REES Vol. 40, 1972; F. T. Epstein, ed.

    With the volume for 1967, Ohio State University takes over the preparation
and publication of the annual bibliography. I urge contributors and users who
generously and liberally offered assistance during my editorship to transfer
that assistance by sending bibliographical data about publications since 1967
to the bibliography's new Editor, Professor Kenneth E. Naylor, Department of
Slavic Languages and Literatures, Ohio State University, 216 N. Oval Drive,
Columbus, Ohio 43210.

Fritz T. Epstein

TABLE OF CONTENTS

PART TWO — RUSSIA AND THE SOVIET UNION

JOURNALS CONSULTED IN
PREPARATION OF THE BIBLIOGRAPHY

TITLE	ABBREVIATIONS USED
About the House	
The Academy of Political Science, Proceedings	Proc Acad Poli Sci
ACEN News (Bulletin of the Association of Captive European Nations)	
Acoustical Society of America, Journal	
Acta Sociologica	Acta Soc
Administrative Science Quarterly	
Agricultural History	
Agriculture Abroad	Ag Abroad
American Academy of Political and Social Sciences, Annals	Ann Am Acad Pol Soc Sci
American Anthropologist	Am Anthro
American Archivist	
American Association of University Professors, Bulletin	AAUP Bull
American Bar Association Journal	Am Bar Assoc J
American Choral Review	
American Civil Liberties Union Newsletter	ACLU Newsletter
American Documentation	
American Economic Review	Am Econ R
American Economist	Am Econ
American Ethnological Society, Proceedings	
American Heritage	
American Historical Review	Am Hist R
American Imago	
American Institute for Planning, Journal	J Am Inst Plan
American Jewish Historical Quarterly	Am Jew Hist Q
American Jewish Yearbook	Am Jew Yearb
American Journal of Archeology	
American Journal of Economics and Sociology	Am J Econ Soc
American Journal of International Law	Am J Int Law
American Journal of Philology	
American Journal of Physical Anthropology	
American Journal of Psychoanalysis	
American Journal of Science	
American Journal of Sociology	
American Musicological Society, Journal	
American Oriental Society, Journal	
American Philosophical Society, Proceedings	
American Political Science Review	Am Pol Sci R
The American Psychoanalytical Association, Journal	
American Psychologist	Am Psych
American Quarterly	

American Scholar	Am Scholar
American Sociological Review	Am Soc R
American Speech	
Annals of the American Academy of Political and Social Sciences	Ann Am Acad Pol Soc Sci
Annals of the Association of American Geographers	Ann Assoc Am Geog
Anthropologica	
Anthropological Linguistics	Anthro Ling
Anthropological Quarterly	Anthro Q
Antiquity	
Archives Internationales d'Histoire des Sciences	
Arctic	
Arctic Anthropology	Arctic Anthro
Art and Literature	Art Lit
Art in America	
Art Journal	
Asian Survey	Asian Sur
ASTE [Association for the Study of Soviet-Type Economies] Bulletin	ASTE Bull
Association of American Geographers, Annals	Annals Assoc Am Geog
Association of Captive European Nations, Bulletin	ACEN News
Atlantic Monthly	
Audio Record Review	
Audio-Visual Communications Review	Audio-Visual Communications R
Australian Journal of Politics and History	Austral J Pol Hist
Austrian History Yearbook	Austrian H Yearb
Balkan Studies	Balk St
Baltic Review	Balt R
Bankers Magazine	Bank Mag
Behavioral Science	
Book Week	
Books Abroad	Books Abr
British Journal of Aesthetics	Brit J Aesth
The British Journal of Criminology	Brit J Crim
British Journal of Educational Studies	
British Journal of Industrial Relations	Brit J Ind Rel
Bucknell Review	Buck R
Bulgarian Review	Bulg R
Bulletin of the Atomic Scientists	Bull Atom Sci
Bulletin of the Institute of Historical Research (London University)	Bull Inst Hist Research
Bulletin of the Institute for the Study of the USSR	Bull Inst St USSR
Bulletin of the International Commission of Jurists	Bull Inst Commis Jur
Bulletin of the International Social Security Association	Bull Int Soc Sec Assoc
Bulletin of the New York Public Library	Bull NYPL
Bulletin of the Oxford University Institute of Economic Statistics	Bull Ox U Inst Econ Stat
Byzantinische Zeitschrift	
Cahiers d'Histoire Mondiale	
Cahiers du Monde Russe et Soviétique	

California Law Review	
Canadian Geographer	Can Geog
Canadian Modern Language Review	
Canadian Slavic Studies	Can Slav St
Canadian Slavonic Papers	Can Slav Pap
The Canadian Yearbook of International Law	Can Yearb Int Law
Catholic Historical Review	
The Catholic World	Cath W
Centennial Review	
Central Asian Journal	Cent Asian J
Central Asian Review	Cent Asian R
Central European Federalist	Cent Eur Fed
Central European Journal/Sudeten Bulletin	Cent Eur J/Sud Bull
Chicago Review	Chicago R
China Mainland Review	China Mainland R
China Quarterly	China Q
Chinese Culture	
The Christian Century	
Church History	Church H
The Classical Journal	Classical J
Classical Philology	
Classical Quarterly	
Classical Review	
College and Research Libraries	
Columbia Journal of World Business	Columbia J W Bus
Columbia University Forum	Col U Forum
Commentary	
Comparative Education Review	Comp Ed R
Comparative Literature	Comp Lit
Comparative Studies in Society and History	Comp St Soc Hist
Contemporary Psychology	Contemp Psych
Contemporary Review	Contemp R
Contrat Social	
Cooperation and Conflict: Nordic Studies in International Politics	
Critical Quarterly	
Criticism	
Current Anthropology	Cur Anthro
Current History	Cur Hist
Current Musicology	
Daedalus	
The Dancing Times	
Diogenes	
Dissent	
Downbeat	
Drama Critique	
Drama Survey	
Dumbarton Oaks Papers	Dumb Oaks Pap
Duquesne Review	Duquesne R
East Europe	East Eur
East European Quarterly	East Eur Q
Eastern World	East World

Econometrica
Economia Internazionale   Econ Inter
Economic Development and Cultural Change   Econ Dev Cult Change
Economic Geography   Econ Geog
Economic History Review   Econ Hist R
Economic Journal
Economic Record   Econ Record
Economics of Planning   Econ Plan
Educational Record   Educ Record
Encounter   Enc
Engineering Economist
English Dance and Song
English Historical Review   Eng Hist R
Ethics
Ethnohistory
Ethnology
Ethnomusicology
Explorations in Entrepreneurial History
External Affairs   Exter Aff

Federal Accountant
Film Culture   Film Cult
Folklore Institute, Journal   J Folklore Inst
Foreign Affairs   For Aff
Foreign Language Courier
Fortune
Foundations of Language
The French Review   Fr R

Gazette: International Journal for
    Mass-Communications Studies
Geographical Journal   Geog J
Geographical Magazine   Geog Mag
Geographical Review   Geog R
Geography   Geog
George Washington Law Review   George Washington
                                                        Law R

The German Quarterly
The Germanic Review   Ger R
Government and Opposition
Gypsy Lore Society, Journal   J Gyp Lore Soc

Harper's Magazine   Harper's
Harvard Business Review   Harvard Bus R
Harvard Educational Review
Harvard Law Review   Harvard Law R
Hi Fi/Musical America
Hi-Fi Stereo Review
Hispanic American Historical Review   Hisp Am Hist R
Hispanic Review
The Historian   Hist
Historical Journal   Hist J
Historische Zeitschrift   HZ
History and Theory   Hist and Theory

History Today	Hist Today
Howard Law Review	Howard Law R
Hudson Review	Hudson R
Human Biology	
Human Organization	Human Org
Human Relations	Human R
Hungarian Quarterly	Hung Q
Impact of Science on Society	Impact Sci on Soc
Indian Journal of Political Science	Ind J Poli Sci
Indian Journal of Public Administration	Ind J Pub Admin
Indo-Iranian Journal	
Industrial and Labor Relations Review	Indus Lab Rel R
Industrial Relations	
Information	
Inquiry (Oslo)	
The Instrumentalist	
Intercom	
International Affairs (London)	Int Aff
International and Comparative Law Quarterly	Int Comp Law Q
International Commission of Jurists, Bulletin	Bull Int Commis Jur
International Commission of Jurists, Journal	J Int Commis Jur
International Conciliation	Int Concil
International Folk Music Council, Journal	
International Journal	Int J
International Journal of Agrarian Affairs	
International Journal of American Linguistics	Int J Am Ling
International Journal of Comparative Psychology	
International Journal of Comparative Sociology	
International Journal of Psycho-Analysis	
International Journal of Slavic Linguistics and Poetics	Int J Slav Ling Poet
International Labor Review	Int Lab R
International Language Review	Int Lang R
International Monetary Fund Staff Papers	
International Music Educator	
International Organization	Int Org
International Philosophical Quarterly	Int Phil Q
International Relations	Int Rel
International Review of Administrative Science	Int R Admin Sci
International Review of Applied Linguistics on Language Teaching	IRAL
International Review of Education	Int R Ed
International Review of History and Political Science	Int R Hist Poli Sci
International Review of Social History	Int R Soc Hist
International Social Science Journal	Int Soc Sci J
International Social Security Association, Bulletin	Int Soc Sec Assoc Bull
International Studies	Int St
ISIS: International Review devoted to the history of science and its cultural influences	ISIS
Italian Quarterly	
Italica	

Jahrbücher für Geschichte Osteuropas	Jahrb Gesch Osteur
Japan Quarterly	
Jazz	
Jewish Social Studies	Jew Soc St
Jews in Eastern Europe	
Johns Hopkins Studies in Historical and Political Science	
Journal of Aesthetics and Art Criticism	J Aes Art Crit
Journal of Agricultural Economics	
Journal of the American Musicological Society	
Journal of the American Institute of Planning	J Am Inst Plan
Journal of Applied Behavioral Science	J of Applied Behavioral Science
Journal of Asian Studies	J Asian St
Journal of Business	
Journal of Conflict Resolution	J Conf Resol
Journal of Contemporary History	J Contemp Hist
Journal of Criminal Law, Criminology and Police Science	
Journal of Croatian Studies	J Croat St
Journal of Developing Areas	J Dev Areas
Journal of Economic History	J Econ Hist
Journal of English and Germanic Philology	
Journal of Farm Economics	
Journal of the Folklore Institute	J Folklore Inst
Journal of Geography	J Geog
Journal of the Gypsy Lore Society	J Gyp Lore Soc
Journal of Historical Studies	
Journal of the History of Ideas	J Hist Ideas
Journal of Human Relations	J Hum Rel
Journal of Industrial Arts Education	J Industrial Arts Ed
Journal of International Affairs	J Int Aff
Journal of the International Commission of Jurists	J Int Commis Jur
Journal of Marketing	J Marketing
Journal of Marriage and the Family	J Marriage and the Family
Journal of Modern History	J Mod Hist
Journal of Parapsychology	
Journal of Peace Research	
Journal of Philosophy	J Philosophy
Journal of Political Economy	J Pol Econ
Journal of Politics	J Poli
Journal of Religion	J Rel
Journal of Research in Music Education	
Journal of Secondary Education	J Secondary Ed
Journal of Sex Research	
Journal of Social Issues	
Journal of Social Psychology	
Journal of Speech and Hearing Research	
Journal of Theological Studies	J Theol St
Journalism Quarterly	Jour Q
Kenyon Review	
Kritika	
Kyklos	

Labor Developments Abroad	Lab Dev Abroad
Land Economics	
Language	Lang
Language and Speech	
Language Learning	
Language Quarterly	Lang Q
Law and Contemporary Problems	Law Contemp Prob
Library of Congress Quarterly	Q J Lib Cong
Library Trends	
Lingua	
Linguistics	
Literature and Philosophy	
Literary Review	Lit R
Lituanus	Litua
London Times Literary Supplement	TLS
London University, Institute of Historical Research, Bulletin	
Making Music	
Mariner's Mirror	
Medieval Studies	
Medium Aevum	
Michigan Slavic Materials	Mich Sl Mat
Middle East Journal	
Middle Eastern Studies	Mid East St
Midstream	
Midwest Journal of Political Science	Midwest J Pol Sci
Military Affairs	Mil Aff
Military Review	Mil R
Minerva. Review of Science Learning and Policy	
Modern Age	Mod Age
Modern Drama	
Modern Fiction Studies	Mod Fict St
Modern Language Association, Publications	PMLA
Modern Language Journal	Mod Lang J
Modern Language Notes	
Modern Language Quarterly	
Modern Language Review	
Modern Philology	
Monthly Bulletin of Agricultural Economics and Statistics	Mo Bull Agric Econ Stat
Monthly Commentary on Indian Economic Conditions	Mo Commentary Ind Econ Cond
Monthly Labor Review	Mo Lab R
Munich, Institute for the Study of the USSR, Bulletin	Bull Inst St USSR
Music and Letters	
Music and Musicians	
Music in Education	
Music Journal	
Music Library Association, Notes	
Music Review	
Musical Events	
Musical Opinion	
The Musical Quarterly	Mus Q

The Musical Times
Muslim World

Names
Nation
National Geographic Magazine   Nat Geog
Nederlands Tijdschrift voor International Recht
New Leader   New Lead
New Left Review
New Republic
New Review   New R
The New Scholasticism
New York Public Library, Bulletin
New York Review of Books   NY Rev of Books
New York Times Book Review   NY Times Book Rev
New York Times Magazine   NY Times Magazine
Novyi Zhurnal

Opera News
Operational Research Quarterly
Orbis
Osteuropa   Osteur
Osteuropa-Naturwissenschaft   Osteur Naturwiss
Osteuropa-Recht   Osteur Recht
Osteuropa-Wirtschaft   Osteur Wirt
Oxford University, Institute of Economic Statistics,
   Bulletin
Oxford University, Institute of Statistics Bulletin

Pacific Affairs   Pac Aff
Pacific Historical Review   Pac Hist R
Parliamentary Affairs
The Partisan Review   Part R
Pavilion
Pennsylvania Law Review
Pennsylvania School Journal   Penn School J
Personalist
Personnel Psychology   Pers Psych
Perspection
Perspectives of New Music
PEP [Political and Economic Planning]
Phi Delta Kappan
Philological Quarterly
Philosophical Review
Philosophy and Phenomenological Research   Phil Phenom Res
Philosophy of Science
Phonetica
Poland and Germany   Pol Ger
Polish Affairs   Polish Aff
Polish-American Studies   Pol Am St
Polish Review   Pol R
Political Science   Poli Sci
Political Science Quarterly   Poli Sci Q
Political Studies

Political Quarterly	Poli Q
Population Index	
Population Review	
Population Studies	
Problems of Communism	Prob Comm
Problems of the Peoples of the USSR	Prob Peop USSR
Proceedings of the Academy of Political Science	Proc Acad Poli Sci
Proceedings of the American Philosophical Society	
Professional Geographer	Prof Geog
Psychoanalysis and the Psychoanalytic Review	
Psychoanalytic Quarterly	
Psychological Review	Psych R
Public Administration Review	
Public Finance	
Public Opinion Quarterly	Pub Op Q
Publications of the Modern Language Association	PMLA
Quarterly Journal of Economics	Quart J Econ
Quarterly Journal of Speech	Q J Speech
Quarterly Journal of Studies on Alcohol	Q J St Alcohol
Quarterly Journal of the Library of Congress	Q J Lib Cong
Quarterly Review	
Queen's Quarterly	Queen's Q
Records and Recording	
Regional Science Association Papers	
Renaissance News	Ren News
The Reporter	
Review of Economic Studies	
Review of Economics and Statistics	R Econ Stat
Review of Educational Research	
Review of Metaphysics	
Review of Politics	R Poli
Review of Social Economy	R Soc Econ
Review of Soviet Medical Science	R Sov Med Sci
Revue des Études Slaves (Paris)	
Revue Historique	
Romance Philology	
Romanic Review	
Royal Central Asian Journal	Roy Cent Asian J
Rural Sociology	
Russian Review	Russ R
Saeculum	
St. Vladimir's Seminary Quarterly	St. Vladimir's Sem Q
Saturday Review	Sat Rev
Scando-Slavica	
School Review	
Science	Sci
Science and Culture	
Science and Society	Sci Soc
Scientific American	Sci Am
Slavic and East European Journal	Slav East Eur J
Slavic and East European Studies (Études Slaves et Est-Européenes)	Sl East Eur St

Slavic Review	Slav R
Slavonic and East European Review	Slav East Eur R
Social and Economic Studies	
Social Forces	Soc Forces
Social Problems	
Social Research	
Social Service Revue	
Social Work	
The Socialist Register	
Sociologica	
Sociological Analysis	
Sociologie du Travail	
Sociologus	
Sociology and Social Research	
Sociology of Education	
Sociometry	
South Atlantic Quarterly	Sou Atl Q
Southern Economic Journal	Sou Econ J
Southern Journal of Philosophy	
Southern Quarterly	Sou Q
Southwestern Journal of Anthropology	Sou J Anthropology
Southwestern Social Science Quarterly	Sou Soc Sci Q
Soviet Life	
Soviet Psychology and Psychiatry	
Soviet Studies	Sov St
Special Libraries	Spec Lib
Speculum	Spec
Strad	
Studia Linguistica	
Studia Musicologica	
Studies in Philology	St Philol
Studies in Short Fiction	St Short Fict
Studies in Soviet Thought	St Sov Thought
Studies on Romanticism	St Romant
Studies on the Left	
Studies on the Soviet Union	St Sov Un
Studio International	
Survey; a Journal of Soviet and East European Studies	Sur
Symposium	Symp
Teachers College Record	
Technology and Culture	
Tempo	
Texas Studies in Literature and Language	
Tijdschrift voor economische en social Geografie	Tijd Econ Soc Geog
Times Literary Supplement	TLS
Transatlantic Review	Trans R
Tri-Quarterly (Northwestern University)	
Tulane Drama Review	Tu Dr R
The Ukrainian Quarterly	Ukr Q
Ukrainian Review	Ukr R
United States Naval Institute Proceedings	USNIP

University of California Publications in Linguistics
University of California Publications in Modern
 Philology
University of Toronto Quarterly   Univ of Toronto Q
Ural-Altaische Jahrbücher

Verbal Learning and Behavior
Virginia Journal of Education   Virg J Ed
Virginia Quarterly Review   Virg Q R

Welt der Slaven   Welt Slav
Weltwirtschaftliches Archiv   Welt Arch
Western Economic Journal   West Econ J
The Western Political Quarterly West Poli Q
Wiener Slavistisches Jahrbüch
World
World Affairs
World Justice
World Politics   W Poli
World Today   W Today

Yale Economic Essays
Yale Law Journal
Yale Review   Yale R
Yale University Library Gazette Yale U Lib Gaz
Yearbook of Psychoanalysis

One. The Soviet Union and East Europe

I. GENERAL

BIBLIOGRAPHY AND REFERENCE

1. Ashraf, Shawkat, V. K. Arora, and S. K. Arora. "India and World Affairs: An Annual Bibliography, 1964." Int St, VII, 3 (Jan), 468-514. [See No. 294]

2. Blake, John B. "Ninety-first Critical Bibliography of the History of Science and its Cultural Influences (To January 1966)." ISIS, LVII, 4 (Winter), 576-644.

3. Canadian Slavonic Papers, VII (1965). Review, Max Oppenheimer, Jr., Slav East Eur J, X, 3 (Fall), 361-362.

4. "Complete List of Institute Publications." Bull Inst St USSR, XIII, 12 (Dec), 50-60.

5. Clarke, James F. "English Histories of Bulgaria." Balk St, VII, 1, pp. 175-183.

6. Dumbarton Oaks Papers, No. 19 (1965). Review, John E. Rexine, Balk St, VII, 2, p. 492.

6a. Dumbarton Oaks Papers, No. 20 (1966). Review, Speros Vryonis, Jr., Am Hist R, LXXIV, 2 (Dec 1968), 557-558.

7. Epstein, F. T. et al. American Bibliography of Russian and East European Studies for 1963. [See ABREES, 1965, No. 5] Review, Robert W. Simmons, Jr., Slav East Eur J, X, 4 (Winter), 492-494.

7a. Epstein, F. T., ed., and Cynthia H. Whittaker, assoc. ed. American Bibliography of Russian and East European Studies for 1964. Bloomington, Ind.: Indiana U Press, 119p. (Russian and East European Series, 34).

8. Hammond, Thomas T., ed. Soviet Foreign Relations. [See ABREES, 1965, No. 7] Reviews, F. L. Carsten, Slav East Eur R, XLIV, 103 (Jul), 530; Melvin Croan, Russ R, XXV, 2 (Apr), 199-200; Fritz T. Epstein, Slav R, XXV, 1 (Mar), 173-174; correspondence, ibid., pp. 175-176.

9. Lencek, Rado L. A Bibliographic Guide to the Literature on Slavic Civilizations. NY: Dept. of Slavic Languages, Columbia U, 66p. Reviews, A. Helliwell, Slav East Eur R, XLVI, 107 (Jul 1968), 553-554; Benjamin A. Stolz, Slav East Eur J, XII, 1 (Spring 1968), 118-119.

10. "List of Books and Articles Published by Scandinavian Slavists and Baltologists (1965-1966)." Scando-Slavica, XII, pp. 176-179.

11. "List of Books and Articles Published by Scandinavian Slavists and Baltologists (1966-1967)." Scando-Slavica, XIII (1967), 269-273.

12. Miliband, R., and J. Saville, eds. The Socialist Register (1965). NY: Merlin Press, 362p. Review, Royden Harrison, Poli Q, XXXVII, 1, pp. 114-119.

12a. _____. The Socialist Register, (1966). NY: Merlin Press, 320p.

12b. Rocznik Slawistyczny (Yearbook of Slavonic Studies), vol. XXXI, part II. Wroclaw: Ossolineum, 153-480pp. (1970). [Includes works on Slavistics from all countries for the year 1966]

13. Slavs in Canada. Proceedings of the First National Conference on Canadian Slavs. Inter-University Committee on Canadian Slavs, Vol. I, 171p. Edmonton, Alberta. Review, W. T. Zyla, Ukr Q, XXIV, 1 (Spring 1968), 86-88.

3

14. Trefousse, H. L., ed. The Cold War. [See ABREES, 1965, No. 10] Review, Frederick H. Hartmann, J Poli, XXVIII, 2 (May), 455-457.

See also: 326, 327, 493, 990

SOVIET AND EAST EUROPEAN STUDIES IN THE WEST

15. Armstrong, John A. "Slavic Studies in Western Europe: Some Personal Observations." Can Slav Pap, VII, pp. 55-67.

16. Bolsover, G. H. "The School of Slavonic and East European Studies: The First Fifty Years. III (Since 1947)." Slav East Eur R, XLIV, 102 (Jan), 18-30. [See also items 20, 23]

17. Dossick, Jesse J., comp. "Doctoral Dissertations on Russia, the Soviet Union and Eastern Europe Accepted by American, Canadian and British Universities, 1965-66." Slav R, XXV, 4 (Dec), 710-717.

17a. The same, 1966-67, Slav R, XXVI, 4 (Dec), 705-712.

18. Fischer, George. American Research on Soviet Society. Guide to Specialized Studies since World War II by Sociologists, Psychologists and Anthropologists in the United States. NY: Columbia U, Bureau of Applied Social Research, 82p.

19. Gross, Feliks. "Area Studies at New York University." Pol R, XI, 3 (Summer), 29-44.

20. Jopson, N. B. "The School of Slavonic and East European Studies: The First Fifty Years. I (1922-1937)." Slav East Eur R, XLIV, 102 (Jan), 1-7. [See also 16, 23]

21. Kirkconnell, Watson. "Letters in Canada: 1965-Publications in Other Languages." Univ of Toronto Q, XXXV, 4 (Jul), 537-550.

21a. Andrusyshen, C. H. The same (1966), ibid. XXXVI, 4 (Jul 1967), 545-556.

22. Mehlinger, Howard. "Area Studies and the Secondary Schools." Educ Record, XLVII, 2 (Spring), 244-252.

22a. Miller, Richard I. Teaching about Communism. [See ABREES, 1965, No. 269] Review, Howard Mehlinger, Slav R, XXVI, 3 (Sept 1967), 523-524.

23. Rose, W. J. "The School of Slavonic and East European Studies: The First Fifty Years. II (1937-1947)." Slav East Eur R, XLIV, 102 (Jan), 8-17. [See also 16, 20]

24. Rosen, Nathan. "All's Well That Ends Badly." Slav East Eur J, X, 1 (Spring), 46-65. [Russian language proficiency of graduate students]

25. Timberlake, Charles E. "The Slavic Department of the Helsinki University Library." Slav R, XXV, 3 (Sept), 513-522.

See also: 326, 327, 577, 990

BIOGRAPHY

26. Nettl, J. P. Rosa Luxemburg. 2 vols. London: Oxford U Press, 1006p. Reviews, Werner T. Angress, J Mod Hist, XXXIX, 4 (Dec 1967), 471-472; Hannah Arendt, NY Rev of Books, VII, 5, Oct 6, pp. 21-26; Abraham Ascher, Prob Comm, XV, 11-12 (Nov-Dec), 78-80; Samuel H. Baron, Russ R, XXVI, 1 (Jan 1967), 88; F. L. Carsten, Slav East Eur R, XLV, 105 (Jul 1967), 560-562; Lewis Coser, Dissent, XIII, 5 (Sept-Oct), 544-548; Leon Dennen, East Eur, XVI, 11 (Nov 1967), 57-60; J. K. Eaton, Poli Q, XXXVIII, 1 (Jan-Mar 1967), 105-110; Louis Fischer, Book Week, III, 49 (Jul 14), p. 11; George Lichtheim, Enc, XXVI (Jun), 55; Boris Sapir, Slav R, XXVII, 1 (Mar 1968), 146-148; Rudolf Schlesinger, Sov St, XVIII, 2 (Oct), 225-251; corr., ibid., XIX, 3 (Jan 1968), 453-457; Carl E. Schorske, Am Hist R, LXXIII, 4 (Apr 1968), 1140-1141; Z.A.B. Zeman, Survey, no. 60 (Jul), 167-171; TLS, May 5, p. 377.

II. HISTORY

26a. Cambridge Medieval History, Vol. IV, Part I: Byzantium and its Neighbors. J. M. Hussey, ed., Cambridge: Cambridge U Press, 1168p. Reviews, Victor Terras, Slav East Eur J, XII, 2 (Summer), 261-2; Norman Tobias, Balk St, VIII, 2, pp. 499-502; P. D. Whitting, Slav East Eur R, XLVI, 107 (Jul 1968), 515-517; Virg Q R, XLII (Autumn), 153.

27. Degras, Jane, ed. Communist International Documents, 1919-1943. Vol. 3, 1929-1943. [See ABREES, 1965, No. 28] Reviews, John C. Campbell, Russ R, XXV, 3 (Jul), 317-318; Alexander Dallin, Survey, no. 59 (Apr), 117-120.

28. Deutscher, Isaac. Ironies of History; Essays on Contemporary Communism. London: Oxford U Press, 278p. Reviews, Cyril E. Black, Virg Q R, XLIII (Spring 1967), 342; Jesse D. Clarkson, Russ R, XXVII, 3 (Jul 1968), 355-356; Henry Hanak, Slav East Eur R, XLVI, 107 (Jul 1968), 547-549; Walter Laqueur, NY Rev of Books, Apr 20, 1967, p. 23; H. W. Morton, Am Pol Sci R, LXI, 4 (Dec 1967), 1125; Myron Rush, Commentary, XLIII (Jun 1967), 84; James D. Young, Poli Q, XXXVIII, 3 (Jun-Aug 1967), 214-215; TLS, Dec 1, p. 1117.

28a. Gatzke, Hans. The Present in Perspective. A Look at the World Since 1945. London: John Murray; Chicago: Rand McNally, 221p. Review, V. G. Irinin, Novaia i Noveishaia Istoriia, no. 1 (Jan-Feb 1967), 164-165.

29. Lavrin, Janko. "Yury Krizhanich." Russ R, XXV, 4 (Oct), 369-382.

30. Prusek, Jaroslav. "The Steppe Zone in the Period of Early Nomads and China of the 9th-7th Centuries B.C." Diogenes, no. 54 (Summer), 23-46.

31. Rogger, Hans, and Eugen Weber, eds. The European Right. [See ABREES, 1965, No. 32] Reviews, Elliott P. Fagerberg, J Poli, XXVIII, 2 (May), 434-436; Klemens von Klemperer, Am Hist R, LXXI, 2 (Jan), 546-548; Gordon Wright, Poli Sci Q, LXXXI, 2 (Jun), 317-318; Francis D. Wormuth, West Poli Q, XIX, 1 (Mar), 192.

See also: 1770

III. INTERNATIONAL RELATIONS: POLITICS, ECONOMICS, LAW

GENERAL

32. Dean, Arthur H. Test Ban and Disarmament: The Path of Negotiations. NY: Harper & Row, for the Council of Foreign Relations, 156p. Reviews, Elie Abel, Book Week, May 8, pp. 2-12; Lincoln P. Bloomfield, Ann Am Acad Pol Soc Sci, no. 368 (Nov), 172-173; W. R. Frye, NY Times Book Rev, Jul 25, p. 10; J Am Hist, LIII (Sept), 424.

33. Eubank, Keith. The Summit Conferences. Norman: U of Oklahoma Press, 225p. Reviews, Thomas Barman, Int Aff, XLIV, 1 (Jan 1968), 80-82; Herbert Feis, Am Hist R, LXXIII, 1 (Oct 1967), 101-102; B. M. Ziegler, Ann Am Acad Pol Soc Sci, 371 (May 1967), 216.

34. Gross, Feliks. World Politics and Tension Areas. NY: NY Univ Press, 377p. Reviews, Theodore Caplow, Poli Sci Q, LXXXII, 4 (Dec 1967),

633; L. A. D. Dellin, East Eur, XVI, 6 (Jun), 48; Louis Kreisberg, Am Soc R, XXXII, 1 (Feb 1967), 130; W. W. Kulski, Pol R, XIII, 1 (Winter 1968), 98-100; H. H. Ransom, Sat Rev, XLIX, Jun 11, p. 53; TLS, Nov 10, p. 1018.

35. Hangen, Welles. The Muted Revolution: East Germany's Challenge to Russia and the West. NY: Alfred A. Knopf, 231p. Reviews, R. V. Burks, East Eur Q, I, 4 (Jan 1968), 414-416; Viktor Meier, Prob Comm, XVI, 4 (Jul-Aug 1967), 58-61; Philip Shabecoff, NY Times Book Rev, Nov 13, p. 10; Ronald Steel, Book Week, IV, 5, Oct 9, p. 5.

36. Koczy, Leon. "Millennium of the Formation of the Frontier Between Eastern and Western Europe." Cent Eur Fed, XIV, 2 (Dec), 5-10.

37. Roucek, Joseph S. "Geopolitical Trends Behind the Iron Curtain." Cent Eur J, XIV, 9 (Sept), 267-279.

38. Strzetelski, Stanislaw. "The Critical Decade, 1965-1975." Pol R, XI, 2 (Spring), 65-81.

INTRA-BLOC RELATIONS

39. Allen, Robert V. "Recent Developments in the History of the Soviet Union and Eastern Europe." Ann Am Acad Pol Soc Sci, no. 65 (May), 147-160.

40. Anderson, Stephan S. "Soviet Relations with East Europe." Curr Hist, LI, 302 (Oct), 200-205.

41. Aron, Raymond. "On Polycentrism." Survey, no. 58 (Jan), 10-18.

42. Aspaturian, Vernon T. The Soviet Union in the World Communist System. Stanford: Hoover Institution on War, Revolution and Peace, 96p. Reviews, John A. Armstrong, Russ R, XXVI, 1 (Jan 1967), 90; Harry Hanak, Slav East Eur R, XLVI, 107 (Jul 1968), 541-542; Nish Jamgotch, Jr., Am Pol

Sci R, LXII, 2 (Jun 1968), 690-691.

43. C(oser), L(ewis). "Tito, Rankovic, and All That." Dissent, XIII, 5 (Sept-Oct), 470-471.

44. Croan, Melvin. "Moscow and Eastern Europe." Prob Comm, XV, 9-10 (Sept-Oct), 60-64. [1956-1966]

45. Devlin, Kevin. "A Movement Transformed: Some Consequences and Lessons." Ibid., 48-59. [1965-1966]

46. Erasmus (pseud). "Polycentrism and Proliferation." Survey, no. 58 (Jan), 67-72.

47. Keep, John L. H. "Belgrade and Moscow: A Calculating Courtship." Orbis, X, 3 (Fall), 754-781.

48. Lyon, Peter. "Neutralism and Polycentrism." Survey, no. 58 (Jan), 35-42

49. Mayer, Peter. "International Fraternity vs. National Power: A Contradiction in the Communist World." R Poli, XXVIII, 2 (Apr), 193-209.

50. Mosely, Philip E. "Eastern Europe in World Power Politics." Mod Age, XI, 2 (Spring 1967), 119-136.

51. Pethybridge, Roger. The Development of the Communist Bloc. [See ABREES, 1965, No. 54] Reviews, Robert Bass, East Eur, XV, 4 (Apr), 51-53; Myron Rush, Slav R, XXVII, 3 (Sept 1968), 492-494.

52. Scott, John. The Soviet World: Growth, Disintegration and Reform: A Report to the Publisher of TIME, the Weekly Newspaper. NY: Time, 90p.

53. Wolfe, Thomas W. "The Warsaw Pact in Evolution." W Today, XXII, 5 (May), 191-198.

SINO-SOVIET RELATIONS

54. Americus (pseud). "A Realistic view of Soviet-Chinese Relations." Ukr Q, XXII, 1 (Spring), 63-72.

55. Bromke, Adam, ed. The Communist States at the Crossroads Between Moscow and Peking. [See ABREES, 1965, No. 39] Reviews, Ivan Avacumovic, Pac Aff, XXXVIII, 3-4 (Fall-Winter 1965-66), 363-364; Robert Bass, East Eur, XV, 4 (Apr), 51-53; TLS, May 25, 1967, p.434.

56. Clemens, Walter C., Jr. "The Nuclear Test Ban and Sino-Soviet Relations." Orbis, X, 1 (Spring), 152-183.

57. Cohen, Warren I. "American Observers and the Sino-Soviet Friendship Treaty of August, 1945." Pac Hist R, XXXV, 3 (Aug), 347-350.

58. Cottingham, Chester T. "The Impact of Recent Reverses in Chinese Foreign Policy Upon the Sino-Soviet Dispute." Bull Inst St USSR, XIII, 2 (Feb), 15-25.

59. Devlin, Kevin. "Workers of the World Disunite." Orbis, X, 3 (Fall), 782-802.

60. Doolin, Dennis J. Territorial Claims in the Sino-Soviet Conflict. [See ABREES, 1965, No.1003] Reviews, W.J.Drew, Sov St, XVIII, 1 (Jul), 120-122; John Erickson, China Q, no. 26 (Apr-Jun), 193-194.

61. Ermath, Fritz. "Moscow and the Chinese Missile." East Eur, XV, 12 (Dec), 2-6.

62. Fairbank, John K. "How to Deal with the Chinese Revolution." NY Rev of Books, VI, 2, Feb 19, 10-15.

63. Fokkema, D.W. Literary Doctrine in China and Soviet Influence, 1956-1960. [See ABREES, 1965, No. 329] Reviews, Merle Goldman, China Q, no. 27 (Jul-Sept), 170-172; C. T. Hsia, J Asian St, XXV, 4 (Aug), 747-750; TLS, Mar 17, p. 224.

64. "Foreign Relations." China Mainland R, XI, 3 (Dec), 216-217.

65. Garthoff, Raymond L., ed. Sino-Soviet Military Relations. NY:

Praeger, 285p. Reviews, Matthew P. Gallagher, Slav R, XXVII, 1 (Mar 1968), 138-9; R.T.Gill, East Eur, XVI, 3 (Mar 1967), 55-6; H.Hedley, Russ R, XXII, 2 (Apr 1967), 190; Geoffrey Shillinglaw, Int Aff, XLIV, 1 (Jan 1968), 154-5; Daniel Tretiak, China Q, no.32 (Oct-Dec 1967), 179-180; Thomas W. Wolfe, Prob Comm, XVII, 2 (Mar-Apr 1968), 66.

66. _____. "A Soviet Critique of China's 'Total Strategy'." Reporter, XXXIV, 10 (May), 48-50.

67. Gittings, John. "China and the Cold War." Survey, no. 58 (Jan), 196-208.

68. Griffith, William E. "Sino-Soviet Relations, 1964-5." China Q, no. 25 (Jan-Mar), 3-143.

69. _____. The Sino-Soviet Split. [See ABREES, 1965, No. 1007] Review, Peter Lyon, Political Studies, XIV, 2 (Jun), 262-263.

70. Halperin, Morton H. "Sino-Soviet Relations and Arms Control: An Introduction." China Q, no. 26 (Apr-Jun), 118-122.

71. Hudson, G.F. "China and the Communist Movement." Survey, no. 58 (Jan), 59-66.

72. Hyer, Paul. "The Re-evaluation of Chinggis Khan: Its Role in the Sino-Soviet Dispute." Asian Sur, VI, 12 (Dec), 696-705.

73. Isenberg, Irwin. The Russian-Chinese Rift: Its Impact on World Affairs. NY: H.W.Wilson, 221p.

74. Kashin, A. "The Generation Problem in China and its Implications for Sino-Soviet Relations." Bull Inst St USSR, XIII, 8 (Aug), 18-27.

75. _____. "The Soviet Leaders and the Chinese Dilemma." St Sov Un, VI, 1, pp. 10-19.

76. _____. "The Geopolitical Aspect of the Sino-Soviet Dispute." Bull Inst St USSR, XIII, 1 (Jan), 37-49.

77. Kyozo, Mori. "The Two

Communisms." Japan Q, XIII, 1 (Jan-Mar), 46-53

78. Labedz, Leopold, and G. R. Urban, eds. The Sino-Soviet Conflict. [See ABREES, 1965, No. 49] Review, Richard Rowson, East Eur, XV, 4 (Apr), 54-55.

79. London, Kurt L. "The Sino-Soviet Conflict." Cur Hist, LI, 302 (Oct), 206-212.

80. Moseley, George. A Sino-Soviet Cultural Frontier: The Ili Kazakh Autonomous Chou. Cambridge, Mass.: East Asian Research Center, Harvard U., 171p. (Harvard East Asian Monographs, 22). Review, Yi Chu Wang, Am Hist R, LXXIII, 4 (Apr 1968), 1106-7.

81. Prybyla, Jan S. "Soviet and Chinese Aid to North Vietnam." China Q, no. 27 (Jul-Sept), 84-100.

82. Ray, Hemen. "Sinkiang: The Sino-Soviet Game." Contemp R, CCIX, 1206 (Jul), 15-19.

83. Rupen, Robert A. "Vietnam and the Sino-Soviet Dispute: A Summary." St Sov Un, VI, 2, 99-118.

84. Schultz, Karl A. "The Sino-Soviet Rift: A Perspective." Int R Hist Poli Sci, III, 1 (Jun), 25-40.

85. Schurmann, Franz. "What is Happening in China?" NY Rev of Books, VII, 6, Oct 20, pp. 18-25.

86. Sonnenfelt, Helmut. "The Chinese Factor in Soviet Disarmament Policy." China Q, no. 26 (Apr-May), 123-135.

87. Swearingen, Roger, ed. Soviet and Chinese Communist Power in the World Today. NY: Basic Books, 138p. Review, Jonathan Harris, Am Pol Sci R, LXII, 1 (Mar 1968), 311-312.

88. Wheeler, Geoffrey. "Soviet and Chinese Policies in the Middle East." W Today, XXII, 2 (Feb), 64-78.

89. Young, Oran R. "Chinese Views on the Spread of Nuclear Weapons." China Q, no. 26 (Apr-Jun), 136-170.

90. Zablocki, Clement J., ed. Sino-Soviet Rivalry, Implications for U.S. Policy. NY: Praeger, 240p. Reviews, Geoffrey Shillinglaw, Int Aff, XLIV, 3 (Jul 1968), 601-603; East Eur, XVI, 4 (Aug 1967), 56; Reginald F. Zelnik, East Eur Q, I, 2 (Jun 1967), 164-167.

See also: 182, 215, 286, 293, 474, 495, 619, 646, 669, 704

FOREIGN RELATIONS
OF THE BLOC

90a. Brzezinski, Zbigniew, ed. Africa and the Communist World. Stanford: Stanford U Press, 272p. (1965) Review, Harry Hanak, Slav East Eur R, XLVI, 107 (Jul 1968), 549-550.

91. McWhinney, Edward, ed. Law, Foreign Policy and the East-West Detente. Toronto: U Toronto Press, 123p.

91a. Schatten, Fritz. Communism in Africa. NY: Praeger, 352p. Reviews, David L. Morison, Prob Comm, XVI, 1 (Jan-Feb 1967), 66; S. Volin, Novyi Zhurnal, no. 88 (1967), 288-291.

92. Schmitt, Karl M. Communism in Mexico. A Study in Political Frustration. Austin: U Texas Press, 290p. (1965) Review, Martin C. Needler, Hisp Am Hist R, XLVI, 3 (Aug), 327-329.

93. Zabih, Sepehr. The Communist Movement in Iran. Berkeley: U California Press, 286p. Reviews, H. L. Hoskins, Ann Am Acad Pol Soc Sci, CLXXIV (Nov 1967), 243; T. Cuyler Young, Am Hist R, LXXIII, 3 (Oct 1967), 189.

See Part II, VII-International

Communism and Intra-Bloc
Party Relations

COLD WAR AND CO-EXISTENCE

94. Abel, Elie. The Missile Crisis. Philadelphia: Lippincott, 220p. Reviews, Michael Amrine, Book Week, Mar 6, p. 3; Anthony T. Bouscaren, Ukr Q, XXII, 3 (Autumn), 272-274; I. F. Stone, NY Rev of Books, Apr 14, p. 12; NY Times Book Rev, Feb 20, p. 3; TLS, Jun 9, p. 514.

95. Allen, Richard V. Peace or Peaceful Coexistence? Chicago: American Bar Association, 233p. Review, Lev E. Dobriansky, Ukr Q, XXII, 4 (Winter), 368-371.

96. Anderson, Evelyn. "Germany in the Cold War." Survey, no. 58 (Jan), 177-186.

97. Barnet, Richard J., and Marcus G. Raskin. After Twenty Years: Alternatives to the Cold War in Europe. [See ABREES, 1965, No. 78] Review, Max Beloff, Prob Comm, XV, 4 (Jul-Aug), 46-50.

98. Bedriy, Anatol W. "The Cold War Educational Gap." Ukr R, XIII, 3 (Autumn), 71-73. [U.S. knowledge about communism]

99. Beezley, P. C., ed. United Nations Fact Book, Number 2. Linden, N.J.: Bookmailer, 140p.

100. Bonham-Carter, Mark. "Roads to European Unity." Survey, no. 58 (Jan), 149-152.

101. Brzezinski, Zbigniew K. "American Globalism." Survey, no. 58 (Jan), 19-29.

102. Cornides, Wilhelm. "German Unification and the Power Balance." Survey, no. 58 (Jan), 140-148.

103. Donnelly, Desmond. "Containment and After." Survey, no. 58 (Jan), 30-34.

104. _____. The Struggle for the World. [See ABREES, 1965, No. 79] Review, Frederick H. Hartmann, J Poli, XXVIII, 2 (May), 455-457.

105. Dulles, Eleanor L., and Robert D. Crane, eds. Détente: Cold War Strategies in Transition. [See ABREES, 1965, No. 80] Reviews, Willard F. Barber, West Poli Q, XXI, 1 (Mar 1968), 153-154; Peter Calvocoressi, Poli Q, XXXVII, 2 (Apr-Jun), 217-219; Ciro Elliott Zoppo, Ann Am Acad Pol Soc Sci, CCCLXIII (Jan), 155-158

106. Fleming, D. F. "The Costs and Consequences of the Cold War." Ann Am Acad Pol Soc Sci, CCCLXVI (Jul), 127-138.

107. Gasteyger, Curt. "Nuclear Prospects and Foreign Policy." Survey, no. 58 (Jan), 73-81.

108. Griffith, William E. "The German Problem and American Policy." Survey, no. 61 (Oct), 105-117.

109. Herz, Martin F. Beginnings of the Cold War. Bloomington, Ind.: Indiana U Press, 214p. Reviews, Harland B. Moulton, Orbis, XII, 1 (Spring 1968), 326-331; Myron Rush, Slav R, XXVII, 3 (Sept 1968), 492-494; Jolene Scholten, Cent Eur J/Sud Bull, XIV, 7-8 (Jul-Aug), 253-254.

110. Jelenski, K. A. "The European Revival." Survey, no. 58 (Jan), 89-100.

111. Kaplan, Morton A. "Strategy of Survival." Survey, no. 58 (Jan), 82-88.

112. Kennan, George F. "Europe in East-West Relations." Survey, no. 58 (Jan), 118-127.

113. Kim, Young Hum, ed. Patterns of Competitive Coexistence: U.S.A. vs. U.S.S.R. NY: Putnam, 484p. Review, Solomon B. Levine, Mo Lab R, LXXXIX, 12 (Dec), 1405.

114. Knapp, Wilfred. "Cold War Origins." Survey, no. 58 (Jan), 153-158.

115. Korey, William. "Zimmerwald: Some Contemporary Echoes." Prob Comm, XV, 1-2 (Jan-Feb), 49-53.

116. Lerche, Charles O. The Cold War — And After. [See ABREES, 1965, No. 86] Review, Frederick H. Hartmann, J Poli, XXVIII, 2 (May), 455-457.

117. Manning, Clarence A. "Coexistence: American and Soviet Styles." Ukr Q, XXII, 4 (Winter), 334-342.

118. McLellan, David S. The Cold War in Transition. NY: Macmillan, 149p. Reviews, Willard F. Barber, West Poli Q, XX, 2, pt. 1 (Jun 1967), 488-490; Warren B. Walsh, Russ R, XXVI, 1 (Jan 1967), 93.

119. Mende, Erich. "German Reunification and European Security." Cent Eur J, XIV, 11 (Nov), 331-335.

120. "Neutralizing the Iron Curtain." Ukr Q, XXII, 4 (Winter), 293-299.

121. Shulman, Marshall D. Beyond the Cold War. New Haven: Yale U Press, 111p. Reviews, East Eur, XV, 4 (Apr), 55-56; Max Beloff, Prob Comm, XXI, 2 (Spring), 211-217; Howard R. Swearer, Sov St, XIX, 4 (Apr 1968), 595; W. J. Thorbecke, Sat Rev, XLIX, Jan 22, p. 39.

122. Smith, Jean Edward. "Berlin Confrontation." Virg Q R, XLII, 3 (Summer), 349-365.

123. Stolte, Stefan C. "Who Will Bury Whom." Bull Inst St USSR, XIII, 5 (May), 19-25.

IV. PUBLIC AFFAIRS, LAW AND GOVERNMENT

124. Labedz, Leopold. "Sociology and Social Change." Survey, no. 60 (Jul), 18-39.

125. Meyden, Hartmut. "The Demographic Effects of Relaxed Abortion Laws in Soviet Bloc Countries." R Sov Med Sci, III, 2, pp. 33-44.

126. Skilling, H. Gordon. "Interest Groups and Communist Politics." West Poli Q, XVIII, 3 (Apr), 435-451.

127. Wilhelm, Donald, Jr. The West Can Win: A Study of Science and World Power. NY: Praeger, 208p. Reviews, TLS, Jun 2, 498; corr., Jun 16, p. 541; NY Times Book Rev, Apr 3, p. 34.

V. ECONOMICS

GENERAL

128. Bronfenbrenner, Martin. "The Marxian Macro-Economics Model: Extension from Two Departments." Kyklos, XIX, 2, pp. 201-218.

129. Goldman, Marshall I. "Communist Foreign Aid: Successes and Shortcomings." Cur Hist, LI, 300 (Aug), 78-87.

130. Mieczkowski, Bogdan. "The Study of Communist Living Standards." Cent Eur Fed, XIV, 1 (Jul), 29-35.

131. Orlowski, Miroslaw, and Zbigniew Pirozynski. "Problems of Financing Education in Socialist Countries." Pub Fin, XXI, 1-2 (Summer), 121-164. "Comments" by J. B. D. Derksen, ibid., 121-164.

132. Perlo, Victor. "Notes on Marxian Economics in the United States: Comment." Am Econ R, LVI, 1 (Mar), 187-8.

133. Petrov, Vladimir. Money and Conquest: Allied Occupation Currencies in World War II. Johns Hopkins Studies in Historical and Political Science, vol. LXXXIV, no. 2. Baltimore: Johns Hopkins Press, 282p. Reviews, Arthur Schweitzer, J Econ Hist, XXVIII, 3 (Sept 1968), 493-495; Victor B. Sullam, Prob Comm, XVII, 2 (Mar-Apr 1968), 69-70.

134. Rabinowitch, Eugene. "The Second Challenge." Bull Atom Sci, XXII, 5 (May), 25-27.

135. Sawyer, Carole A. Communist Trade with Developing Countries, 1964-5. NY: Praeger, 126p. Reviews, Roger E. Kanet, Slav R, XXVI, 4 (Dec 1967), 693-695; Paul Marer, East Eur. XVI, 7 (Jul 1967), 60; David L. Morison, Prob Comm, XVI, 4 (Jul-Aug 1967), 74-75.

See also: 1465

INTRA-BLOC ECONOMIC RELATIONS

136. Arbib, Michael A. "A Partial Survey of Cybernetics in Eastern Europe and the Soviet Union." Behav Sci, XI, 3 (May), 193-216.

137. Bregman, Alexander. "The Communist Car: An Upside-Down Status Symbol." Reporter, XXXIV, 9, May 5, 30-31.

138. Feddersen, Berend H. "Markets Behind the Iron Curtain." J Marketing, XXXI, 3 (Jul 1967), 1-5.

139. Frisch, Ragnar. "Rational Price Fixing in a Socialist Society." Econ Plan, VI, 2, pp.97-124.

140. Köhler, Heinz. Economic Integration in the Soviet Bloc — with an East Germany Case Study. Praeger Special Studies in International Economics and Development. NY: Praeger, 402p.

140a. Kutt, Aleksandr. Soviets Have Robbed Satellites of Nearly $13 Billion." ACEN News, no. 122, (Mar-Apr), 20-24.

141. Montias, John M. "Problems of Integration." Review article on M. Kaser, Comecon. [See ABREES, 1965, No. 106] W Poli, XVIII, 4 (Jul), 715-716.

142. Moyer, Red. "Marketing in the Iron Curtain Countries." J Marketing, XXX, 4 (Oct), 3-9.

143. Olgin, C. "Cybernetics and the Political Economy of Communism." Bull Inst St USSR, XIII, 10 (Oct), 3-21.

144. Rajkiewicz, Antoni. "Industrialization and Structural Changes in Employment in the Socialist Countries." Int Lab R, XCIV, 3 (Sept), 286-302.

145. Stolte, Stefan. "Comecon through Soviet Eyes." St Sov Un, V, 3, pp. 37-45.

146. Wyczalkowski, Marcin R. "Communist Economics and Currency Convertibility." International Monetary Fund Staff Papers, XIII, 2 (Jul), 155-197.

EAST-WEST TRADE RELATIONS

147. Dunning, E. G., and E. I. Hopper. "Industrialism and the Problem of Convergence: A Critical Note." Social Research, XIV, 2 (Jul), 163-186; "A Reply," by Goldthorpe, John H., ibid., 187-198.

148. Goldman, Marshall I., and Alice Conner. "Businessmen Appraise East-West Trade." Harvard Bus R, XLIV, 1 (Jan-Feb), 6-29.

149. Kaser, Michael C. "Trends in East-West Trade." W Today, XXII, 3 (Mar), 100-106.

150. Laato, Erleki. "Finnish Trade with East and West." Econ Plan, VI, 3, pp. 193-210.

151. Laun, John I. "East-West Trade Conference, Stanford University." Am J Int Law, LX, 4 (Oct), 817-8.

152. McKitterick, Nathaniel. East-West Trade: The Background of U.S. Policy. NY: Twentieth Century Fund, 59p. Review, Jerzy Hauptmann, Cent Eur J/Sud Bull, XIV, 10 (Oct), 324-326.

153. Nove, Alec. "Something There Is That Doesn't Love a Trade Wall." Columbia J W Bus, I, 1 (Winter), 15-26.

154. Schwartz, Harry. "Straws in the Trade Winds." Columbia J W Bus, I, 1 (Winter), 27-32.

155. Tinbergen, J., Linnemann, H., and J. P. Pronk. "The Meeting of the Twain." Columbia J W Bus, I, 3 (Summer), 139-149.

156. Uren, Philip E., ed. East-West Trade: A Symposium. Toronto: Canadian Institute of International Affairs, 181p. Review, Abraham Rotstein, Int J, XXI, 4 (Autumn), 527-531.

157. Wilczynski, J. "Dumping in Trade Between Market and Centrally Planned Economies. Lessons from Australia's Experience with the Socialist Bloc." Econ Plan, VI, 3, pp. 211-227.

VI. PHILOSOPHY, IDEOLOGY AND RELIGION

MARXISM

158. Aptheker, Herbert. Marxism and Alienation. [See ABREES, 1965, No. 204] Review, Nelson F. Norman, West Poli Q, XLX, 3 (Sept), 534-535.

158a. Babic, Ivan. "Blanshard's Reduction of Marxism." J Philosophy, LXIII, no. 23 (Dec 8), 745-756. Branko Ozbolt and Ante Starcevic, trs. [Comment on Blanshard's article, item 158b]

158b. Blanshard, Brand. "Reflections on Economic Determinism." J Philosophy, LXIII, no. 7 (Mar 31), 169-178.

159. Bochenski, J. M. "On Philosophical Dialogue." St Sov Thought, VI, 4, pp. 243-259.

160. Bukharin, Nikolai. The ABC of Communism. Ann Arbor: U Michigan Press, 422p. Review, Alfred G. Meyer, Am Pol Sci R, LXI, 1 (Mar 1967), 171-172.

161. Ciolkosz, Adam. "Marxism

and the Individual." East Eur, XV, 5 (May), 16-22. Discussion of Adam Schaff, Marksizm a jednostka ludzka (Marxism and the Individual). (1965) Review, Robert A. Rupen, Am Pol Sci R, LX, 3 (Sept), 703-705.

162. Csikszentmihalyi, Mihaly. "Marx: A Socio-Psychological Evaluation." Mod Age, XI, 3 (Summer 1967), 272-282.

163. DeGeorge, Richard T. Patterns of Soviet Thought: The Origins and Development of Dialectical and Historical Materialism. Ann Arbor: U Michigan Press, 294p. Reviews, Frederick C. Barghoorn, Ann Am Acad Pol Soc Sci, 376 (Mar 1968), 163; David Dinsmore Comey, Slav R, XXVII, 4 (Dec 1967), 695-696; Eugene Kamenka, Prob Comm, XVII, 3 (May-Jun 1968), 49-53.

164. Demaitre, Edmund. "The Wonders of Marxology." Prob Comm, XV, 7-8 (Jul-Aug), 29-35.

165. Desan, Wilfred. The Marxism of Jean-Paul Sartre. [See ABREES,

1965, No. 145] Review, Donald Clark, Phil Phenom Res, XXVI, 3 (Mar), 459-461.

166. Drachkovitch, Milorad M., ed. Marxist Ideology in the Contemporary World: Its Appeals and Paradoxes. NY: Praeger, for the Hoover Institution, 192p. Review, Carl J. Friedrich, Slav R, XXVII, 2 (Jun 1968), 333-334.

167. Drachkovitch, Milorad M., ed. Marxism in the Modern World. [See ABREES, 165, No. 146] Reviews, James Joll, Eng Hist R, no. 326, p. 222; Thomas Molnar, Mod Age, X, 2 (Spring), 209-212; John Plamenatz, Slav East Eur R, XLV, 104 (Jan 1967), 262-264; Stanley Rothman, Prob Comm, XV, 4 (Jul-Aug), 51-54; Louis Wasserman, West Poli Q, XIX, 2 (Jun), 384-386; TLS, Mar 24, p. 239.

168. Dupré, Louis. The Philosophical Foundations of Marxism. NY: Harcourt, Brace and World, 240p. Review, Eugene Kamenka, Prob Comm, XVII, 3 (May-Jun 1968), 49-53.

169. Dworkin, Gerald. "Marx and Mill: A Dialogue." Phil Phenom Res, XXVI, 3 (Mar), 403-414.

170. Elliot, George F. "Proletarian Revolution and the Mass Strike." Sou Soc Sci Q, XLVII, 1 (Jun), 44-50.

171. Feuer, Lewis S. "The Influence of the American Communities upon Engels and Marx." West Poli Q, XIX, 3 (Sept), 456-474.

172. Gottheil, Fred M. Marx's Economic Predictions. Evanston, Ill.: Northwestern U Press, 216p. Reviews, Ben B. Seligman, Prob Comm, XVI, 3 (May-Jun 1967), 58-61; R. Joseph Monsen, J Econ Hist, XXVIII (Mar 1968), 137-138; Murray Wolfson, Ann Am Acad Pol Soc Sci, No. 372 (Jul 1967), 189-190; TLS, Apr 27, 1967, p. 350.

173. Gregor, A. James. A Survey of Marxism. [See ABREES, 1965, No. 153] Review, Bernard S. Morris, Poli Sci Q, LXXXI, 2 (Jun), 318-320.

174. Hampsch, George H. The Theory of Communism: An Introduction. [See ABREES, 1965, No. 156] Review, Eugene Kamenka, Prob Comm, XVII, 3 (May-Jun, 1968), 49-53.

175. Hirozowicz, Maria. "Ideologies and Traditions: The Marxist Approach." Int Soc Sci J, XVIII, 1, pp. 11-21.

176. Hodges, Donald Clarke. "Engels' Contribution to Marxism." The Socialist Register, 1965, 297-310. [See item 12]

177. _____. "The Young Marx — A Reappraisal." Phil Phenom Res, XXVII, 2 (Dec), 216-229.

178. Hook, Sidney. "Marx's Second Coming." Prob Comm, XV, 7-8 (Jul-Aug), 26-29; also in NY Times Book Rev, May 22, p. 2. [Views of Marx in the twentieth century]

179. Howe, I., ed. The Basic Writings of Trotsky. NY: Vintage, 427p. (1965). Review, Robert E. Dowse, Political Studies, XIV, 3 (Oct), 389-397.

180. Kirschenmann, P. "On the Kinship of Cybernetics to Dialectical Materialism." St Sov Thought, VI, 1, pp. 37-41.

181. Lichtheim, George. "Marxism and Marxology: The Transmutations of a Doctrine." Prob Comm, XV, 7-8 (Jul-Aug), 14-25.

182. Lowe, Donald M. The Function of "China" in Marx, Lenin and Mao. Berkeley: U California Press, 200p. Reviews, James P. Harrison, Prob Comm, XVI, 7-8 (Jul-Aug 1967), 70-71; A. E. Kane, Ann Am Acad Pol Soc Sci, CCCLXX (Mar 1967), 238; F. H. Tucker, Am Hist R, LXXII, 4 (Apr 1967), 1052.

183. McLean, Edward B. "Rosa Luxemburg's Conception of Proletarian Revolution." Int R Hist Poli Sci, III, 3 (Dec), 44-63.

184. Miliband, R. "Marx and the State." The Socialist Register, 1965, 278-296. [See item 12]

185. O'Malley, Joseph J. "History and Man's 'Nature' in Marx." R Poli, XXVIII, 4 (Oct), 508-527.

186. O'Neill, John. "Marxism and Mythology." Ethics, LXX, 1 (Oct), 38-49.

187. Odajnik, Walter. Marxism and Existentialism. [See ABREES, 1965, No. 220] Review, Lev E. Dobriansky, Ukr R, XXII, 3 (Autumn), 275-277.

188. Polin, Raymond. The Marxian Foundations of Communism. Chicago: Regnery, 203p. Review, Eugene Kamenka, Prob Comm, XVII, 3 (May-Jun 1968), 49-53.

189. Schlesinger, Rudolf. "Marxism without an Organizing Party: Personal Observations on Rosa Luxemburg's Work." Sov St, XVIII, 2 (Oct), 225-251. [Also discusses Nettl, item 26]

190. Schotte, Bob. Review of Lucien Sebag, Marxisme et Structuralisme. Paris: Payot, 1964; in Am Anthro, LXVIII, 5 (Oct), 1255-56.

191. Vigor, P. H. A Guide to Marxism and Its Effects on Soviet Development. NY: Humanities Press, 253p. Reviews, East Eur, XVI, 3 (Mar 1967), 56; Allen Kassof, Am Soc R, XXXI, 4 (Dec), 888; John Plamenatz, Slav East Eur R, XLV, 104 (Jan 1967), 262-264; TLS, Mar 24, p. 239.

192. Wetter, Gustav A. "Communism and the Problem of Intellectual Freedom." St Sov Un, V, 4, pp. 1-12.

193. _____. "Freedom of Thought and Ideological Coexistence." St Sov Thought, VI, 4, pp. 260-273.

194. Wolfe, Bertram D. Marxism: One Hundred Years in the Life of a Doctrine. [See ABREES, 1965, No. 193] Reviews, Samuel H. Baron, J Mod Hist, XXXVIII, 2 (Jun), 234; Thomas Molnar, Mod Age, X, 2 (Sept), 209-212; Stanley W. Page, Russ R, XXV, 1 (Jan), 78-79; Stanley Rothman, Prob Comm, XV, 4 (Jul-Aug), 51-54.

195. _____. Strange Communists I Have Known. [See ABREES, 1965, No. 24] Review, J. Miller, Sov St, XVIII, 3 (Jan 1967), 383-384; TLS, Sept 8, p. 836.

See also: 1193, 1206, 1208, 1480, 1482, 1486

LENINISM

196. Blakeley, Thomas J. "Marxist-Leninist Scientific Atheism." Inquiry (Oslo), IX, 1, pp. 30-46.

197. Jordan, Z. A. "The Dialectical Materialism of Lenin." Slav R, XXV, 2 (Jun), 259-286.

198. Possony, Stefan T., ed. Lenin Reader. Hoover Institution Studies, No. 15. Chicago: Henry Regnery, 561p. Review, Robert V. Daniels, Prob Comm, XVII, 2 (Mar-Apr 1968), 65-66; NY Times Book Rev, Oct 9, p. 50.

199. Vardy, Alexander. "Parapsychology Versus Marxism-Leninism." R Sov Med Sci, III, 2, pp. 59-62.

See also: 527, 1486

CONTEMPORARY THEORY AND IDEOLOGY

200. Alavi, Hamza. "Peasants and Revolution." The Socialist Register, 1965, 241-277. [See item 12]

201. Charle, Edwin. "The Concept of Neo-Colonialism and Its Relation to Rival Economic Systems." Soc Econ St, XV, 4 (Dec), 329-337.

202. Hodges, Donald Clark. "Socialist Humanism and the Morals Race." Buck R, XIV, 2 (May), 114-130.

203. Hoover, Calvin. Memoirs of Capitalism, Communism and Nazism. [See ABREES, 1965, No. 214] Reviews, R. Murray Haven, Soc Econ J, XXXIII, 2 (Oct), 274-276; Edward S. Mason, Am Econ R, LVI, 4, pt. 1 (Sept), 885-887; C. B. Robson, J Poli, XXVIII, 3 (Aug), 707-708.

204. Jordan, Z. A. "Socialism, Alienation, and Political Power." Survey, No. 60 (Jul), 119-133.

205. Lasswell, Harold, and Daniel Lerner, eds. World Revolutionary Elites: Studies in Coercive Ideological Movements. Cambridge, Mass.: M. I. T. Press, 468p. Reviews, John H. Hedley, Russ R, XXVI, 2 (Apr 1968), 200-201; D. A. Rustow, W Poli, XVIII (Jul), 690.

206. Quester, George H. "On the Identification of Real and Pretended Communist Military Doctrine." J Conf Resol, X, 2 (Jun), 172-179.

207. Urban, Pavel. "What is 'Scientific Communism'?" Bull Inst St USSR, XIII, 9 (Sept), 26-30.

208. Wetter, Gustav A. Soviet Ideology Today. Peter Heath, tr. NY: Praeger, 334p. Reviews, David Dinsmore Comey, Sov St, XIX, 2 (Oct 1967), 278-281; D. D. Comey, Slav R, XXVI, 2 (Jun 1967), 337-8; Eugene Kamenka, Prob Comm, XVII, 3 (May-Jun 1968), 49-53; TLS, Aug 4, p. 704.

INTERNATIONAL COMMUNISM

209. Atkinson, James D. The Politics of Struggle: The Communist Front and Political Warfare. Chicago: Regnery, 192p. Reviews, A. T. Bouscaren, Ann Am Acad Pol Soc Sci, CCCLXXI (May 1967), 230; Wright Miller, Int Aff, XLIV, 1 (Jan 1968), 85-86.

210. Black, C. E., and T. P. Thornton, eds. Communism and Revolution: The Strategic Uses of Political Violence. [See ABREES, 1965,

No. 223] Review, O. J. F., Bull Inst St USSR, XIII, 4 (Apr), 57-58.

211. Devlin, Kevin. "The Catholic-Communist 'Dialogue'." Prob Comm, XV, 5-6 (May-Jun), 31-38.

212. Drachkovitch, Milorad M., and Branko Lazitch, eds. The Comintern: Historical Highlights, Essays, Recollections, Documents. NY: Praeger (for the Hoover Institution), 430p. Reviews, George Barr Carson, Jr., Am Hist R, LXXIII, 2 (Dec 1967), 441; F. L. Carsten, Prob Comm, XVI, 5-6 (May-Jun 1967), 61-62; James W. Hulse, Hist, XXX, 2 (Feb 1968), 269-270; Robert H. McNeal, Russ R, XXVI, 3 (Jul 1967), 310-311; Bernard S. Morris, East Eur Q, I, 3 (Sept 1967), 293-295; A. Z. Rubinstein, Ann Am Acad Pol Soc Sci, CCCLXXI (May 1967), 229; Anthony Sylvester, East Eur, XVI, 9 (Sept 1967), 53-54; TLS, Apr 27, 1967, 350.

213. Drachkovitch, Milorad M., ed. The Revolutionary Internationals, 1864-1943. Stanford: Stanford U Press, 256p. Reviews, James Joll, Eng Hist R, no. 83 (1966), 636; George Lichtheim, Slav East Eur R, XLVI, 106 (Jan 1968), 247-248; Kaethe Mengelberg, Poli Sci Q, LXXXII, 4 (Dec 1967), 670; Alfred G. Meyer, Ann Am Acad Pol Soc Sci, no. 369 (Jan 1967), 198; TLS, Feb 2, 1967, p. 89.

214. Griffith, William E., ed. Communism in Europe: Continuity, Change and the Sino-Soviet Dispute, Vol. II. [See ABREES, 1964, No. 1410 for Vol. I] Cambridge, Mass.: M. I. T. Press, 503p. Reviews, R. V. Burks, Slav R, XXVI, 2 (Jun 1967), 326-328; Herbert J. Ellison, J Mod Hist, XXXIX, 4 (Dec 1967), 483-484; Jacques Freymond, Poli Sci Q, LXXXIII, 2 (Jun 1968), 335-336; John Gillespie, J Poli, XXIX, 2 (May 1967), 431-432; Andrew Gyorgy, Midwest J Pol Sci, XII, 1 (Feb 1968), 136-138; Ghita Ionescu, Int Aff, XLIV, 2 (Apr 1967), 341-342; Bernard S. Morris, Prob Comm, XVII, 5-6 (May-Jun 1968), 57-58; H. E. Salisbury, Sat

Rev, XLIX, June 11, 52; Geoffrey Stern, Sov St, XIX, 3 (Jan 1967) 451-452.

215. Hayward, J. E. S. "Leninizing China and Sinicizing Lenin." Political Studies, XIV, 1 (Feb), 95-99.

216. Labedz, Leopold. "Foreign Policy in a Polycentric World: Twenty Years After." Survey, No. 58 (Jan), 3-9.

217. _____., ed. International Communism After Khrushchev. [See ABREES, 1965, No. 236] Reviews, A. T. Bouscaren, Ann Am Acad Pol Soc Sci, CCCLXIV (Mar), 203-204; Peter J. Fliess, J Poli, XVIII, 3 (Aug), 686-687; Frank Knopfelmacher, Austral J Pol Hist, XII, 1 (May), 107-109.

218. Lowenthal, Richard. World Communism: The Disintegration of a Secular Faith. NY: Oxford U Press, 296p.

219. Lubasz, Heinz, ed. Revolutions in Modern European History. NY: Macmillan, 136p.

220. McNeal, Robert H. "The Legacy of the Comintern." Int J, XXI, 2 (Spring), 199-204.

221. Moore, Barrington, Jr. Social Origins of Dictatorship and Democracy: Lord and Peasant in the Making of the Modern World. Boston: Beacon Press, 578p. Reviews, G. A. Almond, Am Pol Sci R, LXI, 3 (Sept 1967), 768; Reinhard Bendix, Poli Sci Q, LXXXII, 4 (Dec 1967), 625; C. E. Black, Am Hist R, LXXII, 4 (Jul 1967), 1338; Joseph Featherstone, New Republic, CLVI, Jan 7, 1967, 34; W. L. Gundersheimer, The Reporter, XXXVI, Mar 9, 1967, 58; Edith M. Link, J Econ Hist, XXVII, 2 (Jun 1967), 261-2; G. D. Ness, Am Soc R, XXXII (Oct 1967), 818; Gilbert Shapiro, ibid., 821; J. H. Plumb, NY Times Book Rev, Oct 9, p. 10; Michael Rogin, Book Week, Jan 1, 1967, p. 5; H. L. Stinchcombe, Harvard Educational

Review, XXXVII, 3 (Sept 1967), 290; Lawrence Stone, NY Rev of Books, IX, Aug 24, 1967, p. 31; Virg Q R, XLIII (Autumn 1967), 154; TLS, Dec 21, 1967, p. 1231; C. V. Woodward, Yale R, LVI (Mar 1967), 450.

222. Morris, Bernard S. International Communism and American Policy. NY: Atherton Press, 179p. Reviews, Anthony T. Bouscaren, J Poli, XXX, 2 (May 1968), 546-548; F. L. Carsten, Prob Comm, XVI, 1-2 (Jan-Feb 1967), 61; Wright Miller, Int Aff, XLIV, 1 (Jan 1968), 85-86.

223. Rubinstein, Alvin Z. Communist Political Systems. Englewood Cliffs, N.J.: Prentice-Hall, 399p. Review, Harry Hanak, Slav East Eur R, XLV, 105 (Jul 1967), 572-573.

224. Sworakowski, Witold S. The Communist International and its Front Organizations. [See ABREES, 1965, No. 9] Reviews, John C. Campbell, Russ R, XXV, 3 (Jul), 317-318; F. L. Carsten, Slav East Eur R, XLV, 104 (Jan 1967), 266-267.

See also: 26, 27, 28, 1209, 1212

ANTI-COMMUNISM IN THE WEST

225. Bedriy, Anatol W. "For a New U.S. Foreign Policy." Ukr R, XIII, 1 (Spring), 33-37.

226. Dobriansky, Lev E. "The Traditional Captive Nations Week." Ukr Q, XXII, 2 (Summer), 107-121.

227. Hyde, Douglas A. Dedication and Leadership: Learning from the Communists. South Bend, Ind.: U Notre Dame Press, 157p.

228. Miller, Donald Lane. Strategy for Conquest. A Study of Communist Propaganda Techniques. Washington: Public Affairs Press, 74p. Review, Vernon C. Warren, Jr., West Poli Q, XX, 1 (Mar 1967), 234-235.

RELIGION-GENERAL

229. Ciszek, Walter J. "Religion Under Communism." ACEN News, no. 123 (May-Jun), 3-5.

230. Kindermann, Adolf. "Churches Under Communist Persecution." Cent Eur J/Sud Bull, XIV, 5 (May), 153-163.

VII. LINGUISTICS

SLAVIC AND BALTIC GENERAL

231. Akhmanova, O. S., I. A. Mel'chuk, R. M. Frumkin, and E. V. Paducheva. Exact Methods in Linguistic Research. David C. Hays, Dolores V. Mohr, trs. The Rand Corporation. Berkeley, Los Angeles: U California Press, 186p. (1963) Review, Stanley Newman, Rom Philol, XIX, 4 (May), 594-596.

232. Bidwell, Charles E. "A Note on the Reflexes of Borrowed Velar Plus Front Vowel in Early Post-Common Slavic." St Philol, LXIII, 4 (Jul), 589-592.

233. Buch, Tamara, and Zuzanna Topolinska. "Remarks on the Syntactic Influences of German on Neighboring Non-German Dialects." Int J Slav Ling Poet, X, pp. 103-110.

234. Fishman, Joshua A. et al., eds. Language Loyalty in the United States: The Maintenance and Perpetuation of Non-English Mother Tongues by American Ethnic and Religious Groups. The Hague: Mouton, 478p. (Janua Linguarum, Series Maior, 21). Review, J. B. Rudnyckyj, Lang, XLIV, 1 (Mar 1968), 198-201.

235. Hamm, Josip. "Entrophy in Slavic Morphology." Int J Slav Ling Poet, X, pp. 39-51.

236. Leont'ev, A. A. Iazykoznanie i psikhologiia. Moscow: Nauka, 80p. [Linguistics and Psychology] Review, G. Koolemans Beynen, Slav East Eur J, XII, 2 (Summer 1968), 229.

237. Lightner, Theodore M. "On the Phonology of the Old Church Slavonic Conjugation." Int J Slav Ling Poet, X, pp. 1-28.

238. Mareš, F. V. The Origin of the Slavic Phonological System. [See ABREES, 1965, No. 298] Review, William A. Schmalstieg, Slav East Eur J, X, 3 (Fall), 351-354.

239. Otrebski, Jan. "Jan Otrebski's Works on Baltic Linguistics." L. Dambriunas, comp. Litua, XII, 3 (Feb), 74-80.

240. Schmalstieg, William A. "The Preposition 'S' and the Instrumental." Slav East Eur J, X, 2 (Summer), 179-180.

240a. Senn, Alfred. "The Relationships of Baltic and Slavic," in Ancient Indo-European Dialects. Henrik Birnbaum and Jaan Puhvel, eds. Proceedings of the Conference on Indo-European Linguistics Held at the University of California, Los Angeles, April 25-27, 1963. Berkeley and Los Angeles: U of California Press, pp. 139-151.

241. Shevelov, G. Y. A Prehistory of Slavic: The Historical Phonology of Common Slavic. [See ABREES, 1965, No. 302] Reviews, Horace G. Lunt, Slav East Eur J, X, 1 (Spring), 85-92; Joseph A. Van Campen, Int J Slav Ling Poet, pp. 52-81.

242. Stang, C. S. "'Metatonie Douce' in Baltic." Int J Slav Ling Poet, X, pp. 111-119.

See also: 990, 1839

URALIC-ALTAIC-GENERAL

242a. Bako, Elemer. "The Minor Finno-Ugric Languages." Q J Lib Cong, XXIII, 2 (Apr), 117-138.

243. Collinger, Björn. An Introduction to the Uralic Languages. [See ABREES, 1965, No. 307] Review,

G. F. Cushing, Slav East Eur R, XLVI, 106 (Jan 1968), 220-221.

243a. Decsy, Gyula. Yurak Chrestomathy. Bloomington, Ind.: Indiana U Press, 489p. [Indiana U Publications, Uralic and Altaic Series, 50]

See also: 1597

VIII. LITERATURE AND THE ARTS

COMPARATIVE LITERATURE

244. De Groot, Adrian. Saint Nicholas: A Psychoanalytic Study of His History and Myth. The Hague: Mouton, 211p. (1965) Review, Gustav Bychowski, American Imago, XXIII, 3 (Fall), 277-278.

245. Demaitre, Ann. "The Great Debate on Socialist Realism." Mod Lang J, L, 5 (Apr), 263-268.

246. Edgerton, William B. "Puškin, Mickiewicz and a Migratory Epigram." Slav East Eur J, X, 1 (Spring), 1-8.

247. Erlich, Victor. The Double Image: Concept of the Poet in Slavic Literatures. Johns Hopkins Press, 160p. (1965) Review, Max Reiser, J Aes Art Crit, XXIV, 3 (Spring), 453.

248. Gerschenkron, Erica, and Alexander Gerschenkron. "The Illogical Hamlet: A Note on Translatability." Texas Studies in Literature and Language, VIII, 3 (Fall), 301-336. [Discusses translations into Polish, Serbo-Croatian and Russian]

249. Herling-Grudzinski, Gustav. "Kafka in Russia." Dissent, XIII, 4 (Jul-Aug), 396-400.

250. Jakobson, Roman. Selected Writings, Vol. IV: Slavic Epic Studies. The Hague: Mouton, 751p. Reviews, Milimir Drazic, Books Abr, XLII, 2 (Spring 1968), 335-336; Felix J. Oinas, Slav East Eur J, XII, 2 (Summer 1968), 219-222.

251. Kostka, Edmund K. Schiller in Russian Literature. [See ABREES, 1965, No. 332] Reviews, W. H. Bruford, Slav East Eur R, XLV, 105 (Jul 1967), 537-539; Simon Karlinsky, Slav East Eur J, X, 1 (Spring), 108-110; Charles A. Passage, Ger R, XLI, 2 (Mar), 143-145; Heinrich A. Stammler, Russ R, XXV, 1 (Jan), 90-92; TLS, Mar 17, p. 224.

252. Kozintsev, Grigori. Shakespeare: Time and Conscience. [Nash Sovremennik: Villiam Shekspir] Joyce Vining, tr. NY: Hill and Wang, 276p. Review, Alfred Harbage, NY Times Book Rev, Aug 7, p. 4. [Kozintsev was director of the Soviet film "Hamlet"] [See also: 1392]

253. Poggioli, Renato. The Spirit of the Letter. Essays in European Literature. London: Oxford U Press, 373p. Review, TLS, Jun 23, p. 547.

254. Preminger, G. A., ed. Encyclopedia of Poetry and Poetics. Princeton, N.J.: Princeton U Press, 906p. (1965) Review, Robert W. Simmons, Jr., Slav East Eur J, X, 2 (Summer), 231-233.

255. Vočadlo, O. "Shakespeare and the Slavs." Slav East Eur R, XLIV, 102 (Jan), 36-50.

See also: 492, 980, 1021, 1050, 1058-1061, 1063, 1069, 1084, 1117, 1144, 1169, 1170, 1172, 1490, 1491

CULTURAL — POLITICAL PROBLEMS

256. Christopherson, Jens A.

The Meaning of "Democracy" as used in European Ideologies from the French to the Russian Revolution: An Historical Study in Political Language. NY: Humanities Press, 389p. Review, Thomas I. Cook, Am Hist R, LXXIII, 5 (Jun 1968), 1510-1512.

YIDDISH

See: 1244, 1252, 1260, 1708, 1718

Two. Russia and the Soviet Union

I. GENERAL REFERENCE AIDS AND BIBLIOGRAPHIES

BIBLIOGRAPHIES

257. Brožek, Josef, and Margaret Maria Brožek. "Recent Russian Books in Psychology." Contemp Psych, XI, 7 (Jul), 364-367.

258. _____, and Jiri Hoscovec. "Sovietica in English: In the Press, in the Works, on the Drawing Board, A Note." Contemp Psych, XI, 8 (Aug), 382-383.

259. Brožek, J., and J. Hoscovec. "Recent Russian Books in Psychology." Contemp Psych, XI, 9 (Sept), 460-461.

260. Carlton, Robert G., ed. Latin America in Soviet Writings: A Bibliography. Vol. I, 1917-1958; Vol. II, 1959-1964. Baltimore: Johns Hopkins Press, 257 and 311p. (The Library of Congress, Hispanic Foundation Publications, 1, 2.) Leo Okinshevich, compiler.

261. Maichel, Karol. Guide to Russian Reference Books, Vol. II (History, Auxiliary historical sciences, Ethnography and Geography). J. S. G. Simmons, ed. Stanford: Hoover Institution on War, Revolution and Peace, Stanford U Press, 297p. (Bibliographical Series, 10). Reviews, Fritz T. Epstein, Slav R, XXV, 2 (Jun), 370-372; Dorothy Libby, Am Anthro, LXVIII, 1 (Feb), 285-286.

262. _____, compiler. Soviet and Russian Newspapers at the Hoover Institution: A Catalog. Stanford: Hoover Institution, 245p. (Hoover Institution Bibliographical Series, XXIV). Review, A. Helliwell, Slav East Eur R, XLVI, no. 106 (Jan 1968), 270.

263. Vladimirov, Lev. "Soviet Centralized Bibliography: Its Strengths and Weaknesses." Coll Res Lib, XXVII, 3 (May), 185-190.

264. Widener Library. Russian History Since 1917. "Widener Library Shelflist, no. 4." Cambridge, Mass.: Harvard U Press, 698p. Review, Fritz T. Epstein, Slav East Eur J, XXII, 2 (Summer 1968), 264.

265. Zvorykin, Anatoly A. "A Structural Analysis of Publications in the Field of Social Studies in the Soviet Union, 1960-1965." Social Research, XXXIII, 4 (Winter), 552-561.

See also: 291, 499, 560

BIOGRAPHICAL AND AUTOBIOGRAPHICAL MATERIALS

266. Almedingen, Edith Martha. The Emperor Alexander I. NY: Vanguard Press, 257p. Reviews, Hans Kohn, Sat Rev, XLIX, Sept 17, p. 38; Hugh Ragsdale, Russ R, XXVI, 2 (Apr 1968), 196-197; TLS, Jun 4, 1964, p. 490.

267. Bashkirtseff, Marie. Marie and the Duke of H: The Daydream Love Affair of Marie Bashkirtseff. Doris Langley Moore, ed. Philadelphia: Lippincott, 304p. Reviews, Anne Freemantle, NY Times Book Rev, Oct 25, p. 10; TLS, Jul 28, p. 669. [Excerpts from the diary of Marie Bashkirtseff]

268. Blackstock, Paul W. "'Books for Idiots': False Soviet 'Memoirs'." Russ R, XXV, 3 (Jul), 285-296.

269. Hackel, Sergei. One of Great Price. The Life of Mother Maria Skobtsova, Martyr of Ravensbrück. London: Darton, Longman and Todd, 136p. Review, Hélène Iswolsky,

Russ R, XXVI, 1 (Jan 1967), 82. [See item 285]

270. Katz, Martin. Mikhail N. Katkov: A Political Biography, 1818-1887. The Hague: Mouton, 195p. Reviews, Hugh Seton-Watson, Slav East Eur R, XLVI, 106 (Jan 1968), 267-269; Edward C. Thaden, Russ R, XXVII, 1 (Jan 1968), 103-104.

Khrushchev

271. Achminov, Herman. "The Activities of a Soviet Leader." Bull Inst St USSR, XIII, 1 (Jan), 16-28.

272. Chamberlin, William Henry. "The Trend After Khrushchev: Immobilism." Russ R, XXV, 1 (Jan), 3-9.

273. Conquest, Robert. Russia After Khrushchev. [See ABREES, 1965, No. 866] Reviews, M. Hookham, Int Aff, XLII, 2 (Apr), 307-308; Louis Nemzer, Russ R, XXV, 2 (Apr), 184-187; P. B. Reddaway, Sov St, XVIII, 1 (Jul), 96-98.

274. Crankshaw, Edward. Khrushchev: A Career. NY: Viking, 320p. Reviews, Richard T. Davies, Prob Comm, XVI, 4 (Jul-Aug 1967), 64-66; Walter Dushnyck, Ukr Q, XXII, 4 (Winter), 364-366; Henry Krisch, Poli Sci Q, LXXXIII, 1 (Mar 1968), 106-107; Carl A. Linden, Slav R, XXVI, 3 (Sept 1967), 492-493; Philip E. Mosely, Mod Age, XI, 1 (Winter 1966-1967), 110-111; Myron Rush, Am Pol Sci R, LXI, 1 (Mar 1967), 199; Harrison Salisbury, NY Times Book Rev, Jun 19, p.1+; D.W. Treadgold, Am Hist R, LXXII, 2 (Apr 1967), 1041-1042; Robert C. Tucker, Book Week, CXI, no. 40, Jun 12, p.3; Paul Wilkinson, Contemp R, CCIX, no. 1211 (Dec), 328-329; TLS, Oct 27, p.971-972.

275. Deutscher, Isaac. "The Failure of Khrushchevism." The Socialist Register, 1965, pp.30-44. [See item 12]

276. Kenez, Peter. "Khrushchev:

Before and After." Prob Comm, XV, 6 (Nov-Dec), 71-77.

277. Linden, Carl A. Khrushchev and the Soviet Leadership. Baltimore: Johns Hopkins Press, 270p. Reviews, Violet Conolly, Slav East Eur R, XLVI, 106 (Jan 1968), 261-262; Roger A. Kanet, Russ R, XXII, 3 (Jul 1967), 312-313; George A. Lanyi, East Eur, XVI, 4 (Apr 1967), 55-56; Roger Pethybridge, Sov St, XIX, 2 (Oct 1967), 285-286; Sidney I. Ploss, Am Pol Sci R, LXI, 4 (Dec 1967), 1151; Myron Rush, Poli Sci Q, LXXXIII, 3 (Sept 1968), 447-449; Myron Rush, Slav R, XXVII, 3 (Sept 1968), 492-494; TLS, May 4, 1967, p.371.

278. Page, Martin, and David Burg. Unpersoned: The Fall of Nikita Sergeyevitch Khrushchev. London: Chapman and Hall, 174p. Reviews, R.W. Pethybridge, Poli Q, XXXVII, 3 (Jul-Sept), 344-346; P. B. Reddaway, Sov St, XVIII, 1 (Jul), 96-98.

279. Seton-Watson, Hugh. "The Khrushchev Era." Survey, 58 (Jan), 187-195.

---

280. Littauer, Vladimir S. Russian Hussar. [See ABREES, 1965, No. 382] Review, TLS, Jun 2, 498.

281. Lukashevich, Stephen. Ivan Aksakov. [See ABREES, 1965, No. 384] Reviews, Edward J. Brown, Slav R, XXVI, 4 (Dec 1967), 698-699; Joseph Frank, Russ R, XXVI, 1 (Jan), 78-80; Maurice Friedberg, Slav East Eur J, XI, 1 (Spring 1967), 95-96; Hugh Seton-Watson, Slav East Eur R, XLVI, 106 (Jan 1968), 267-269; TLS, May 19, p.458.

281a. Maiskii, Ivan Mikhailovich. Spanish Notebooks. Ruth Kisch, tr. London: Hutchinson, 208p. [Notes of a Russian diplomat during the Spanish Civil War]

282. Nicolaevsky, Boris I. Power and the Soviet Elite. [See ABREES,

1965, No. 386] Reviews, Frederick C. Barghoorn, Ann Am Acad Pol Soc Sci, CCCLXV (May), 182-183; Stephen Cohen, Dissent, XIII, 4 (Jul-Aug), 435-438; Michael Edo, J Int Aff, XX, 1, 189-191; Henry Lane Hull, Mil Aff, XXX, 2 (Summer), 106; Naum Jasny, Sov St, XVIII, 1 (Jul), 105-107; R.W. Pethybridge, Poli Q, XXXVII, 3 (Jul-Sept), 344-346; Leonard Schapiro, NY Rev of Books, VII, 4, Sept 22, pp. 13-14; Joel Schwartz, Am Pol Sci R, LX, 2 (Jun), 439-440; Robert Slusser, Slav R, XXV, 3 (Sept), 529-531; Robert C. Tucker, Russ R, XXV, 3 (Jul), 306-307; Thomas W. Wolfe, Prob Comm, XV, 3 (May-Jun), 43-46; TLS, Feb 17, p. 118.

282a. Kristof, Ladis K.D. "Boris I. Nicolaevsky, 1887-1966." Russ R, XXV, 3 (Jul), 324-327.

283. Odom, W.E. "Sverdlov: Bolshevik Party Organizer." Slav East Eur R, XLIV, 103 (Jul), 421-443. [On Yakov Mikhailovich Sverdlov]

284. Penkovskii, Oleg. The Penkovskiy Papers. [See ABREES, 1965, No. 389] Reviews, Yaroslav Bilinsky, J Poli, XXVIII, 3 (Aug), 688-689; George A. Brinkley, R Poli, XXVIII, 2 (Apr), 253-255; Hugo Dewar, Prob Comm, XV, 4 (Jul-Aug), 54-57; Max Frankel, Atlantic Monthly, CCXVII May, p. 131; Nikolai Galay, Bull Inst St USSR, XXII, 6 (Jun), 41-48; Stefan T. Possony, Mod Age, X, 2 (Spring), 215-217; John S. Reshetar, Am Pol Sci R, LX, 2 (Jun), 401-408; Paul R. Willging, J Int Aff, XX, 2, 369-371; Thomas W. Wolfe, J Mod Hist, XXXVIII, 2 (Jun), 236-238; Richard Wraga, Russ R, XXV, 4 (Oct), 416-418; East Eur, XV, 4 (Apr), 56.

285. Smith, Stratton. The Rebel Nun: The Moving Story of Mother Maria of Paris. Springfield, Ill.: Templegate, 252p. Review, Hélène Iswolsky, Russ R, XXVI, 1 (Jan 1967), 82. [See item 269]

Stalin

286. Brandt, Conrad. Stalin's Failure in China. NY: W.W. Norton, 226p.

287. Payne, Robert. The Rise and Fall of Stalin. [See ABREES, 1965, No. 388] Review, R.H. McNeal, Russ R, XXV, 3 (Jul), 304-305; Francis B. Randall, Slav R, XXV, 2 (Jun), 343-344; TLS, Feb 17, p. 118.

288. Rigby, T.H., ed. Stalin. Englewood Cliffs, N.J.: Prentice Hall, 189p. Reviews, Robert V. Daniels, Prob Comm, XVII, 2 (Mar-Apr 1968), 65-66; Ralph Carter Elwood, Int J, XXII, 1 (Autumn 1966-67), 142-143; J. Miller, Sov St, XIX, 2 (Oct 1967), 282-283; Joseph S. Roucek, Ukr Q, XXII, 3 (Autumn), 277-280.

289. Ulam, Adam. The Bolsheviks. [See ABREES, 1965, No. 394] Reviews, George A. Brinkley, R Poli, XXX, 3 (Jul 1968), 378-383; Alexander Dallin, Ann Am Acad Pol Soc Sci, no. 367 (Sept), 188; Robert V. Daniels, Russ R, XXV, 3 (Jul), 303-304; Walter Dushnyck, Ukr Q, XXII, 2 (Summer), 179-181; Barry Hollingsworth, Slav East Eur R, XLVI, 106 (Jan 1968), 255-256; Walter Laqueur, Commentary, XLI (Mar), 100; Arthur P. Mendel, Am Hist R, LXXII, 1 (Oct), 245; Max Nomad, Sat Rev, XLVIII, Nov 20, 1965, p. 39; Alec Nove, NY Rev of Books, VII, Sept 22, pp. 25-28; Joseph A. Petrus, J Poli, XXI, 1 (Feb 1967), 183-185; Henry L. Roberts, NY Times Book Rev, Dec 26, 1965, p. 3; Tibor Szamuely, Survey, no. 60 (Jul), 164-167; TLS, Jan 12, 1967, p. 30.

290. West, Rebecca. The Birds Fall Down. NY: Viking, 435p. Reviews, Mary Ellmann, Atlantic Monthly, CCXVIII, 12 Dec, pp. 68-71; William J. Shanahan, Books Abr, XLI, 4 (Feb 1967), 468. [Novel about the activities of the spy Azef]

290a. Yarmolinsky, Avrahm. A Russian's American Dream: A Memoir on William Frey. Lawrence: U Kansas Press, 147p. (1965) Review, Robert F. Byrnes, Slav East Eur J, X, 3 (Fall), 370. [Memoir on the utopian thinker V. Gejns, who assumed the name Frey when he emigrated to America]

291. Yeremenko, A. I. The Arduous Beginning. Vic Schneiderson, tr. Moscow: Progress Publications, 329p. Review, Michael Parrish, Slav R, XXVII, 1 (Mar 1968), 139-141.

292. Zeman, Z. A. B. Merchant of Revolution. [See ABREES, 1965, No. 398] Reviews, Richard Wraga, Russ R, XXV, 2 (Apr), 192-193; Harold Shukman, Slav East Eur R, XLV, 104 (Jan 1967), 254-256. [On the career of Alexander Helphand (Parvus)]

See also: 499

RESEARCH ON THE USSR

293. Ahmad, S. H. "Survey of Recent Research: The Sino-Soviet Conflict." Int St, VII, 4 (Apr), 595-606.

294. Charavorty, A. R. "Russian Studies in India." Russ R, XXV, 3 (Jul), 297-302. [See No. 1]

295. Laqueur, Walter, and Leopold Labedz. State of Soviet Studies. [See ABREES, 1965, No. 405] Review, Albert Parry, Russ R, XXV, 2 (Apr), 206-207.

296. McNeal, Robert H. "The Study of Bolshevism: Sources and Methods." Int J, XXI, 4 (Autumn), 521-526.

297. Social Sciences in the U.S.S.R. Paris, The Hague: Mouton, 297p. Review, W. Rex Crawford, Ann Am Acad Pol Soc Sci, 371 (May 1967), 265-267; Allen H. Kassof, Slav R, XXVI, 2 (Jun 1967), 330-331.

See also: 297, 670

II. TRAVEL AND DESCRIPTION

298. Gorin, Arkadi V., as told to Leo Heiman. "Two Faces of Soviet Tourism." Ukr Q, XXII, 1 (Spring), 13-24.

299. Hall, Calvin. "Driving and Camping in Russia." Am Psych, XXI, 3 (Mar), 244.

300. Hammond, Thomas T. "An American in Moscow, Russia's Capital." Nat Geog, CXXIX, 3 (Mar), 297-352.

301. Kreusler, A. A. A Teacher's Experience in the Soviet Union. [See ABREES, 1965, No. 422] Review, Thomas D. Brandt, Slav East Eur J, X, 3 (Fall), 371-373.

302. Latham, Peter. Travel, Business, Study and Art in the U.S.S.R.

London: Blackie, 383p. [paper] Review, Sov St, XVIII, 4 (Apr 1967), 538-539.

303. McElheny, Victor K. "What the French President Saw: A Gallic View of Novosibirsk." Sci, CLIII, no. 3731 (Jul 1), 45-46.

304. Wraget, P., ed. U.S.S.R. [See ABREES, 1965, No. 437] Reviews, George Feifer, Book Week, III, 38, May 29, p. 12; R. N. North, Sov St, XVIII, 1 (Jul), 122-123.

305. Soloukhin, Vladimir. A Walk in Rural Russia. Stella Miskin, tr. NY: Dutton, 254p. Reviews, NY Times Book Rev, Apr 30, 1967, p. 32; TLS, Mar 9, 1967, p. 200.

See also: 1177

III. THE LAND

GENERAL GEOGRAPHY

306. Gibson, James R. "Archival Research on the Historical Geography of Russia." Prof Geog, XVIII, 3 (May), 164-167.

307. Hooson, David. The Soviet Union: People and Regions. Belmont, Calif.: Wadsworth Publishing Co., 376p. Review, Robert A. Lewis, Slav R, XXVI, 2 (Jun 1967), 331-334.

308. Kingsbury, Robert, and Robert N. Taaffe. An Atlas of Soviet Affairs. [See ABREES, 1965, No. 443] Review, B. Ross Guest, Russ R, XXV, 4 (Oct), 429-430.

309. Pounds, Norman J.G. Europe and the Soviet Union. 2nd ed. NY: McGraw-Hill, 528p. Review, W.H. Parker, Sov St, XVIII, 3 (Jan 1967), 392-393.

See also: 76

PHYSICAL GEOGRAPHY

310. Barr, Brenton M. "The Importance of Regions in Analyses of the Soviet Forest Resource." Can Geog, X, 4, 234-239. [A reply to R. M. Bone, no. 311; see also 314]

311. Bone, Robert M. "The Soviet Forest Reserve." Can Geog, X, 2, pp. 94-116. [See also 310 and 314]

312. Borisov, A. A. Climates of the U.S.S.R. Cyril A. Halstead, ed. R. A. Ledward, tr. [See ABREES,

1965, No. 445] Reviews, B. Ross Guest, Prof Geog, XVIII, 3 (May), 178-179; Theodore Shabad, Slav R, XXV, 2 (Jun), 366-367.

ECONOMIC GEOGRAPHY

313. Hutchings, Raymond. "Geographic Influences on Centralization in the Soviet Economy." Sov St, XVII, 3 (Jan), 286-302.

314. Tseplyaev, V.P. The Forests of the U.S.S.R. A. Gourevitch, tr. Israel Program for Scientific Translations, 1965; NY: Davey, 527p. Review, David J.M. Hooson, Sci, CLIV, no. 3747 (Oct 21), 574-575. [See also 310 and 311]

REGIONS AND CITIES

315. Hall, Peter. The World Cities. London: Weidenfeld and Nicolson, 256p. [Discusses Moscow] Review, Geog J, CXXXII, 3 (Sept), 429-430.

316. Hoyt, Homer. "Growth and Structure of Twenty-One Great World Cities." Land Economics, XL, 1 (Feb), 53-64.

317. Swithinbank, Charles. "A Year with the Russians in Antarctica." Geog J, CXXXII, 4 (Dec), 463-475. [See also 310]

See also: 80, 468, 498, 511, 556, 566, 791, 1301

IV. ARCHAEOLOGY, DEMOGRAPHY, ETHNOGRAPHY

317a. Allen, Robert V. "Alaska Before 1867 in Soviet Literature." Q J Lib Cong, XXIII, 3 (Jul), 243-250.

318. Armstrong, Terence E. Russian Settlement in the North. [See ABREES, 1965, No. 461] Reviews, `C. L. Drage, Slav East Eur R, XLVI, 106 (Jan 1968), 242-243; Raymond H. Fisher, Russ R, XXV, 4 (Oct), 418-419; George A. Lensen, J Asian St, XXV, 3 (May), 539-540; I. Norman Smith, Int J, XXV, 4 (Autumn), 566-567.

319. Berelson, Bernard, et al., eds. Family Planning and Population Programs. A Review of World Developments. Chicago: U Chicago Press, 848p.

320. Hajenko, F. "Unemployment and Manpower Migration in the USSR." Bull Inst St USSR, XIII, 6 (Jun), 27-34.

321. Hewes, Gordon W. Review, S. V. Bruk and V. S. Appenchenko, eds. Atlas narodov mira. Am Anthro, LXVIII, 2 (Apr), 532-534.

322. Lewis, Robert A., and J. William Leasure. Population Changes in Russia and the U.S.S.R.: A Set of Comparable Territorial Units. San Diego: San Diego State College Press, 43p. Review, Chauncey D. Harris, Slav R, XXVI, 3 (Sept 1967), 501.

323. _____. "Regional Population Changes in Russia and the U.S.S.R. Since 1851." Slav R, XXV, 4 (Dec), 663-668.

323a. Okladnikov, Aleksei P. The Soviet Far East in Antiquity: An Archaeological and Historical Study of the Maritime Region of the U.S.S.R. Henry M. Michael, ed. Toronto: U Toronto Press, 280p. (1965) [Anthropology of the North: Translations from Russian Sources, vol. 6]

324. Sakoff, Alexandre N. "Rural Population and Agricultural Labor Force in the U.S.S.R." Mo Bull Agric Econ Stat, XV, 7-8 (Jul-Aug), 1-10.

See also: 414, 433, 777, 778, 1283, 1314

V. THE NATION, CIVILIZATIONS AND POLITICS

THE NATIONAL QUESTION

325. Zelenetsky, Oleh. "Historical View of Soviet Russian Nationalities Policy." Ukr R, XIII, 1 (Spring), 78-83.

See also: 1216

UKRAINICA

1. Bibliography

326. Bedriy, Anatol W. "Problems of Acquisition of Materials on Ukraine in the Humanities and Social Sciences." Ukr R, XIII, 3 (Autumn), 45-78.

327. _____. "Survey of Holdings by the Columbia Libraries on Ukraine (in the field of social sciences)." Ukr R, XIII, 4 (Winter), 93-96.

See also: 13, 21, 21a

2. History and Foreign Relations

328. Andrusiak, Nicholas. "Ukraine in the Twentieth Century: A Brief Survey." Ukr Q, XXII, 2 (Summer), 152-163.

329. Bohdaniuk, Volodymyr. "Ukrainian Thermopylae (The Battle of Kruty - 29.1.1918)." Ukr R, XIII, 1 (Spring), 3-6.

330. _____. "Symon Petlura — National Hero of Ukraine." Ukr R, XIII, 2 (Summer), 6-12.

331. Donzow, D. "Why was Petlura Murdered?" Ukr R, XIII, 3 (Autumn), 55-61.

332. Harvey, Elizabeth Anne. "The Norman Conquest of England and its Connection with Old Ukraine." Ukr R, XIII, 4 (Winter), 33-53.

333. Kuchar, Roman V. "Marginal Remarks on a Notorious Fallacy." Ukr R, XIII, 1 (Spring), 38-42. [On literature of Kievan times]

334. Mackiw, Theodore. "Ukraine as seen by the 'London Gazette' (1665-1965)." Ukr R, XIII, 1 (Spring), 71-77.

335. Martin, Neil A. "The Brotherhood of SS. Cyril and Methodius, 1845-1846." Ukr Q, XXII, 3 (Autumn), 260-271.

336. Nakashidze, Niko. "And Yet Not Conquered! Ukrainian Nationalism and the A. B. N. Attacked in the Soviet Press." Ukr R, XIII, 1 (Spring), 7-16. [Anti-Bolshevik Bloc of Nations]

337. Ohloblyn, Alexander. "Michael Hrushevsky — Foremost Ukrainian Historian. On the Centennial of His Birth, 1866-1966." Ukr Q, XXII, 4 (Winter), 322-333.

338. Pidhainy, Oleh Semenovych. The Formation of the Ukrainian Republic. The Ukrainian Republic in the Great East-European Revolution, vol. 1. Toronto: New Review Books, 685p. Review, Arthur E. Adams, Am Hist R, LXXII, 4 (Jul 1967), 1451-1452.

339. Shankowsky, Lew. "Ukrainian Liberation Struggle." Ukr R, XIII, 2 (Summer), 13-31.

340. Stetzko, Slava. "Ukraine and the Unity of Europe." Ukr R, XIII, 4 (Winter), 2-7.

341. Trembicky, Walter. "National Coat-of-Arms and Flag of Ukraine." Ukr Q, XXII, 4 (Autumn), 343-350.

3. Politics, government and law

342. Bohdaniuk, Volodymyr. "Further Trials of Ukrainian Intellectuals." Ukr R, XIII, 4 (Winter), 90-93.

343. Roucek, Joseph S. "Revival of Stalinism." Ukr Q, XXII, 3 (Autumn), 225-236.

344. Strauss, Wolfgang. "Moscow's Achilles' Heel: Ukraine." Ukr R, XIII, 2 (Summer), 51-53.

4. Education

345. Yendyk, R. "The Ukrainian Technico-Economic Institute in Munich Marks its 20th Anniversary." Ukr R, XIII, 2 (Summer), 56-59.

5. Language and Literature

346. Franko, Ivan. "Easter Day" and "The Idyll." Vera Rich, tr. Ukr R, XIII, 3 (Autumn), 22-26.

347. Gaboda, Mary. "Ivan Franko's First Love." Ukr R, XIII, 4 (Winter), 54-65.

348. Görlich, Joachim G. "Ukrainian Literature between Persecution and Thaw." Ukr R, XIII, 2 (Summer), 49-50.

349. Kotsyubynsky, Mykhaylo. "The Christmas Tree." [story] Ukr R, XIII, 4 (Winter), 72-78.

350. Kuchar, Roman V. "R. Volodymyr: Poems." Ukr R, XIII, 1 (Spring), 45-48. [Volodymyr is Kuchar's pseudonym]

351. Malaniuk, Euhen. "Ivan Franko as a Manifestation of the Intellect." Ukr R, XIII, 3 (Autumn), 16-21.

352. Nytchenko, D. "Extinction of Ukrainian Literature and Arts under

Russian Occupation." Ukr R, XIII, 4 (Winter), 8-16.

353. Pelenski, Jaroslaw. "Recent Ukrainian Writing." Survey, no. 59 (Apr), 102-112.

354. Rich, Vera. "Elizabeth, the Wise-King's Daughter." [poem] Ukr R, XIII, 3 (Autumn), 2. [On the daughter of Yaroslav the Wise]

355. _____. "Ivan Franko and the English Poets." Ukr Q, XXII, 2 (Summer), 122-128.

356. Siehs, Karl. "A Great European Mind: Ivan Yakovych Franko. On the occasion of the fiftieth anniversary of his death." Ukr R, XIII, 3 (Autumn), 3-15.

357. Slavutych, Yar. "Taras Shevchenko in Literary Criticism." Proceedings of the IVth Congress of the International Comparative Literature Association. The Hague: Mouton, 317-320.

357a. _____. Ukrainian Literature in Canada. Edmonton, Alberta: Slavuta, 15p.

358. _____. "Ukrainian Onomastics II." Names, XIV, 3 (Sept), 161-168. [See item 362]

359. Symonenko, Vasyl. "A Dairy Which Horrified Moscow." Ukr Q, XXII, 2 (Summer), 164-168. [Excerpts from Symonenko's diary]

360. _____. "From Vasyl Symonenko's Diary." Ukr R, XXII, 1 (Spring), 48-52.

361. _____. "The Law Court;" "Loneliness." Ukr R, XXII, 2 (Summer), 48. [poems]

362. Zyla, Wolodymyr T. "Ukrainian Onomastics I." Names, XIV, 2 (Jun), 109-120. [See item 358]

See also: 1003, 1403

6. Philosophy

363. D(ziuba), I(van). "Ivan

Dziuba on Hryhory Skovoroda." Ukr R, XIII, 3 (Autumn), 67-70.

7. Arts, Music, Folklore

364. Lutsiv, Volodymyr. "Kobza-Bandura and 'Dumy' and Their Significance in the History of the Ukrainian People." Ukr R, XIII, 1 (Spring), 53-70. [Music and epic poetry]

365. Pauls, John P. Great Maecenas of the Arts Glorified by Painters." Ukr R, XIII, 4 (Winter), 17-32. [Ivan Mazeppa]

366. Senkiv, Ivan. "Traditional Christmas Festivities in Ukraine." Ukr R, XIII, 4 (Winter), 66-71.

BALTICA

The Baltic Countries

367. Anderson, Edgar. "Toward the Baltic Union, 1920-1927." Litua, XII, 2 (Summer), 30-56.

368. Balkunas, John. "Baltic Exiles Continue Struggle for Freedom." Ukr Q, XXII, 2 (Summer), 129-136.

369. Dunn, Stephen P. Cultural Processes in the Baltic Area Under Soviet Rule. Institute of International Studies, Research Series no. 11. Berkeley: U of California Press, 92p. Review, R. Beermann, Sov St, XIX, 2 (Oct 1967), 300-301.

370. "Postscript on U.S. Recognition of the Baltic States in 1922." Litua, XII, 1 (Spring), 90-91.

371. R(emeikis), T(homas) P. "Party Congresses in the Baltic Republics." Litua, XII, 1 (Spring), 84-89.

372. Schnorf, Richard A. "The Baltic States in U.S.-Soviet Relations, 1939-1942." Litua, XII, 1 (Spring), 33-53.

373. _____. "The Baltic States in U.S.-Soviet Relations: The Years of Doubt, 1943-1946." Litua, XII, 4 (Winter), 58-75.

374. "Soviet Colonialism in the Baltic States." Balt R, no. 32 (Oct), 4-17.

375. Tarulis, Albert N. American-Baltic Relations, 1918-1922. [See ABREES, 1965, No. 559] Reviews, Louis L. Gerson, Am Hist R, LXXI, 2 (Jan), 516-517; Alfred Erich Senn, J Mod Hist, XXXVIII, 1 (Mar), 110-111.

376. Vardys, V. Stanley. "How the Baltic Republics Fare in the Soviet Union." For Aff, XL, 3 (Apr), 512-517.

See also: 239, 242, 481, 515

Estonia

377. Ivask, George. "Eight Estonian Poets." Balt R, no. 21 (Apr), 17-21. [Review article on Ivask's Acht Estnische Dichter (Stockholm, 1965). Ants Oras, tr. Deals with Betti Alver, Bernard Kangro, Uku Masing, Aleksis Rannit, Gustav Suits, Heiti Talvik, Marie Under, Henrik Visnapuu]

378. Jürma, Mall. Basic Course in Estonian. The Hague: Mouton, 399p. Indiana U Publications, Uralic and Altaic Series, 54. Review, Felix J. Oinas, Slav East Eur J, XII, 1 (Spring 1968), 102-103.

379. _____. "Literature in Estonia." Balt R, 32 (Oct), 28-40.

380. Lehiste, Ilse. Consonant Quality and Phonological Units in Estonian. Uralic and Altaic Series, 65. Bloomington, Ind.: Indiana U Press, 73p. Reviews, Robert T. Harms, Lang, XLIV, 2, pt.1 (Jun 1968), 407-409; Elizabeth T. Uldall, Lingua, XX, 3 (Oct 1968), 327-329.

380a. Oinas, Felix J. Basic Course in Estonian. Bloomington, Ind.: Indiana U Press, 408p. (Indiana U Publications, Uralic and Altaic Series, 54). Reviews, Mall Jürma, Slav East Eur J, XII, 1 (Spring 1968),

102-103; Ilse Lehiste, Lang, XLIV, 2, pt. 1 (Jun 1968), pp. 409-411.

380b. Vahter, Arthur, and L. Normet. Music in the Estonian S.S.R. Tallinn: Eesti Raamat, 46 p. (1965)

Latvia

381. Fetler, James. "The Dust of Yuri Serafimovich." Atlantic Monthly, CXVII, 6, Jun, pp. 63-69. [Short story about the Russian colony in San Francisco by a Latvian émigré]

382. Lazdina, Tereza Budina. Teach Yourself Latvian. London: English Universities Press, 341p. Review, Pauline B. Alksnis, Slav East Eur R, XLV, 104 (Jan 1967), 264-265.

383. Remeikis, Thomas. "A Latvian in the Politbureau: A Political Portrait of Arvids Pelše." Litua, XII, 1 (Spring), 81-83.

383a. Zeps, Valdis J. "Latvian rība 'boletus edulis'." Slav East Eur J, X, 3 (Fall), 313-315.

Lithuania

384. Dambriunas, Leonardas, Antanas Klimas, and William R. Schmalstieg. Introduction to Modern Lithuanian. Brooklyn, N.Y.: Franciscan Fathers Press, 471p. Reviews, B. Ciplijauskaite, Slav East Eur J, XII, 1 (Spring 1968), 103-104; Theodore M. Lightner, Int J Slav Ling Poet, XII (1969), 202-204.

385. Ford, Gordon B. "The Unjustifiable Nasal Vowels in Vilentas' Enchiridion." Welt Slav, XI, 1-2, pp. 176-179. [Lithuanian document of 1579 by Baltramiejus Vilentas]

386. Ivinskis, Zenonas. "The Lithuanian Revolt Against the Soviets in 1941." Litua, XII, 2 (Summer), 5-19. [Part of an article from Vardys, V., ed. Lithuania Under the Soviets.] [See ABREES, 1965, No. 621, and 1966, 401]

387. Jonaitis, Demie. "Two Poems." Litua, XII, 2 (Summer), 70-71.

388. Kavolis, Vytautas. "Faith in Exile: The Decomposition and Re-constitution of God in the Poetry of Algimantas Mackus." Litua, XII, 3 (Fall), 5-14.

389. Matulis, Anatole C. Lithu-anian Culture in Modern German Prose Literature. Vienna: R. Spies, 166p. Review, George W. Radimersky, Litua, XII, 2 (Summer), 77-79.

390. ____. "Lithuanian Folk-song as a Philosophical 'Leitmotif' in German Literature: Ernst Wie-chert [1887-1950]." Litua, XII, 4 (Winter), 49-55.

391. Mekas, Jonas. "Two Poems." Clark Mills, tr. Litua, XII, 1 (Spring), 70-73.

392. Ostrauskas, Kostas. "The Gravediggers [Excerpt from the play]." Litua, XII, 3 (Fall), 15-24.

393. Rubikas, Jonas. "Lysenko in Lithuania: Some Revelations Twenty Years After." Litua, XII, 3 (Fall), 65-67.

394. Savasis, Jonas. "Child, School, and God in Lithuania." ACEN News, 123 (Mar-Jun), 6-12.

395. ____. "Religious Persecu-tion in Lithuania." Balt R, 31 (Apr), 22-63; 32 (Oct), 41-55. [Digest of the author's book, item 368]

396. ____. The War Against God in Lithuania. NY: Manyland Books. Review, Daniel L. Flaherty, Litua, XII, 2 (Summer), 75-76.

397. Schmalstieg, William R. "An English-Speaker Studies Lithua-nian." Litua, XII, 3 (Fall), 68-70.

397a. Senn, Alfred. Handbuch der Litauischen Sprache, I: Gram-matik. Heidelberg: Carl Winter, 495p. Reviews, Friedrich Scholz, Int J Slav Ling Poet, XII (1969), 194-202;

Valdis J. Zeps, Slav East Eur J, XII, 4 (Winter 1968), 493.

398. Škėma, Antanas. "Three Poems." Aldona and Robert Page, and Mariejo Fonsale, trs. Litua, XII, 4 (Winter), 24-25.

399. Šilbajoris, Rimvydas. "The Tragedy of Creative Consciousness in the Literary Heritage of Antanas Škėma." Litua, XII, 4 (Winter), 5-23.

399a. Stukas, Jack J. Awakening Lithuania: A Study on the Rise of Modern Lithuanian Nationalism. Mad-ison, N.J.: Florham Park Press, 187p.

400. Tautrimas, R. "Cultural Discrimination in Lithuania: The Problem of the Cultural Press." Litua, XII, 1 (Spring), 21-32.

401. Vardys, Vitas Stanley, ed. Lithuania Under the Soviets. [See ABREES, 1965, No. 621] Reviews, David T. Cattell, West Poli Q, XIX, 1 (Mar), 205-206; Robert H. Herrick, Int J, XXI, 2 (Spring), 264-265; Tibor Payzs, Am Pol Sci R, LX, 1 (Jan), 157-158; Bronius B. Vaskelis, Russ R, XXV, 1 (Jan), 106. [See also 386]

402. Vaštokas, R. "Image of the Partisan." Litua, XII, 4 (Winter), 26-48. [Partisan theme in Lithuanian literature]

403. Velaikis, Jonas. "Lithuanian Literature Under the Soviets." Litua, XII, 3 (Fall), 25-43.

404. Venclova, Antanas. "Return to the Capital: Memoirs." Litua, XII, 3 (Fall), 44-54.

405. XY. "A Nightmare or Real-ity: Excerpts from Lithuanian Under-ground Literature." Litua, XII, 1 (Spring), 5-20.

CENTRAL ASIA

406. Allworth, Edward. Central Asian Publishing. [See ABREES, 1965, No. 629] Review Panas Fedenko, St Sov Un, V, 4, 139-141.

407. Bacon, Elizabeth E. Central Asians Under Russian Rule. A Study in Culture Change. Ithaca: Cornell U Press, 273p. Reviews, Owen Lattimore, Ann Am Acad Pol Soc Sci, CCCLXXI (May 1967), 232; Alexander G. Park, Slav R, XXVI, 2 (Jun 1967), 349-350; Richard A. Pierce, Am Pol Sci R, LX, 3 (Sept 1967), 832; J. W. Strong, Pac Aff, XL, 1 (Spring-Summer 1967), 200; Donald W. Treadgold, Am Hist R, LXX, 3 (Jul 1967), 1449; Geoffrey Wheeler, Prob Comm, XVI, 5 (Sept-Oct 1967), 135.

408. Bairamov, E. "Points to Keep in Mind When Talking with Devotees of Islam." Prob Peop USSR, no. 26 (Winter 1966), 31-38.

409. Bennigsen, Alexandre, and Chantal Lemercier-Quelquejay. "The History of the Kazakh Press, 1900-1920." Cent Asian R, XIV, 2, pp. 151-163. [Tr. from the book of the authors, La Presse et le mouvement national chez les musulmans de Russie avant 1920 (Paris, 1964)] Review, Serge A. Zenkovsky, Slav R, XXV, 2 (Jun), 339-341.

410. Davletshin, Tamurbek. "Soviet Colonialism in Turkestan." St Sov Un, V, 3, pp. 28-37.

411. Dunn, Stephen P. "Comments on Krader's Review of 'Peoples of Siberia'." Am Anthro, LXVIII, 2 (Apr), 519-521. [M. G. Levin and L. P. Potapov, Narody Sibiri, 1956. [See ABREES, 1964, No. 172] Review, L. Krader, Am Anthro, LXVII, 2 (Apr 1965), 575-577].

412. Evans, Hubert. "New Soviet Books." Mid East St, II, 2 (Jan), 157-163; II, 4 (Jul), 367-372; III, 1 (Oct), 68-73.

413. _____. "Russian Research on Ulugh Beg." Cent Asian R, XIV, 3, pp. 270-273.

414. Frumkin, Gregoire, "Archaeology in Soviet Central Asia. VII. Turkmenistan." Cent Asian R, XIV, 1, pp. 71-90.

415. Frye, Richard N. Bukhara. [See ABREES, 1965, No. 637] Reviews, Richard R. Antoun, Ethnohistory, XIII, 3-4 (Summer-Fall), 192-194; Gustav Glaesser, East and West, N.S., XVI, 3-4 (Sept-Dec), 345-347.

415a. Glaesser, Gustav. Review of Akademiia Nauk SSSR. Institut iazykoznaniia. Iazyki narodov SSSR. Vol. I: Indo-European languages, II: Turkic languages. In: East and West, N.S., XVI, 3-4 (Sept-Dec), 349-352.

416. Higgins, Humphrey. "Petr Kuz'mich Kozlov (1863-1935) and the Discovery of Karakhoto." Cent Asian R, XIV, 4, pp. 330-340.

417. _____. "Obruchev's Travels in Mongolia." Cent Asian R, XIV, 2, pp. 123-138.

418. Khalfin, N. A. The Joining of Central Asia to Russia. [Prisoedinenie Srednei Azii k Rossii, 1965] Reviews, Hubert Evans, Cent Asian R, XIV, 4, pp. 350-351; TLS, Jul 21, p. 632.

419. _____. Russia's Policy in Central Asia, 1857-1868. Hubert Evans, tr. London: Central Asian Research Center, 107p. (1964) Reviews, Richard A. Pierce, Mid East J, XX, 2 (Spring), 245-246; D. S. M. Williams, Slav East Eur R, XLIV, 102-103 (Jan-Jul), 232.

420. Klein, Richard C. "Chellean and Acheulean on the Territory of the Soviet Union; a Critical Review of Evidence as Presented in the Literature." Am Anthro, special publication, vol. LXVIII, 2, pt. 2, (Apr), 1-45.

421. Knobloch, Edgar. "Glimpses of Central Asia." Cent Asian R, XIV, 1, pp. 55-61.

422. Krader, Lawrence. Peoples of Central Asia. Bloomington, Ind.: Indiana U Press, 319p. (Uralic and Altaic Series, 26) Review, Allen Hetmanek, Mid East J, XX, 2 (Spring), 243-245.

423. Lawson, Joan. "Kazakh

Woman's Dance." The Dancing Times, LVI, 669 (Jun), 479-483.

424. Margulan, A. "Chokan Chingisovich Valikhanov." Cent Asian R, XIV, 1, pp. 25-31.

425. Musakhanova, Kh. "Political Work Among Uzbek Women." Prob Peop USSR, no. 27 (Autumn), 13-19.

426. Newth, J. A. "The Communist Party of Uzbekistan, 1959: A Brief Statistical Note." Sov St, XVII, 4 (Apr), 484-489.

427. Nove, Alec, and J. A. Newth. The Soviet Middle East: A Communist Model for Development. NY: Praeger, 160p. Reviews, Charles W. Hostler, Middle East Journal, XXI, 4 (Autumn 1967), 533-534; Harry N. Howard, Middle East Journal, XXI, 4 (Autumn 1957), 539; Charles Issawi, Slav R, XXVI, 3 (Sept 1967), 503-505; Joseph S. Roucek, Russ R, XXVI, 3 (Jul 1967), 313; Ann Sheehy, Survey, no. 67 (Apr 1968), 145-150; Gerald B. Sperling, Can Slav St, II, 1 (Spring 1968), 123-126; Nicolas Spulber, Ann Am Acad Pol Soc Sci, 373 (Sept 1967), 264; Charles K. Wilber, Sov St, XIX, 1 (Jul 1967), 137-138; TLS, Jun 15, 1967, p. 522.

428. Pahlen, Count K. K. Mission to Turkestan 1908-1909. (1964) [See ABREES, 1964, No. 106] Reviews, Edward Allworth, Slav R, XXV, 1 (Mar), 158-159; Marvin L. Entner, J Asian St, XXV, 3 (May), 542; Gare Le Compte, Mid East J, XX, 3 (Summer) 406-407.

429. Schuyler, Eugene. Turkestan: Notes of a Journey in Russian Turkestan, Kokand, Bukhara and Kuldja. Geoffrey Wheeler, ed. NY: Praeger, 340p.

430. Shapiro, Jane P. "Political Rehabilitation in Soviet Central Asian Party Organizations." Cent Asian R, XIV, 3, pp. 199-209.

431. Sheehy, Ann. "The Andizhan Uprising of 1898 and Soviet Historiography." Cent Asian R, XIV, 2, pp. 139-150. [Turkestan]

432. _____. "Labour Problems and Employment in Kazakhstan and Central Asia." Cent Asian R, XIV, 2, pp. 164-177.

433. _____. "Population Trends in Central Asia and Kazakhstan, 1959-1965." Cent Asian R, XIV, 4, pp. 317-329.

434. _____. "The Tashkent Earthquakes." Cent Asian R, XIV, 3, pp. 261-269.

435. Shimoniak, Wasyl. "Bolshevism in Turkestan: The Establishment of the Soviet Regime in Central Asia, 1917-1939." Ukr Q, XXII, 4 (Autumn), 351-363.

436. Sjoberg, Andrée F. Uzbek Structural Grammar. Bloomington, Ind.: Indiana U Press, 158p. [Indiana U Publications, Uralic and Altaic Series, 18] Review, Paul Friedrick, Lang, XLII, 3, pt. 1 (Sept), 703-704.

437. Stackelberg, Georg von. "The Tenacity of Islam in Soviet Central Asia." St Sov Un, 4, pp. 91-101.

438. Vernadsky, George V. "Historical Background of Russo-Kalmyk Relations," pp. 11-50, in Kalmyk-Oirat Symposium. Arash Bormanshinov and John R. Krueger, eds. Philadelphia: Society for the Promotion of Kalmyk Culture, 227p.

439. Wheeler, Geoffrey. The Peoples of Soviet Central Asia. A Background Book. London: Bodley Head, 126p. Reviews, Mary Holdsworth, Sov St, XIX, 2 (Oct 1967), 296-299; Robert A. Rupen, Am Pol Sci R, LXI, 3 (Sept 1967), 831; John W. Strong, Pac Aff, XXXIX, 1-2 (Spring-Summer), 175-176; TLS, Jul 21, p. 632.

440. Williams, D. S. M. "Native Courts in Tsarist Central Asia." Cent Asian R, XIV, 1, pp. 6-19.

441. Zhdanko, T. "Sedentarisation of the Nomads of Central Asia, including

Kazakhstan, under the Soviet Regime."
Int Lab R, XVIII, 6 (Jun), 611-621.

See also: 698, 723, 778, 815,
828, 861, 1286

OTHER NATIONS

442. The Balavariani (Barlaam
and Josaphat): A Tale from the Christian East Translated from the Old
Georgian. David Marshall Lang, tr.
Berkeley: U California Press, 187p.
Review, TLS, Nov 24, p. 1103.

443. "The Chechen-Ingush."
Jews in Eastern Europe, III, 5 (Oct),
9-10.

444. Ebeling, C.L. "The Grammar of Literary Avar." Studia Caucasica, II, 58-100.

444a. Erdelyi, Istvan. The Art of
the Avars. Budapest: Corvina, 69p.

444b. Hoogasian-Villa, Susie, ed.
100 Armenian Tales and Their Folkloristic Relevance. Detroit: Wayne
St U Press, 602p. Review, Nina G.
Garsoïan, Slav East Eur J, XI, 3 (Fall
1967), 366-369.

445. Householder, Fred W., Jr.,
and Mansour Lofti. Basic Course in
Azerbaijani. Bloomington, Ind.: Indiana U Press, 275p. (1965) (Uralic
and Altaic Series, 45) Review, Jiri
Kramsky, Lingua, XIX, 4 (Mar 1968),
443-445.

446. "Jews, Armenians and
Others: Two Soviet Views on Repatriation." Jews in Eastern Europe,
III, 5 (Oct), 15-22.

447. "Jews as a Soviet Nationality: A Comparative Study." Jews in
Eastern Europe, III, 5 (Oct), 3-9.

448. Khaidakov, S.M. "The
Dialect-division of Lak." Studia Caucasica, II, 9-18.

449. Lang, David Marshall. The
Georgians. NY: Praeger, 244p. "Ancient People and Places, no. 51."
Reviews, Nina G. Garsoïan, Slav R,
XXVII, 1 (Mar 1968), 133-135; Firuz
Kazemzadeh, Russ R, XXVII, 1 (Jan

1968), 104-105; A.O. Sarkissian, Am
Hist R, LXXIII, 2 (Dec 1967), 540-541;
TLS, Jan 5, 1967, p.12.

450. Murphy, George G.S. Soviet
Mongolia. A Study of the Oldest Political Satellite. Berkeley: U California Press, 224p. Reviews, W.B.Ballis,
Ann Am Acad Pol Soc Sci, 373 (Sept
1967), 266; George Ginsburgs, Am Pol
Sci R, LXII, 1 (Mar 1968), 291-292;
W. Jackson, J Dev Areas, I, 3 (Apr
1967), 407-408; Owen Lattimore, Poli
Sci Q, LXXXII, 2 (Jun 1967), 302-304;
G. LeCompte, Can Slav St, II, 4 (Winter 1968), 615; Jack Minkoff, J Econ
Hist, XXVIII, 1 (Mar 1968), 146; Geoffrey Wheeler, Sov St, XIX, 2 (Oct
1967), 306-307.

451. Riasanovsky, Valentin A.
Customary Law of Nomadic Tribes of
Siberia and Fundamental Principles
of Mongol Law. Bloomington, Ind.:
Indiana U Press, Uralic-Altaic Series
43, 343p. Reviews, Lawrence Krader
and Roberte Hamayon, Am Anthro,
LXVIII, 5 (Oct), 1285-1286; Robert A.
Rupen, J Asian St, XXV, 3 (May), 542-544.

452. Rondière, Pierre. Siberia.
London: Constable, 205p. Review,
Sov St, XVIII, 4 (Apr 1967), 537.

453. Rupen, Robert A. The
Mongolian People's Republic. Stanford: Hoover Institution, Stanford
University Press, 205p. Review, C.
R. Bowden, Roy Cent Asian J, LI, 4
(Oct), 327-328.

454. Simonian, Victor, as told to
Leo Heiman. "From Erevan to Eternity." Ukr Q, XXII, 2 (Summer), 137-151. [Colonel Georges Artunyan,
Communist agent and nationalist]

455. "The Soviet Germans."
Jews in Eastern Europe, III, 5 (Oct),
10-15.

456. Toumanoff, C. "Armenia
and Georgia," in Cambridge Medieval
History, vol. IV, pt. 1, 593-637. [See
no. 26a]

See also: 80, 791, 818, 862,
1336, 1864

VI. HISTORY

GENERAL SURVEYS

457. Almedingen, Edith Martha. The Romanovs: Three Centuries of an Ill-fated Dynasty. NY: Holt, Rinehart & Winston, 333p. Reviews, Jesse D. Clarkson, Slav R, XXVI, 2 (Jun 1967), 317-318; Clarence A. Manning, Ukr Q, XXIV, 3 (Summer 1968), 179-181; TLS, Aug 18, p. 739.

458. Daniels, Robert V. Russia. Englewood Cliffs, N.J.: Prentice-Hall, 152p. (1965) Review, John C. Campbell, Russ R, XXV, 1 (Jan), 97-98.

459. Freeborn, Richard. A Short History of Modern Russia. NY: Morrow, 288p. Reviews, Herbert J. Ellison, Slav R, XXVI, 3 (Sept 1967), 484-485; W.V. Wallace, Sov St, XVIII, 4 (Apr 1967), 534-535.

460. Hoetzsch, Otto. The Evolution of Russia. Rhys Evans, tr. London: Thames and Hudson, 213p. Reviews, J. Keep, Eng Hist R, LXXXIII, no. 327 (Apr 1968), 388; TLS, Oct 20, p. 962.

461. Laqueur, Walter. Russia and Germany. [See ABREES, 1965, No. 703] Reviews, C. G. Anthon, Am Hist R, LXXI, 4 (Jul), 1323; Alexander Dallin, Russ R, XXV, 4 (Oct), 413-414; Klaus Epstein, Mod Age, X, 2 (Spring), 196-198; Hans W. Gatzke, Jahrb Gesch Osteur, XIV, pp. 607-608; Harry Hanak, Political Studies, XIV, 2 (Jun), 272-273; Calvin B. Hoover, Virg Q R, XLII, 2 (Spring), 319-322; Richard Lowenthal, NY Rev of Books, VI, 3, Mar 3, pp. 28-29.

462. Oliva, L. Jay. Russia and the West from Peter to Khrushchev. London: Harrap, 289p. Reviews, Charles C. Adler, Can Slav St, I, 1 (Spring 1967), 148-9; TLS, Apr 28, p. 359.

463. Pokrovsky, M. N. History of Russia from the Earliest Times to the Rise of Commercial Capitalism. Jesse D. Clarkson and M. R. M. Griffiths, tr. and ed. Bloomington, Ind.: Indiana U Prints and Reprints, Russian and East European Series, vol. 6, 383p.

464. Raeff, Marc, ed. Plans for Political Reform in Imperial Russia, 1730-1905. Englewood Cliffs, N.J.: Prentice-Hall, 159p. Reviews, Ralph T. Fisher, Jr., Russ R, XXVI, 4 (Oct 1967), 418; John Keep, Slav East Eur R, XLV, 104 (Jan 1967), 251-253; Lionel Kochan, Eng Hist R, LXXXII, 4 (Oct 1967), 846-847; Anatole G. Mazour, Slav R, XXVII, 1 (Mar 1968), 135-136.

464a. Senn, Alfred Erich. Readings in Russian Political and Diplomatic History. Homewood, Ill.: Dorsey Press, vol. 1, 235p. and vol. II, 255p.

464b. Westwood, J. N. Russia 1917-1964. NY: Harper & Row, 208p. (Harper's Twentieth Century Nation Series, 1).

See also: 306, 338, 1175, 1176

GENERAL MONOGRAPHS

465. Chevigny, Hector. Russian America. [See ABREES, 1965, No. 694] Reviews, John Boojamra, St Vlad Sem Q, X, 3, 171-173; Alton S. Donnelly, Pac Aff, XXXVIII, 3-4 (Fall-Winter, 1965-1966), 362-363; James R. Gibson, Slav R, XXVI, 3 (Sept 1967), 502-503; TLS, Sept 22, p. 877.

466. Evans, Hubert. "Sixty Years of Drang nach Osten: The Soviet View of Germany's Approach to Persia." Cent Asian R, XIV, 4, pp. 341-349.

498. Ledyard, John. John Ledyard's Journey through Russia and Siberia, 1787-1788: The Journal and Selected Letters. Stephen D. Watrous, ed. Madison, Wis.: U Wisconsin Press, 293p. Reviews, George J. Demko, Slav R, XXVII, 2 (Jun 1968), 340; C. L. Drage, Slav East Eur R, XLVI, 106 (Jan 1968), 242-243; Walther Kirchner, Am Hist R, LXXII, 4 (Jul 1967), 1448; Albert Parry, Russ R, XXVI, 3 (Jul 1967), 316-317; NY Times Book Rev, Mar 19, 1967, p. 37.

499. Longworth, Philip. The Art of Victory: The Life and Achievements of Field-Marshal Suvorov, 1729-1800. [See ABREES, 1965, No. 383] Reviews, Gerald G. Govorchin, Russ R, XXVII, 1 (Jan 1968), 97-98; Barbara Jelavich, Am Hist R, LXXII, 1 (Oct), 241-242; Hans Kohn, Sat Rev, XLIX, Sept 17, 38; P. S. Squire, Slav East Eur R, XLV, 104 (Jan 1967), 250-251; TLS, Nov 9, 1965, p. 1122.

500. Raeff, Marc, ed. Origins of the Russian Intelligentsia: The Eighteenth Century Nobility. NY: Harcourt, Brace & World, 248p. Review, George W. Simmonds, Slav R, XXVII, 2 (Jun 1968), 317.

See also: 495a, 600

1801-1855

501. Brett-James, Anthony. 1812. NY: St. Martin's Press, 312p. Reviews, J. H. Plumb, NY Rev of Books, VII, 7 (Nov 3), pp. 20-22; TLS, May 19, p. 459.

502. Chandler, David. The Campaigns of Napoleon. London: Macmillan, 1172p. Reviews, Gordon Craig, Book Week, IV, 11, November 20, p. 9; J. H. Plumb, NY Rev of Books, VII, 7, November 3, 20-22.

503. Connelly, Owen. Napoleon's Satellite Kingdoms. NY: Free Press, 387p.

504. Curtiss, John Shelton. The Russian Army under Nicholas I, 1825-1855. [See ABREES, 1965, No. 729] Reviews, Henry Armani, Mil Aff, XXX, 2 (Summer), 109; Hugh Seton-Watson, Slav East Eur R, XLIV, 103 (Jul), 512-513; Edward D. Sokol, Russ R, XXV, 3 (Jul), 307-308.

505. _____. "Russian Sisters of Mercy in the Crimea, 1854-1855." Slav R, XXV, 1 (Mar), 84-100.

506. de Ségur, Count Philippe Paul. Napoleon's Russian Campaign. J. David Townsend, tr. NY: Time, Inc., 295p.

507. Jelavich, Barbara. Russia and the Greek Revolution of 1843. Munich: R. Oldenbourg, 124p. Reviews, Douglas Dakin, Balk St, VIII (1967), 161-164; Stephen Fischer-Galati, Am Hist R, LXXIII, 4 (Apr 1968), 1203-1204; Troian Stoianovich, Can Slav St, II (Spring 1968), 126-128; Stephen G. Xydis, Slav R, XXVII, 2 (Jun 1968), 330-331.

508. McGrew, Roderick E. Russia and the Cholera. [See ABREES, 1965, No. 732] Reviews, John Duffy, Ann Am Acad Pol Soc Sci, 364 (Mar), 212-213; Raymond H. Fisher, Russ R, XXV, 3 (Jul), 308-309; Barry Hollingsworth, Slav East Eur R, XLV, 105 (Jul 1967), 559-560; Sidney Monas, Slav R, XXV, 2 (Jun), 335-336.

509. Manceron, Claude. Austerlitz: The Story of a Battle. George Unwin, tr. NY: W. W. Norton, 318p. Review, Charles A. Le Guin, West Poli Q, XX, 1 (Mar 1967), 230-231.

510. Oliver, Daria. The Burning of Moscow, 1812. Michel Heron, tr. NY: Thomas Y. Crowell, 221p. Reviews, Albert J. Schmidt, Am Hist R, LXXIII, 2 (Oct 1967), 542-543; TLS, Dec 1, 1967, p. 1117.

511. Papmehl, K. A. "The Regimental School Established in Siberia by Samuel Bentham." Can Slav Pap, VII, pp. 153-168.

512. Raeff, Marc. The Decembrist Movement. Englewood Cliffs, N.J.: Prentice-Hall, 180p. Reviews, Arthur E. Adams, Russ R, XXVI, 1 (Jan 1967), 95; John Keep, Slav East Eur R, XLV, 104 (Jan 1967), 251-253; Lionel Kochan, Eng Hist R, LXXXII, 4 (Oct 1967), 846-847; Anatole G. Mazour, Slav R, XXVII, 1 (Mar 1968), 135-136.

513. Russell, W.H. Dispatches from the Crimea, 1854-1856. Nicolas Bentley, ed. NY: Hill and Wang, 286p. TLS, Dec 22, p.1186.

514. Uxkull, Baron Boris (Uexküll, Berend Joh Friedrich). Arms and the Woman: The Intimate Journal of a Baltic Nobleman in the Napoleonic Wars. The Diaries, 1812-1819. Detlev von Uexküll, ed., Joel Carmichael, tr. NY: Macmillan, 319p. Review, NY Times Book Rev, Oct 23, p.18; TLS, Nov 3, p.1007.

515. Wheeler, Mary E. "The Origins of the Russian-American Company." Jahrb Gesch Osteur, XIV, pp.485-494.

516. Woodhouse, C.M. The Battle of Navarino. London: Hodder and Stoughton, 191p. (1965) Review, Douglas Dakin, Balk St, VII, 2, pp. 458-461.

517. Zacek, Judith Cohen. "The Russian Bible Society and the Russian Orthodox Church." Church H, XXXV, 4 (Dec), 411-437.

See also: 1005, 1178, 1183-1185

1855-1900

518. Hookham, Hilda. "The Builders of the Trans-Siberian Railway." Hist Today, XVI, 8 (Aug), 528-537.

519. Alexander II. The Politics of Autocracy: Letters of Alexander II to Prince A.I. Bariatinskii (1857-1864). Alfred J. Rieber, ed. Paris: Mouton, 154p. Reviews, Michel Laran, Revue Historique, CCXXXIX, 1 (Jan-Mar 1968), 194-198; David MacKenzie, Slav R, XXVI, 3 (Sept 1967), 481; Hugh Seton-Watson, Slav East Eur R, XLVI, 106 (Jan 1968), 245-246; Joseph L. Wieczynski, Russ R, XXVI, 3 (Jul 1967), 313; Reginald E. Zelnik, Am Hist R, LXXIII, 1 (Oct 1967), 182-183.

520. Rogger, Hans. "Reflections on Russian Conservatism: 1861-1905." Jahrb Gesch Osteur, XIV, pp.195-212.

521. Standish, J.F. "The Persian War of 1856-57." Mid East St, III, 1 (Oct), 18-45.

522. Tibawi, A.L. "Russian Cultural Penetration of Syria — Palestine in the Nineteenth Century." Roy Cent Asian J, LIII, 2 (Jun), 166-182; 3 (Oct), 309-323.

See also: 856, 1177, 1183, 1192

1900-1917

523. Alexandrov, Victor. The End of the Romanovs. Boston: Little, Brown and Co., 256p. Reviews, Nikolai P. Poltoratzky, Russ R, XXVII, 3 (Apr 1968), 246-248; TLS, Sept 29, p. 902.

524. Dando, William A. "A Map of the Election to the Russian Constituent Assembly of 1917." Slav R, XXV, 2 (Jun), 314-319.

525. Debo, Richard K. "The Making of a Bolshevik: Georgii Chicherin in England, 1914-1918." Slav R, XXV, 4 (Dec), 651-662.

526. Elkin, Boris. "Further Notes on the Policies of the Kerensky Government." Slav R, XXV, 2 (Jun), 323-332. [Reply to M.Vishniak; see below, no. 536]

527. Elwood, Ralph Carter. "Lenin and the Social Democratic Schools for Underground Party Workers, 1909-1911." Poli Sci Q, LXXXI, 3 (Sept), 370-391.

528. Falkus, Malcolm. "Aspects

of Russian Industrialization Before the First World War." Austral J Pol Hist, XII, 3 (Dec), 330-340.

529. Heilbronner, Hans. "An Anti-Witte Diplomatic Conspiracy, 1905-1906: The Schwanebach Memorandum." Jahrb Gesch Osteur, XIV, pp. 347-361.

530. ____. "Count Aehrenthal and Russian Jewry, 1903-1907." J Mod Hist, XXXVIII, 4 (Dec), 337-354.

531. Kochan, Lionel. Russia in Revolution, 1890-1918. NY: New American Library, 365p. Reviews, Paul Avrich, Am Hist R, LXXIII, 2 (Oct 1967), 544-545; Barry Hollingsworth, Slav East Eur R, XLVI, 106 (Jan 1968), 251-253; Walter Laqueur, NY Rev of Books, VIII, Jun 15, 1967, p. 23; James Young, Poli Q, XXXVIII, 4 (Oct-Dec 1967), 451-454; TLS, Feb 2, 1967, p. 89.

532. Rogger, Hans. "Russia in 1914." J Contemp Hist, I, 3, pp. 95-120.

533. Satow, Sir Ernest. Korea and Manchuria between Russia and Japan, 1895-1904: The Observations of Sir Ernest Satow, British Plenipotentiary to Japan (1895-1900) and China (1900-1906). George A. Lensen, ed. Tallahassee: Diplomatic Press, 296p. Reviews, Fukui Fumio, Japan Q, XIII, 3 (Oct-Dec), 536-537; Marius B. Jansen, Am Hist R, LXXII, 1 (Jan 1967), 531; F. C. Jones, Pac Aff, XXXIX, 1-2 (Spring-Summer), 183-184; Shao-Chuan Leng, J Asian St, XXV, 4 (Aug),269-270; John Albert White, Russ R, XXV, 4 (Oct), 426-427.

534. Senn, Alfred Erich. "The Bolshevik Conference in Bern, 1915." Slav R, XXV, 4 (Dec), 676-678.

535. Thompson, Arthur D. "The Reception of Russian Revolutionary Leaders in America, 1904-1906." American Quarterly, XVIII, 3 (Fall), 452-476.

536. Vishniak, Mark. "A Pamphlet in the Guise of a Review." Slav R, XXV, 1 (Mar), 143-149. [Against B. Elkin's review of Robert P. Browder and Alexander F. Kerensky, The Russian Provisional Government (1961), published in Slav R, Dec 1964; see above, no. 526]

537. Williams, Beryl J. "The Strategic Background to the Anglo-Russian Entente of August 1907." Hist J, IX, 3, pp. 360-373.

538. Williams, Robert C. "Russians in Germany, 1900-1914." J Contemp Hist, I, 3, pp. 121-150.

See also: 520, 826, 1085, 1221, 1257, 1258, 1266, 1805

REVOLUTION AND CIVIL WAR 1918-1920

539. Billington, James H. "Six Views of the Russian Revolution." W Poli, XVIII, 3 (Apr), 452-473.

540. Brinkley, George A. The Volunteer Army and Allied Intervention in South Russia, 1917-1921: A Study in the Politics and Diplomacy of the Russian Civil War. Notre Dame: Notre Dame U Press, 446p. Reviews, Firuz Kazemzadeh, Prob Comm, XVI, 3 (May-Jun 1967), 62-63; Murray Polner, Russ R, XXVI, 3 (Jul 1967), 298-300; TLS, Jul 13, 1967, p. 616.

541. Carroll, E. Malcolm. Soviet Communism and Western Opinion, 1919-1921. F. B. M. Hollyday, ed. [See ABREES, 1965, No. 767] Reviews, Ross Horning, Russ R, XXV, 1 (Jan), 96-97; Jesse D. Clarkson, J Mod Hist, XXXVIII, 1 (Mar), 114-115; John E. Jessup, Jr., Mil Aff, XXX, 1 (Spring), 44-45; John M. Thompson, Slav R, XXV, 3 (Sept), 544-545; Richard H. Ullman, Am Hist R, LXXI, 2 (Jun), 517-518.

542. Chamberlin, W. H. The Russian Revolution. Vols. I & II. [See ABREES, 1965, No. 768] Review, [O. J. F.], Bull Inst St USSR, XIII, 3 (Mar), 53-54.

543. Goldston, Robert. The Russian Revolution. Indianapolis: Bobbs-Merrill, 224p. Reviews, Stephan M. Horak, Ukr Q, XXIV, 1 (Spring 1968), 86; Harrison E. Salisbury, NY Times Book Rev, Nov 6, pt. 2, p. 32; Zena Sutherland, Sat Rev, L, Feb 18, 1967, p. 42.

544. Kerensky, Aleksandr F. Russia and History's Turning Point. [See ABREES, 1965, No. 769] Reviews, W. H. Chamberlin, Russ R, XXV, 2 (Apr), 187-188; Leon Dennen, East Eur, XV, 4 (Apr), 53-54; Walter Dushnyck, Ukr Q, XXII, 2 (Summer), 179-181; Roger Pethybridge, Poli Q, XXXVII, 4 (Oct-Dec), 454-455; TLS, Jun 30, pp. 565-566; corr., Oct 27, p. 988, and Nov 10, p. 1023.

545. Narkiewicz, O. A. "Stalin, War Communism and Collectivization." Sov St, XVIII, 1 (Jul), 20-37.

546. Schillinger, Elisabeth Hupp. "British and U.S. Newspaper Coverage of the Bolshevik Revolution." Jour Q, XLIII, 1 (Spring), 10-16.

547. Singleton, Seth. "The Tambov Revolt (1920-1921)." Slav R, XXV, 3 (Sept), 497-512.

See also: 1768

1921-1939

548. Bishop, Donald G. The Roosevelt-Litvinov Agreements. [See ABREES, 1965, No. 776] Reviews, R. A. Divine, J Am Hist, LII (Sept 1965), 407; John N. Hazard, Am J Int Law, LX, 2 (Apr), 419-421; Anthony L. Milnar, Ann Am Acad Pol Soc Sci, CCCLXVII (Sept), 168-169; Dexter Perkins, Am Hist R, LXXI, 2 (Jan), 518-519; Paul Roley, Slav R, XXVII, 1 (Mar 1968), 151-152; John Albert White, Russ R, XXV (Jan), 96.

548a. Brome, Vincent. The International Brigades: Spain, 1936-1939. NY: Morrow, 317p. Review, Joseph Barnes, Book Week, Feb 27, p. 4+.

549. Carr, E. H. Socialism in One Country, Vol. III. Foreign Relations. NY: Macmillan, 1050p. [A History of Soviet Russia, Vol. VII] Reviews, Jesse D. Clarkson, Russ R, XXV, 2 (Apr), 188-190; Hugh Seton-Watson, Political Studies, XIV, 1 (Feb), 115-116.

550. Gruber, Helmut. "Willi Münzenberg's German Communist Propaganda Empire, 1921-1933." J Mod Hist, XXXVIII, 3 (Sept), 278-297.

551. Lubomirski, S. "Prelude to the Molotov-Ribbentrop Pact." Pol Ger, X, no. 38 (Oct-Dec), 10-14.

552. Randall, Francis B. Stalin's Russia. [See ABREES, 1965, No. 785] Frederick C. Barghoorn, Am Hist R, LXXI, 3 (Jul), 1391; George Brinkley, R Poli, XXX, 3 (Jul 1968), 378-383; T. Hunczak, Russ R, XXV, 2 (Apr), 209-210; Bernard S. Morris, Poli Sci Q, LXXXI, 2 (Jun), 318-320; Alec Nove, NY Rev of Books, VII, 4, Sept 22, p. 25; John S. Reshetar, Jr., J Poli, XXVIII, 4 (Nov), 851-852; Louis Wasserman, West Poli Q, XIX, 3 (Sept), 566-567; Bertram Wolfe, Ann Am Acad Pol Soc Sci, 373 (Sept), 182-183.

See also: 31, 281a, 435, 566, 836, 859

WORLD WAR II AND AFTER

553. Abrikossow, Dmitri I. "White Russians in Wartime Japan: Leaves from the Diary of Dmitri Abrikossov." George A. Lensen, tr. [See ABREES, 1965, No. 370, for full citation] Russ R, XXV, 3 (Jul), 268-284.

554. Ainsztein, Reuben. "Stalin and June 22, 1941: Some New Soviet Views." Int Aff, XLII, 3 (Oct), 662-672.

555. Andreyev, Vladimir. "The First Days of the War." Mod Age, XI, 3 (Summer 1967), 236-246.

556. Bell, J. Bowyer. Besieged:

Seven Cities Under Siege. Philadelphia: Chilton Books, 335p. Review, Trumbull Higgins, Am Hist R, LXXII, 3 (Apr 1967), 932. [Includes discussion of the Russian role in the sieges of Madrid, Warsaw, Stalingrad and Berlin]

557. Carell, Paul (pseud of Paul Karl Schmidt). Hitler Moves East. [See ABREES, 1965, No. 789] Review, Michael Parrish, West Poli Q, XIX, 1 (Mar), 154-156.

558. Clark, Alan. Barbarossa: The Russian-German Conflict, 1941-1945. [See ABREES, 1965, No. 790] Reviews, Richard M. Leighton, Am Hist R, LXXI, 2 (Jan), 549-550; Michael Parrish, West Poli Q, XIX, 1 (Mar), 154-156; [A. S.], Ukr R, XIII, 2 (Summer), 89-90. [See item 563]

559. Clark, Douglas. Three Days to Catastrophe. London: Hammond, 228p. Review, Marvin Rintala, Russ R, XXVI, 2 (Apr 1967), 191-192. [Reaction of British and French to Russo-Finnish War]

560. Gripenberg, G.A. Finland and the Great Powers. Memoirs of a Diplomat. [See ABREES, 1965, No. 792] Review, Kent Forster, Int J, XXI, 2 (Spring), 265-266.

561. Hayter, Sir William. The Kremlin and the Embassy. NY: Macmillan, 160p. Reviews, William H. Chamberlin, Russ R, XXVI, 4 (Oct 1967), 416-417; TLS, Aug 24, 1967, p. 754.

562. Higgins, Trumbull. Hitler and Russia: The Third Reich in a Two-Front War, 1937-1943. NY: Macmillan, 310p. Reviews, R. Ainsztein, Int Aff, XLIV, 4 (Oct 1968), 746-747; Hanson Baldwin, NY Times Book Rev, Dec 11, p. 72; Isaac Stone, Russ R, XXVI, 2 (Apr 1968), 200; G. L. Weinberg, Am Hist R, LXXII, 3 (Apr 1967), 965.

563. Lukas, Richard C. "The Impact of 'Barbarossa' on the Soviet Air Force and the Resulting Commit-

ment of United States Aircraft, Jun-Oct 1941." Hist, XXIX, 1 (Nov), 60-80. [See also 558]

564. Morton, Henry W. "U.S.S.R., 1964 — Reminiscences." Russ R, XXV, 1 (Jan), 35-45.

565. Oberländer, Erwin. "The All-Russian Fascist Party." J Cont Hist, I, 1, pp. 158-173.

566. Pavlov, Dmitri V. Leningrad 1941. [See ABREES, 1965, No. 795] Reviews, Max Beloff, Ann Am Acad Pol Soc Sci, CCCLXV (May), 183-184; Robert S. Feldman, Sov St, XIX, 1 (Jul 1967), 144-145; Robert H. McNeal, Russ R, XXV, 3 (Jul), 321; Temira Pachmuss, Slav East Eur J, X, 4 (Winter), 490-492; TLS, Feb 17, p. 118.

567. Pethybridge, R.W. A History of Postwar Russia. NY: New American Library, 263p. Reviews, J. D. White, Sov St, XX, 1 (Jul 1968), 151; TLS, Apr 7, p. 291.

568. Pliyev, I.A. "The Soviet-Mongolian Campaign Against Japan, August, 1945." Cent Asian R, XIV, 4, pp. 306-316. [From Through the Gobi and Khingan (Cherez Gobi i Khingan, 1965)]

569. Ryan, Cornelius. The Last Battle. NY: Simon and Schuster, 571p. Reviews, Eric Larrabee, Book Week, III, 29, Mar 27, p. 1; S. L. A. Marshall, NY Times Book Rev, Mar 27, 1. [Discusses the battle for Berlin, 1945].

570. Starobin, Joseph. "Ten Years that Shook the World: 1956 — A Memoir." Prob Comm, XV, 11-12 (Nov-Dec), 64-70.

571. Theobaris, Athan. "James F. Byrnes: Unwitting Yalta Myth-Maker." Poli Sci Q, LXXXI, 4 (Dec), 581-592.

572. Zawodny, J.K. "Soviet Partisans." Sov St, XVII, 3 (Jan), 368-386. [Includes discussion of J. A. Armstrong, Soviet Partisans in World War II (1964). [See ABREES, 1964, No. 342]

See also: 133, 291, 701

HISTORIOGRAPHY

573. Dedijer, Vladimir. "De-Stalinization." TLS, Sept 8, pp. 837-8.

574. Dorotich, D. "Disgrace and Rehabilitation of M. N. Pokrovsky." Can Slav Pap, VII, pp. 169-181.

575. Fedenko, Panas. "History and Historians." Prob Peop USSR, no. 26, (Winter), 47-48. [Brief report on International Committee of Historical Sciences meeting, Vienna, 1965]

576. Hollingsworth, Barry. "The Napoleonic Invasion of Russia and Recent Soviet Historical Writing." J Mod Hist, XXXVIII, 1 (Mar), 38-52.

577. Langley, Harold D. "Hunt for American Archives in the Soviet Union." Am Archivist, XXIX, 2 (Apr), 265-275. [Efforts of Angus Ward in 1930's]

578. Marko, Kurt. "Ghosts Behind the Ghost — Stalin Under Revision." Survey, no. 60 (Jul), 112-118.

579. "Stalin and the Generals." TLS, Mar 10, p. 196.

580. Strong, J. W. "Continuity and Change in Soviet History." Queen's Q, LXXIII, 3 (Autumn), 333-344.

See also: 72, 431, 554, 566, 615

VII. THE STATE

LAW

581. Beerman, R. "The 'Anti-Parasite Law' of the R.S.F.S.R. Modified." Sov St, XVII, 3 (Jan), 387-388.

582. _____. "An Important Amendment to the Anti-Parasite Law of the R.S.F.S.R." Brit J Crim, VI, 2 (Apr), 210-211.

583. Berman, Harold J., and James W. Spindler. Soviet Criminal Law and Procedures: The R.S.F.S.R. Codes. Cambridge, Mass.: Harvard U Press, Russian Research Center Studies, 50, 509p. Reviews, George Ginsburgs, Slav R, XXV, 3 (Sept), 542-543; Pauline B. Taylor, Russ R, XXV, 3 (Jul), 309-310.

583a. Boim, Leon, Glenn G. Morgan, and Aleksander W. Rudzinski. Legal Controls in the Soviet Union. Leyden: Sijthoff, 339p. (Law in Eastern Europe, vol. 13).

584. Brumberg, Abraham. "'Socialist Legality' On Trial." Reporter, XXXIV, 5 (Mar 10), 34-36.

585. _____. "Traitors in the Dock." Prob Comm, XV, 3-4 (Mar-Apr), 70-78. [Trial of Sinyavskii and Daniel]

586. The Civil Code and the Code of the Civil Procedures of the R.S.F.S.R. (1964) A. K. R. Kiralfy, tr. Leyden: Sijthoff, 280p. (Law in Eastern Europe, vol. 11).

587. Gellhorn, Walter. "Review of Administrative Acts in the Soviet Union." Col Law R, LXVI, 6 (Jun), 1051-1079.

588. Kucherov, Samuel. "The Nature and Status of 'Arbitrazh'." Bull Inst St USSR, XIII, 11 (Nov), 21-40.

589. La Fave, Wayne R., ed. Law in the Soviet Society. [See ABREES, 1965, No. 829] Reviews, Harold J. Berman, Poli Sci Q, LXXXI, 3 (Sept), 378-379; Jurij Fedynskyj, Slav R, XXVII, 2 (Jun 1968), 334-335; Ivo Lapenna, Slav East Eur R, XLV, 104 (Jan 1967), 261; Pauline B. Taylor, Russ R, XXV, 3 (Jul), 320.

590. Mironenko, Yuri. "The Soviet Barrister." St Sov Un, VI, 1, pp. 49-56.

591. _____. "The Evolution of Soviet Family Law." Bull Inst St USSR, XIII, 5 (May), 33-40.

592. Rapp, Fritz. "Open Questions in Contemporary Soviet Theory of Social Law." St Sov Th, VI, 3, pp. 190-201.

593. Revesz, Laszlo. "Open Questions in Contemporary Soviet Philosophy of Law and State." St Sov Th, VI, 3 (Sept), 202-223.

594. Rudden, Bernard. Soviet Insurance Laws. Leyden: Sijthoff, 219p. (Law in Eastern Europe, vol. 12). Review, Robert J. Myers, Prob Comm, XVII, 3-4 (Mar-Apr 1968), 66-67.

595. Singh, Baljit. "Law as a Political Instrument: A Soviet Illustration." World Justice, VII, 4 (Jun), 435-448.

See also: 91, 477-479, 782, 1135, 1136

POLITICS AND GOVERNMENT BEFORE THE REVOLUTION

596. Rigberg, Benjamin. "The Efficacy of Tsarist Censorship Operations, 1894-1917." Jahrb Gesch Osteur, XIV, 3, pp. 327-346.

597. Roucek, Joseph S., and Kenneth V. Lottich. "The Antecedents of Soviet Power." Int R Hist Poli Sci, III, 1 (Jun), 105-120.

598. Zyzniewski, Stanley J. "The Russo-Polish Crucible of the 1860's: A Review of Some Recent Literature." Pol R, XI, 2 (Spring), 23-46.

See also: 464, 475, 476, 486

THE SOVIET REGIME

599. Achminov, Herman. "A De-cade of De-Stalinization." St Sov Un, V, 3, pp. 11-20.

600. Andrews, William G., and Franz D. Scholz, eds. Soviet Institutions and Policies: Inside Views. NY: Van Nostrand, 411p. Review, Derek J. R. Scott, Sov St, XIX, 2 (Oct 1967), 304-5.

601. Armstrong, John A. "Party Bifurcation and Elite Interests." Sov St, XVII, 4 (Apr), 417-430.

602. Avtorkhanov, Abdurakhman. The Communist Party Apparatus. Chicago: Regnery, 422p. Reviews, John A. Armstrong, Russ R, XXVI, 1 (Jan 1967), 79; Anthony T. Bouscaren, Ann Am Acad Pol Soc Sci, CCCLXX (Mar 1967), 217; Michael P. Gehlen, J Poli, XIX, 3 (Aug 1967), 669-671; Henry W. Morton, Slav R, XXVII, 1 (Mar 1968), 159-160; R. S. Sullivant, Am Pol Sci R, LXI (Sept 1967), 816.

603. Barghoorn, Frederick C. Politics in the U.S.S.R. Boston: Little, Brown and Co., 395p. Reviews, Ghita Ionescu, Sov St, XVIII, 4 (Apr 1967), 530-532; Henry W. Morton, Slav R, XXVII, 1 (Mar 1968), 159-160; Richard A. Nordahl, Pub Op Q, XXXII, 2 (Summer 1968), 324-325; Hugh Seton-Watson, Prob Comm, XVI, 4 (Jul-Aug 1967), 53-58.

604. _____. "Changes in Russia: The Need for Perspectives." Prob Comm, XV, 3 (May-Jun), 39-42.

605. _____. "Observations on Contemporary Soviet Political Attitudes." Sov St, XVIII, 1 (Jul), 66-70. [See Alfred G. Meyer, ibid., XVII, 3 (Jan), 273-285]

606. Brzezinski, Zbigniew. "The Soviet Political System: Transformation or Degeneration?" Prob Comm, XV, 1 (Jan-Feb), 1-15. [See also: 620, 621, 623, 632, 635]

607. Brzezinski, Z., and Samuel P. Huntington. Political Power: U.S.A./U.S.S.R. [See ABREES, 1965, No. 862] Reviews, Jacques Freymond,

Poli Sci Q, LXXXI, 1 (Mar), 145-146; J. D. Lees, Political Studies, XIV, 2 (Jun), 246-247; George J. Stansfield, Russ R, XXV, 1 (Jan), 79-81.

608. Churchward, L. G. "Soviet Local Government Today." Sov St, XVII, 4 (Apr), 431-452.

609. Conquest, Robert. "Immobilism and Decay." Prob Comm, XV, 5 (Sept-Oct), 35-37.

610. Dallin, Alexander, and Alan F. Westin. Politics in the Soviet Union: Seven Cases. NY: Harcourt Casebook in Political Science, Harcourt, Brace & World, 296p. Reviews, Frederick C. Barghoorn, Slav R, XXVIII, 1 (Mar 1969), 156-157; Peter Reddaway, Prob Comm, XVII, 2 (Mar-Apr 1968), 61-64.

611. Dobriansky, Lev E. "Old Myths, New Realities About Russia. Freedom Through Understanding." Ukr Q, XXII, 3 (Autumn), 204-224.

612. Dueval, Christian. "The Dismantling of Party and State Control as an Independent Pillar of Soviet Power." Bull Inst St USSR, XIII, 3 (Mar), 3-18.

613. "East Central Europeans in Soviet Labor Camps." ACEN News, 122 (Mar-Apr), 15-17.

614. "Focus on Prisons and Labor Camps." ACEN News, 122 (Mar-Apr), 13-15.

615. Frankel, Jonathan. "Party Genealogy and the Soviet Historians (1920-1938)." Slav R, XXV, 4 (Dec), 563-603.

616. Galli, Giorgio. "Whither Russia? A Bureaucracy under Fire." Prob Comm, XV, 5 (Sept-Oct), 31-35.

617. Kruzhin, Petr. "The Problem of Party Growth and Recruitment." Bull Inst St USSR, XIII, 1 (Jan), 33-36.

618. ____. "Krai and Oblast Party Committee First Secretaries." Ibid., XIII, 4 (Apr), 26-31.

619. Laird, Roy D. "Some Characteristics of the Soviet Leadership System: A Maturing Totalitarian System." Midwest J Pol Sci, X, 1 (Feb), 29-38.

620. Leonhard, Wolfgang. "Whither Russia? Notes on an Agonizing Diagnosis. (Discussion)." Prob Comm, XV, 4 (Jul-Aug), 36-42. [See also nos. 606, 621, 623, 632, 635]

621. Lyons, Eugene. "The Realities of a Vision." [Discussion] Prob Comm, XV, 4 (Jul-Aug), 42-44. [See also nos. 606, 620, 623, 632, 635]

622. Meissner, Boris. "The Soviet Union under Brezhnev and Kosygin." Mod Age, XI, 1 (Winter 1966-67), 7-23.

623. ____. "Whither Russia? Totalitarian Rule and Social Change." [Discussion] Prob Comm, XV, 6 (Nov-Dec), 56-61. [See also nos. 606, 620, 621, 632, 635]

624. Meyer, Alfred G. The Soviet Political System. [See ABREES, 1965, No. 895] Reviews, John A. Armstrong, J Poli, XVIII, 4 (Nov), 850-851; Jurij Borys, Int J, XXII, 1 (Winter 1966-67), 139-140; Michael P. Gehlen, Midwest J Pol Sci, X, 3 (Aug), 399-401; John H. Hodgson, Russ R, XXV, 4 (Oct), 429; Alec Nove, NY Rev of Books, VII, 4, Sept 22, pp. 25-28.

625. Milukas, Alfons. "One Day in a Soviet Labor Camp." ACEN News, 122 (Mar-Apr), 2-6.

626. Moore, Barrington, Jr. Soviet Politics. [See ABREES, 1965, No. 897] Review, Reinhard Bendix, Poli Sci Q, LXXXII, 4 (Dec 1967), 625-627.

627. Morgenthau, Hans. "Alternatives for Change." Prob Comm, XV, 5 (Sept-Oct), 38-40.

628. Mote, Max E. Soviet Local and Republic Elections. [See ABREES, 1965, No. 898] Review, Peter J. Potichnyj, Int J, XXII, 1 (Autumn), 143-144.

629. Parry, Albert. The New Class Divided. NY: Macmillan, 364p.

Reviews, J. M. Gilison, Am Pol Sci R, LXI, 2 (Jun 1967), 537; William Gilman, Book Week, Aug 7, p. 3; Loren R. Graham, Slav R, XXVI, 2 (Jun 1967), 328-329; A. Ivanov, Novyi Zhurnal, no. 84, 290-293; David Joravsky, Prob Comm, XVI, 1 (Jan-Feb 1967), 72-75; Allen H. Kassof, Russ R, XXVI, 2 (Apr 1968), 201; Conway Zirkle, Ann Am Acad Pol Soc Sci, 369 (Jan 1967), 195.

630. Rush, Myron. Political Succession in the U.S.S.R. [See ABREES, 1965, No. 907] Reviews, Frederic J. Fleron, Jr., J Poli, XXVIII, 1 (Feb), 221-223; Robert McNeal, Int J, XXI, 2 (Spring), 258-259; Wright Miller, Int Aff, XLII, 1 (Jan), 132-133; P. B. Reddaway, Sov St, XVIII, 1 (Jul), 96-98.

631. Shaffer, Harry G., ed. The Soviet System in Theory and Practice. [See ABREES, 1965, No. 911] Review, George C. Guins, Russ R, XXV, 2 (Apr), 195-198.

632. Strausz-Hupé, Robert. "Whither Russia? Some Historical Parallels." [Discussion] Prob Comm, XV, 6 (Nov-Dec), 62-63. [See also nos. 606, 620, 621, 623, 635]

633. Strayer, Joseph R. "Problems of Dictatorship: The Russian Experience." For Aff, XLIV, 3 (Jan), 264-274.

634. Szamuely, T. "The Elimination of Opposition between the Sixteenth and Seventeenth Congresses of the C.P.S.U." Sov St, XVII, 3 (Jan), 318-338.

635. Tatu, Michel. "The Beginning of the End?" [Discussion] Prob Comm, XV, 2 (Mar-Apr), 44-47. (Review of M. Garder, L'Agonie du régime en Russie soviétique. (1965) [See also nos. 606, 620, 621, 623, 632]

636. Tucker, Robert, and S. F. Cohen, eds. The Great Purge Trial. [See ABREES, 1965, No. 921a] Reviews, Thomas Molnar, Mod Age, X, 2 (Spring 1968), 209-212; Robert M.

Slusser, Slav R, XXV, 2 (Jun), 353-355; Robert S. Sullivant, Russ R, XXV, 1 (Jan), 104-105.

637. United States Senate, Committee on the Judiciary. The Soviet Empire. A Study in Discrimination and Abuse of Power. (1965) Review, Lev E. Dobriansky, Ukr Q, XXII, 2 (Summer), 177-179.

638. Whiting, Kenneth R. The Soviet Union Today. A Concise Handbook. Rev. ed. NY: Praeger, 434p.

See also: 441, 549, 589, 736, 825, 1129, 1219, 1237, 1284

THE 23RD CPSU CONGRESS, 1966

639. Achminov, H. "The Party Congress: Where Does the Power Really Lie?" Bull Inst St USSR, XIII, 4 (Apr), 20-25.

640. Galay, Nikolai. "Pre-Congress Reshuffle." Bull Inst St USSR, XIII, 1 (Jan), 29-32.

641. _____. "The Twenty-Third Party Congress: The General Significance." Ibid., XIII, 5 (May), 10-13.

642. Hutchings, Raymond. "The 23rd CPSU Congress and the New Soviet Five-Year Plan." W Today, XXII, 8 (Aug), 351-360.

643. Kruzhin, Petr. "The Twenty-Third Party Congress: Personnel Changes." Ibid., XIII, 5 (May), 16-19.

644. Manning, Clarence A. "The Twenty-Third Communist Party Congress." Ukr Q, XXII, 2 (Summer), 169-176.

645. Schapiro, Leonard B. "The Twenty-Third CPSU Congress (1)." Survey, no. 60 (Jul), 72-84.

646. Ulam, Adam. "The Moscow Congress: Prudence and Semantics." Reporter, XXXIV, 9 (May 5), 25-27.

647. Urban, Pavel. "Party Pronouncements on Ideological Conformity." St Sov Un, VI, 1, pp. 35-39.

648. Voronitsyn, S. "Komsomol Problems on the Eve of the Twenty-Third Party Congress." Bull Inst St USSR, XIII, 3 (Mar), 44-48.

649. Wheeler, Marcus. "The Twenty-Third Congress of the CPSU: Problems and Auguries." W Today, XXII, 4 (Apr), 137-141.

650. ____. "Political Aspects of the Twenty-Third Congress of the CPSU." Ibid., XXII, 7 (Jul), 307-314.

See also: 593, 738, 739, 769, 787, 789, 1287

DIPLOMACY AND FOREIGN RELATIONS BEFORE 1917

651. Anderson, M.S. The Eastern Question, 1774-1923: A Study in International Relations. London: Macmillan, 436p. Reviews, Roderic H. Davison, Poli Sci Q, LXXXIII, 1 (Mar 1968), 151-152; H.N.Howard, Ann Am Acad Pol Soc Sci, CCCLXXII (Jul 1967), 144; L.S.Stavrianos, Am Hist R, LXXII, 4 (Jul 1967), 1345; TLS, Nov 10, p.1019.

652. Bestuzhev, I.V. "Russian Foreign Policy, Feb-Jun 1914." Journal of Contemporary History, I, 3 (1914: The Coming of the First World War.), 93-112.

653. Hsü, Immanuel Chung-yueh. The Ili Crisis. [See ABREES, 1965, No. 928] Reviews, Brian L. Evans, Pac Aff, XXXIX, 1-2 (Spring-Summer), 174-175; Leonard Gordon, J Asian St, XXV, 4 (Aug), 752; Ian Nish, Slav East Eur R, XLV, 104 (Jan 1967), 253-254.

654. Lensen, George Alexander, ed. Russia's Eastward Expansion. [See ABREES, 1964, No. 200] Review, Alton S. Donnelly, Pac Aff, XXXVIII, 3-4 (Fall-Winter 1965-66), 362-363.

655. Nish, Ian H. The Anglo-Japanese Alliance. The Diplomacy of Two Island Empires, 1894-1907. London: Athlone Press, 431p. Re-

views, A. Fraser, Eng Hist R, LXXXII, 3 (Oct 1967), 869; H.M.Vinacke, Pac Aff, XXXIX, 1-2 (Spring-Summer), 182; John Albert White, Slav East Eur R, XLVI, 106 (Jan 1968), 248-250; Chitoshi Yanaga, Am Hist R, LXXII, 1 (Jan 1967), 530.

656. Pierce, Richard A. Russia's Hawaiian Adventure. [See ABREES, 1965, No. 931] Reviews, M.S.Anderson, Slav East Eur R, XLIV, 103 (Jul), 511-512; J.C.Beaglehole, Pac Aff, XXXIX, 3-4 (Fall-Winter 1966-67), 416-417; Albert Parry, Russ R, XXV, 1 (Jan), 24-25; John Albert White, Jahrb Gesch Osteur, XIV, pp.278-279.

657. Renzi, William A. "The Russian Foreign Office and Italy's Entrance into the Great War, 1914-1915: A Study in Wartime Diplomacy." Historian, XXVIII, 4 (Aug), 648-668.

658. Stevens, John Knox. "The Franco-Russian Treaty of 1859: New Lights and New Thoughts." Historian, XXVIII, 2 (Feb), 203-223.

659. Thaden, Edward C. Russia and the Balkan Alliance of 1912. University Park, Pa.: Penn State U Press, 192p. Reviews, E.C. Helmreich, Am Hist R, LXXI, 3 (Apr), 1021; L. S. Stavrianos, Ann Am Acad Pol Soc Sci, 373 (Jan), 165; TLS, Sept 29, p.902.

See also: 462, 465, 466, 472, 513, 533

SOVIET DIPLOMACY AND FOREIGN RELATIONS – GENERAL

660. Achminov, Herman. "Foreign Policy and Party Affairs." St Sov Un, VI; 1, pp.1-9.

661. "Cultural and Scientific Cooperation between U.S.S.R. and Other Countries." Int Assoc U Bull, XIV, 3 (Aug), 203-204.

662. Dougherty, James E. "The Non-Proliferation Treaty." Russ R, XXV, 1 (Jan), 10-23.

663. Erickson, John, Edward L. Crowley, and Nikolai Galay, eds. The Military-Technical Revolution: Its Impact on Strategy and Foreign Policy. London: Pall Mall Press, 284p. Review, Alvin Z. Rubinstein, Sov St, XIX, 1 (Jul 1967), 142-143.

664. Eudin, Xenia Joukoff, and Robert M. Slusser, eds. and trs. Soviet Foreign Policy, 1928-1934. Documents and Materials, vols. 1-2. University Park, Pa.: Penn State U Press; vol. 1, 354p.; vol. 2, 434p. (Hoover Institution Publication). Reviews, Melvin Croan, Prob Comm, XVII, 1 (Jan-Feb 1968), 39-40; Harry Hanak, Int Aff, XLIV, 3 (Jul 1968), 564-566; Alfred J. Rieber, Am Hist R, LXXIII, 1 (Oct 1967), 186-187; Ronald R. Rader, J Asian St, XXV, 3 (May), 540-541; TLS, Sept 7, 1967, p. 791.

665. Gliauda, Jurgis. "At the Kremlin with Molotov." Litua, XII, 2 (Summer), 20-29.

666. Hilsman, Roger, and Robert C. Good, eds. Foreign Policy in the Sixties. The Issues and the Instruments. Essays in the Honor of Alfred Wolfers. Baltimore: Johns Hopkins Press, 299p. Reviews, Max Beloff, Sov St, XVII, 4 (Apr), 500-501; D. G. Bishop, Ann Am Acad Pol Soc Sci, CCCLXII (Nov 1965), 151; L. L. Gerson, Poli Sci Q, LXXXI, 1 (Mar), 143.

667. Horelick, Arnold L., and Myron Rush. Strategic Power and Soviet Foreign Policy. Toronto: U Toronto Press; Chicago: U Chicago Press, 225p. Reviews, John A. Armstrong, Prob Comm, XVII, 3 (May-Jun 1968), 54-56; Oleh S. Fedyshyn, J Poli, XXIX, 1 (Feb 1967), 185-187; Harry Hanak, Slav East Eur R, XLVI, 107 (Jul 1968), 540-541; R. T. R. Gill, East Eur, XV, 10 (Oct), 46-47; W. R. Kintner, Ann Am Acad Pol Soc Sci, CCCLXIX (Jan 1967), 164; Kenneth V. Lottich, Ukr Q, XXII, 4 (Winter), 373-374; Malcolm Mackintosh, Sov St, XIX, 1 (Jul 1967), 143-144; Charles

B. Marshall, Am Pol Sci R, LXI, 3 (Sept 1967), 836-7; Robert M. Slusser, Slav R, XXVI, 2 (Jun 1967), 324-326; Virg Q R, XLIII (Winter 1967), 40; Warren B. Walsh, Russ R, XXVI, 1 (Jan 1967), 93; Witold Weynerowski, Int J, XXI, 4 (Autumn), 564-565; Elizabeth Young, Bull Atom Sci, XXII, 12 (Dec), 26; William Zimmerman, J Conf Resol, X, 4 (Dec), 524-528.

668. London, Kurt. The Making of Foreign Policy. Philadelphia: Lippincott, 358p. (1965) Review, Elliot Goodman, Russ R, XXV, 1 (Jan), 101-102.

669. Mackiw, Theodore. "Washington-Peking-Moscow." Ukr R, XIII, 3 (Autumn), 74-75.

670. Manning, Clarence A. "Growing American Knowledge of the Enemy." Ukr Q, XXII, 1 (Spring), 45-52.

671. Pethybridge, Roger. "Russian Foreign Policy." Political Studies, XIV, 2 (Jun), 389-391.

672. Rubinstein, Alvin Z., ed. The Foreign Policy of the Soviet Union. 2nd ed. NY: Random House, 458p. Review, Harry Hanak, Slav East Eur R, XLV, 105 (Jul 1967), 572-573.

673. Russet, Bruce M. "The Apolitics of Strategy." J Conflict Resol, X, 1 (Mar), 122-127. [Review of William W. Kaufmann, The McNamara Strategy. NY: Harper & Row, 1964; and Thomas W. Wolfe, Soviet Strategy at the Crossroads. See ABREES, 1964, No. 813]

674. Zimmerman, W. "Russia and the International Order." Survey, no. 58 (Jan), 209-213.

SOVIET DIPLOMACY AND FOREIGN RELATIONS — WESTERN COUNTRIES

675. "Air-Link Between Canada and the U.S.S.R." Exter Aff, XVIII, 8 (Aug), 322-324. [Statements by Lester Pearson and D. S. Polyansky]

676. Brzezinski, Zbigniew. "Tomorrow's Agenda." For Aff, XLIV, 4 (Jul), 662-670.

677. Cattell, David T. "The U.S.S.R. and the West." Cur Hist, LI, no. 302 (Oct), 193-199.

678. Ducoli, John. "Unity in Diversity or Diversity in Unity. Relations between the Soviet and Italian Communist Parties after Khrushchev and Togliatti." St Sov Un, V, 3, pp. 20-27.

679. Dyck, Leonard. Weimar Germany and Soviet Russia, 1926-1933. A Study in Diplomatic Instability. London: Chatto and Windus, 279p.; NY: Columbia U Press. Reviews, F. L. Carsten, Poli Sci Q, LXXXII, 4 (Dec 1967), 659-660; Louis Fischer, Am Hist R, LXXII, (Apr 1967), 964-965; Hans W. Held, Pol R, XIII, 1 (Winter 1968), 106-109; Josef Korbel, Russ R, XXVI, 3 (Jul 1967), 302-303; R. H. Lutz, Ann Am Acad Pol Soc Sci, CCCLXX (Mar 1967), 215-216; Paul Roley, Slav R, XXVII, 1 (Mar 1968), 151; Kurt Rosenbaum, Am Pol Sci R, LXI, 3 (Sept 1967), 836-838; The Economist, Dec 17, 1966, p. 1251; TLS, Sept 29, 1967, p. 902.

680. _____. "German-Soviet Relations and the Anglo-Soviet Break, 1927." Slav R, XXV, 1 (Mar), 67-83.

681. Groth, A. J. "Churchill and Stalin's Russia." Buck R, XIV, 1 (Feb), 74-94.

682. Halle, Louis J. "The Turning Point." Survey, no. 58 (Jan), 168-176. [American-Soviet relations after 1945]

683. Korbel, Josef. "Soviet-German Relations: the Past and Prospects." Orbis, X, 4 (Winter 1966-1967), 1046-1060.

684. Kulski, W. W. "The U.S.S.R. — France — Germany." Russ R, XXV, 4 (Oct), 343-356.

685. London, Kurt L. "Soviet Policy and the Austrian State Treaty." Orbis, X, 2 (Summer), 622-624. Review of Sven Allard, Diplomat in Wien, 1965]

686. Manning, Clarence A. "The Vision of DeGaulle of France." Ukr Q, XXII, 3 (Autumn), 237-245.

687. Nelson, Bryce. "The Space Treaty: A Step in Easing U.S.-Soviet Tensions." Sci, CLIV, no. 3755 (Dec 16), pp. 1430-1431.

688. Rosenbaum, Kurt. Community of Fate: German-Soviet Diplomatic Relations, 1922-1928. [See ABREES, 1965, No. 962] Reviews, Victor C. Arnold, Hist, XXVIII, 3 (May), 529-530; William B. Ballis, Russ R, XXV, 2 (Apr), 193-195; F. L. Carsten, Slav East Eur R, XLIV, 103 (Jul), 523; M. C. Wren, J Mod Hist, XXXVIII, 1 (Mar), 115-116.

689. Senn, Alfred Erich. The Great Powers, Lithuania and the Vilna Question, 1920-1928. Leiden: E. J. Brill, 242p. Review, Vaclovas Sidzikauskas, Balt R, no. 34 (Nov 1967), 43-46.

690. "Soviet Parliamentarians Visit Canada." Exter Aff, XVIII, 9 (Sept), 395-398.

691. Spittmann, Ilse. "Soviet Union and D.D.R." Survey, no. 61 (Oct), 165-176.

692. Thompson, John M. Russia, Bolshevism and the Versailles Peace. Princeton, N.J.: Princeton U Press, 430p. [Studies of the Russian Institute, Columbia University] Reviews, Abraham Ascher, Prob Comm, XVI, 4 (Jul-Aug 1967), 67-68; George Brinkley, R Poli, XXX, 3 (Jul 1968), 378-383; Jane Degras, Slav R, XXVII, 1 (Mar 1968), 149-151; Panas Fedenko, Bull Inst St USSR, XV, 1 (Jan 1968), 40-43; S. D. Kertesz, Ann Am Acad Pol Soc Sci, 374 (Nov 1967), 226; Walter Laqueur, NY Rev of Books, VIII, Jun 15, 1967, p. 23; Murray Polner, Russ R, XXVI,

3 (Jul 1967), 298-320; Frank Spencer, Int Aff, XLIV, 2 (Apr 1968), 290-291; Richard H. Ullman, Am Hist R, LXXIII, 2 (Oct 1967), 549-550; Rex A. Wade, Sov St, XX, 1 (Jul 1968), 148-149; TLS, Aug 31, 1967, p. 779.

693. Wallace, John E. "Russia and the Munich Conference." Sou Q, V, 1 (Oct), 105-124.

See also: 462, 466, 541, 548, 551, 561, 748

SOVIET DIPLOMACY AND FOREIGN RELATIONS — THIRD WORLD

694. Ballis, William B. "Recent Soviet Relations with Afghanistan." Bull Inst St USSR, XIII, 6 (Jun), 3-13.

695. ____. "Relations between the U.S.S.R. and Vietnam." St Sov Un, VI, 2, pp. 43-56.

696. Chaudhri, Mohammed Ahsen. "Pakistan's Relations with the Soviet Union." Asian Sur, VI, 9 (Sept), 492-500.

697. Crozier, Brian. The Struggle for the Third World. London: Bodley Head, 156p. Review, Lalita P. Singh, Pac Aff, XXXIX, 3-4 (Fall-Winter), 377-378.

698. Evans, Hubert. "Recent Soviet Writings on South and Central Asia." Roy Cent Asian J, LIII, 1 (Feb), 50-59.

699. ____. "New Soviet Books." Mid East St, II, 4 (Jul), 367-372; III, 1 (Oct), 68-73.

700. ____. "Three New Soviet Books on Turkey." Mid East St, II, 3 (Apr), 250-255.

701. "Friendship with the Soviet Union." Japan Q, XIII, 2 (Apr-Jun), 143-145. [Japan and the Soviet Union]

702. Galay, Nikolai. "Moscow Fortifies Its Position in Asia." Bull Inst St USSR, XIII, 3 (Mar), 19-25.

703. Garthoff, Raymond L. "Soviet Intervention in Manchuria, 1945-1946." Orbis, X, 2 (Summer), 520-547.

704. Gopal, S. "India, China and the Soviet Union." Austral J Pol Hist, XII, 2 (Aug), 241-257.

705. "The Gromyko Visit." Japan Q, XIII, 4 (Oct-Dec), 421-424. [Gromyko's visit to Japan, July 24-30, 1966]

706. Haggard, M. T. "Mongolia: New Soviet Moves to Bolster Ruling Group." Asian Sur, VI, 1 (Jan), 13-17.

707. Hayit, Baymirza. Soviet Russian Colonialism and Imperialism in Turkestan. Cologne: Privately printed, 123p. (1965) Review, Garé Le Compte, Mid East J, XX, 1 (Winter), 129-130.

708. Iman, Zafar. "Soviet Asian Policy Today." Contemp R, CCIX, no. 1206 (Jul), 6-14.

709. Kapur, Harish. Soviet Russia and Asia: 1917-1927. NY: Humanities Press, 266p. Reviews, Michael Rywkin, Slav R, XXVII, 1 (Mar 1968), 152-153; Geoffrey Wheeler, Survey, no. 62 (Jan 1967), 183-185; TLS, Jul 21, p. 632.

710. Kashin, Alexander. "The Soviet Offensive in Asia." St Sov Un, V, 3, pp. 1-10.

711. Lowenthal, Richard. "Russia, The One-Party System, and the Third World." Survey, no. 58 (Jan), 43-58.

712. McLane, Charles B. Soviet Strategies in Southeast Asia: An Exploration of Eastern Policy Under Lenin and Stalin. Princeton, N.J.: Princeton U Press, 581p. Reviews, Earl Browder, Poli Sci Q, LXXXII, 1 (Mar 1967), 93-94; S. M. Chiu, Am Hist R, LXXII, (Apr 1967), 1066; Alexander Dallin, J Mod Hist, XL, 2 (Jun 1968), 294-295; R. H. Fifield, Ann Am Acad Pol Soc Sci, CCCLXIX (Jan 1967), 173; T. W. Robinson, Am Pol Sci R, LXI, 2 (Jun 1967), 492; Guy Wint, Sov St, XIX,

4 (Apr 1968), 600-601; TLS, May 11, 1967, p. 394.

713. _____. "Soviet Doctrine and Military Coups in Africa." Int J, XXI, 3 (Summer), 298-310.

714. Moseley, Philip E. "Communist Policy and the Third World." R Poli, XXVIII, 2 (Apr), 210-237.

715. Pennar, Jaan. "The Soviets and Algerian Socialism." Bull Inst St USSR, XIII, 1 (Jan), 3-15.

716. _____. "Moscow and Socialism in Egypt." Prob Comm, XV (Sept-Oct), 41-47.

717. Simon, Sheldon W. "New Soviet Approaches to the Japanese Left." Asian Sur, VI, 6 (Jun), 319-326.

718. Sirc, L. "Changes in Communist Advice to Developing Countries." W Today, XXII, 8 (Aug), 326-335.

719. Taborsky, Edward. "The Less Developed Countries in Soviet Ideology." Sou Soc Sci Q, XLVII, 1 (Jun), 34-43.

720. Vaidyanath, R. "Some Recent Trends in Soviet Policies Towards India and Pakistan." Int St, VII, 3 (Jan), 429-447.

721. Walters, Robert C. "Soviet Economic Aid to Cuba." Int Aff, XLII, 1 (Jan), 74-86.

See also: 90a, 91a, 92, 93, 744, 1273

INTERNATIONAL COMMUNISM AND INTRA-BLOC PARTY RELATIONS

722. Ohanjanian, A. "Taiping Agrarian Policy: Some Chinese and Soviet Views." Pac Aff, XXXIX, 1-2, (Spring-Summer), 128-134.

723. Rupen, Robert A. Mongols of the Twentieth Century. Bloomington, Ind.: Indiana U Press, Uralic and Altaic Series, 37; vol. 1, 510p.,

vol. 2, 167p. Review, John Howard-Gibbon, Pac Aff, XXXIX, 3-4 (Fall-Winter 1966-1967), 381-382.

See also Part I, Section III; particularly Sino-Soviet Relations, 54-90. Also 627, 646

INTERNATIONAL LAW

724. The Status of Refugees in International Law. Leiden: A. W. Sijthoff, (3 vols.) Review, Jacob Robinson, Am J Int Law, LXII, 1 (Jan 1968), 231-232.

725. Grzybowski, Kazimierz. Soviet Private International Law. [See ABREES, 1965, No. 1038] Review, Ivo Lapenna, Sov St, XVIII, 1 (Jul), 111-112.

See also: 696

MILITARY AFFAIRS

726. Erickson, John. "Russians on Soviet Strategy." Prob Comm, XV, 4 (Jul-Aug), 59-62. [Review of books on Soviet strategy in World War II]

727. Galay, Nikolai. "The Relationship Between the Structure of Society and the Armed Forces as Illustrated by the U.S.S.R." Bull Inst St USSR, XIII, 11 (Nov), 3-20, and XIII, 12 (Dec), 3-18.

728. Garder, Michel. A History of the Soviet Army. NY: Praeger, 226p. Reviews, Hanson Baldwin, NY Times Book Rev, Dec 11, p. 72; Charles V. P. von Luttichau, Am Hist R, LXXIII, 1 (Oct 1967), 180-181; Matthew P. Gallagher, Slav R, XXVII, 1 (Mar 1968), 138-139; Thomas W. Wolfe, Prob Comm, XVI, 4 (Jul-Aug 1967), 68; Richard Wraga, Russ R, XXVI, 4 (Oct 1967), 410-411.

729. Garthoff, Raymond L. Soviet Military Policy. A Historical Analysis. NY: Praeger, 284p. Reviews, Alvin D. Coox, West Poli Q,

XXI, 2 (Jun 1968), 346-347; John Shelton Curtiss, Ann Am Acad Pol Soc Sci, 368 (Sept), 183-184; John Erickson, Prob Comm, XVI, 1 (Jan-Feb 1967), 62-63; Oleh S. Fedyshyn, J Poli, XXIX, 1 (Feb 1967), 185-187; Matthew P. Gallagher, Slav R, XXVII, 1 (Mar 1968), 138-139; R. T. Rockingham Gill, East Eur, XV, 6 (Jun), 51-52; Robert H. Johnson, Int J, XXII, 1 (Autumn 1966-1967), 112-113; Kurt London, Russ R, XXV, 4 (Oct), 411-413; Alfred Vagts, Poli Sci Q, LXXXI, 4 (Dec), 682-683; Peter von Wahlde, Sov St, XVIII, 4 (Apr 1967), 529-530; TLS, Oct 20, p. 962.

730. Mostert, Noel. "Russia Bids for Ocean Supremacy." Reporter, XXXIV, 3 (Feb 10), 24-28.

See also: 65, 70, 94, 206, 469, 504, 504a, 563, 612, 663, 851, 894

ARMS CONTROL AND DISARMAMENT

731. Bloomfield, Lincoln P., Walter C. Clemens, Jr., and Franklyn Griffiths. Khrushchev and the Arms Race: Soviet Interests in Arms Control and Disarmament, 1954-1964. Cambridge, Mass.: MIT Press; Arms Control Project, Center for International Studies, MIT, 338p. Reviews, John A. Armstrong, Prob Comm, XVII, 3 (May-Jun 1968), 54-56; E. L. M. Burns, Int J, XXI, 4 (Autumn), 541-542; Herbert S. Dinerstein, Poli Sci Q, LXXXII, 2 (Jun 1967), 301-302; R. T. Rockingham Gill, East Eur, XV, 10 (Oct), 46-47; Philip E. Mosely, Mod Age, XI, 1 (Winter 1966-1967), 110-111; Mike Parrish, West Poli Q, XIX, 4 (Dec), 736-737; Joseph S. Roucek, Russ R, XXVI, 3 (Jul 1967), 309; Robert M. Slusser, Slav R, XXVI, 2 (Jun 1967), 324-326; ibid., XXVI, 4 (Dec 1967), 703-704; correspondence by Walter C. Clemens, Jr.; Ronald Steel, NY Rev of Books, Apr 6, 1967, p. 12.

732. Brown, Neville. "Towards the Super-Power Deadlock." W Today, XXII, 9 (Sept), 366-374.

733. Cook, Don. "The Art of Non-Proliferation." Enc, XXVII, 1 (Jul 1), 3-8.

734. Thomas, John R. "Limited Nuclear War in Soviet Strategy Thinking." Orbis, X, 1 (Spring), 184-212.

See also: 32, 46, 56, 61, 70, 86

ESPIONAGE

735. Deakin, F. W., and G. R. Storry. The Case of Richard Sorge. NY: Harper & Row, 373p. Reviews, Neal Asherson, NY Rev of Books, May 12, p. 18; Ladislas Farago, NY Times Book Rev, May 8, p. 12; Oscar Handlin, Atlantic Monthly, CCXVII, 5 (May), 131; James McKee, Prob Comm, XVII, 1 (Jan-Feb 1968), 38-39; TLS, Jan 27, 1967, p. 55.

736. Lonsdale, Gordon. Spy: Twenty Years in Soviet Secret Service. The Memoirs of Gordon Lonsdale. [See ABREES, 1965, No. 888] Reviews, Hugo Dewar, Prob Comm, XV, 4 (Jul-Aug), 54-57; Max Frankel, Atlantic Monthly, 4 (Apr), 103-108; Stefan T. Possony, Mod Age, X, 2 (Spring), 215-217; Harry Schwartz, NY Times Book Rev, Feb 13, p. 46; Richard Wraga, Russ R, XXV, 4 (Oct), 416-418.

737. Lucas, Norman. The Great Spy Ring. London: Arthur Books, 284p.

738. Seth, Ronald. Unmasked! The Story of Soviet Espionage. [See ABREES, 1965, No. 1078] Review, Hugo Dewar, Prob Comm, XV, 4 (Jul-Aug), 54-57.

739. United States Congress. Senate Committee on the Judiciary. Murder International, Inc.: Murder and Kidnapping as an Instrument of Soviet Policy. (1965) Review, Anatole W. Bedriy, Ukr R, XIII, 2 (Summer), 93-94.

739a. Whiteside, Thomas. An Agent in Place. The Wennerstrom Affair. NY: Viking, 150p.

See also: 284

PUBLIC OPINION, PROPAGANDA AND COMMUNICATIONS

740. Bayley, Richard. "Soviet Journalism and the Assimilation of Science." Jour Q, XLIII, 4 (Winter), 733-738.

741. Buzek, Anthony. How the Communist Press Works. [See ABREES, 1964, No. 1467] Reviews, George Mond, West Poli Q, XIX, 1 (Mar), 152-154; Nikolai P. Poltoratzky, Russ R, XXV, 4 (Oct), 424-425.

742. Dasbach, Anita Mallinckrodt. "U.S.-Soviet Magazine Propaganda: *America Illustrated* and *USSR*." Jour Q, XLIII, 1 (Spring), 73-84.

743. Gayev, A. "The Periodical Press." Bull Inst St USSR, XIII, 1 (Jan), 50-54; 3 (Mar), 49-52; 5 (May), 48-50; 8 (Aug), 38-42; 9 (Sept), 31-36; 10 (Oct), 50-54; 11 (Nov), 56-59; 12 (Dec), 38-41.

743a. Kruzhin, Petr. "The Periodical Press." Bull Inst St USSR, XIII, 2 (Feb), 41-47; 4 (Apr), 49-56; 6 (Jun), 35-40.

744. Grzybowski, Kazimierz. "Propaganda and the Soviet Concept of World Public Order." Law Contemp Prob, XXXI, 3 (Summer), 473-505.

745. Jones, Nancy C. "U.S. News in the Soviet Press." Jour Q, XLIII, 4 (Winter), 687-696.

746. Milenkovitch, Michael M. The View from Red Square: A Critique of Cartoons from Pravda and Izvestia, 1947-1964. NY: Hobbs, Dorman, 162p. [See ABREES, 1965, No. 1087] Reviews, John C. Merrill, Jour Q, XLIII, 4 (Winter), 785-786; Robert C. Richter, Prob Comm, XVI, 3 (May-Jun 1967), 63; Paul-Thomas Szabadsag, Cent Eur Fed, XV, 1 (Jun), 44.

747. Rossbacher, Peter. "The Soviet Journalistic Style." Gazette, XII, 2-3, pp. 201-211.

748. Schwartz, Morton. "The 1964 Presidential Elections through Soviet Eyes." West Poli Q, XIX, 4 (Dec), 663-671.

749. Zoul, Louis. The Soviet Inferno: A Validation of the Soviet Manual of Materialistic Bestiality, Known in Communist Jargon as the Manual on Psycho-political Warfare. NY: Public Opinion, 144p.

See also: 406, 409

VIII. THE ECONOMIC AND SOCIAL STRUCTURE

ECONOMIC HISTORY

750. Balogh, Eva S. "Hesitant Encounter: Episodes from Early Russo-Canadian Trade Relations." Can Slav Pap, VII, pp. 216-232.

751. Crosby, Alfred W., Jr. America, Russia, Hemp and Napoleon. [See ABREES, 1965, No. 1090a] Reviews, Robert G. Albion, J Mod

Hist, XXXIX, 4 (Dec 1967), 461-462; Isaac Stone, Russ R, XXV, 3 (Jul), 318-319.

752. Griffin, Frederick C. "The Formative Years of the Russian Factory Inspectorate, 1882-1885." Slav R, XXV, 4 (Dec), 641-650.

753. Sinzheimer, G. P. G. "The Economics of Russian Serfdom and

the Economics of American Slavery."
Jahrb Gesch Osteur, XIV, pp. 513-528.

See also: 467, 487, 488, 515,
764, 772, 810, 813

GENERAL ECONOMIC STUDIES

754. Ames, Edward. Soviet
Economic Processes. [See ABREES,
1965, No. 1126] Reviews, Alec Nove,
Econ J, LXXVI, 304 (Dec), 886-888;
Frederic L. Pryor, Am Econ R, LVI,
3 (Jun), 597-599.

755. Bergson, Abram. Essays
in Normative Economics. Cambridge,
Mass.: Harvard U Press, 246p. Reviews, William Baumol, J Pol Econ,
LXXIV, 3 (Aug), 410; R.W. Pfouts,
Ann Am Acad Pol Soc Sci, 368 (Nov),
211.

756. Bornstein, Morris, and
Daniel R. Fusfeld, eds. The Soviet
Economy — A Book of Readings. Rev.
ed. Homewood, Ill.: Richard D. Irwin,
Inc., 389p. Review, M.C. Kaser, Sov
St, XVIII, 2 (Oct), 255-256.

757. Campbell, Robert W. Soviet
Economic Power: Its Organization,
Growth and Challenge. 2nd ed. Bos-
ton: Houghton Mifflin Co., 184p.

758. Dobb, Maurice. Soviet
Economic Development Since 1917.
6th ed. NY: International Publishers,
515p.

759. Kuebler, Jeanne. Soviet
Economy: Incentives under Communism. Washington: Editorial Research Reports, II, 2, 18p.

760. Laird, Roy D. "New Trends
and Old Remedies." Prob Comm, XV,
2 (Mar-Apr), 21-28.

761. Nove, Alec. The Soviet
Economy: An Introduction. Rev. ed.
NY: Praeger, 354p. Reviews, Nico-
las Spulber, Ann Am Acad Pol Soc
Sci, 373 (Sept 1967), 264; East Eur,
XV, 6 (Jun), 52; TLS, Jun 15, 1967,
p. 540.

762. Osipov, Gennadii Vasilievich,
ed. Industry and Labour in the U.S.S.R.
Maurice Hookham, tr. London: Tavi-
stock Publications, 297p. Reviews,
Walter Galenson, Am Econ R, LXXVII,
2 (Jun 1967), 690; Alex Inkeles, Ann
Am Acad Pol Soc Sci, 372 (Jul 1967),
194-195; Ghita Ionescu, Government
and Opposition, I, 4 (Aug), 572-574;
M.C. Kaser, Econ J, LXXVI, 304 (Dec),
890-893; TLS, Jul 21, p. 639.

763. Schwartz, Harry. The Soviet
Economy Since Stalin. [See ABREES,
1965, No. 1123] Reviews, Dee Martin
Calligar, Bank Mag, CXLIX, 3 (Sum-
mer), 99-100; Lev E. Dobriansky, Ukr
Q, XXII, 1 (Spring), 80-82; Peter Wiles,
NY Rev of Books, VI, Apr 28, p. 21.

764. Smolinski, Leon. "The Soviet Economy." Survey, no. 59 (Apr),
88-101.

765. Landauer, Carl. Contemporary Economic Systems. [See ABREES,
1964, No. 1000] Review, Esther R.
Taus, Bank Mag, CXLIX, 2 (Spring),
98-99. [Includes discussion of Soviet
and Yugoslav economies]

766. Vaughan, F., and M. Clifford
Vaughan, compilers. Glossary of Eco-
nomics including Soviet Terminology.
NY: Elsevier, 201p. Review, R.E.F.
Smith, Sov St, XIX, 1 (Jul 1967), 147.

767. Wright, Arthur W. "The Soviet Economy." Cur Hist, LI, no. 302
(Oct), 218-225.

See also: 722, 778, 807

ECONOMIC THEORY AND
THE PLANNING SYSTEM

768. Bergson, Abram, Alexander
Erlich, Herbert S. Levine, Warren G.
Nutter, Stanislaw Wellisz, and Henry
L. Roberts, moderator. "Soviet Eco-
nomic Performance and Reform:
Some Problems of Analysis and Prog-
nosis (A Round-Table Discussion)."
Slav R, XXV, 2 (Jun), 222-246.

769. Bergson, Abram. The Economics of Soviet Planning. [See ABREES, 1964, No. 1106] Review, Joseph S. Berliner, Poli Sci Q, LXXXI, 1 (Mar), 120-121.

770. Bernard, Philippe J. Planning in the Soviet Union. I. Nove, tr. NY: Pergamon Press, 309p. Reviews, Philip Hanson, Survey, no. 64 (Jul 1967), 174-175; John P. Hardt, Russ R, XXVI, 3 (Jul 1967), 308-309.

771. Burck, Gilbert. "The Toughest Management Job in the World." Fortune, LXXIV, 1 (Jul 1), 73-79+. [Economic reform in the U.S.S.R.]

772. Bush, Keith. "The Budget and Plan for 1966." Bull Inst St USSR, XIII, 4 (Apr), 32-42.

773. ____. "The New Five-Year Plan." Prob Comm, XV, 4 (Jul-Aug), 1-7.

774. Chayanov, Aleksandr V. The Theory of Peasant Economy (Organizatsiia krest'ianskogo khoziaistva). R. E. F. Smith, tr. South Holland, Ill.: Richard D. Irwin, 317p. Reviews, John Adams, Ann Am Acad Pol Soc Sci, 374 (Nov 1967), 217; Colin Clark, Sov St, XIX, 2 (Oct 1967), 292-293.

775. Davies, R.W. "The Soviet Planning Process for Rapid Industrialization." Econ Plan, VI, 1, pp. 53-67.

776. ____. "Planning a Mature Economy in the U.S.S.R." Econ Plan, VI, 2, pp. 138-153.

777. Dodge, Norton T., and Dana G. Dalrymple. "The Stalingrad Tractor Plant in Early Soviet Planning." Sov St, XVIII, 2 (Oct), 164-168.

778. Eaton, John. Political Economy: A Marxist Textbook. Rev. ed. NY: International Publishers, 254p. [paper] Review, M. Bronfenbrenner, Am Econ R, LVI, 5 (Dec), 1305-1307.

779. "The Economic Reform and its Labor Aspects in the U.S.S.R." Lab Dev Abroad, Jun, pp. 1-9.

780. Felker, Jere L. Soviet Economic Controversies: The Emerging Marketing Concept and Changes in Planning, 1960-1965. Cambridge, Mass.: MIT Press, 172p. Reviews, Gregory Grossman, Poli Sci Q, LXXXIII, 2 (Jun 1968), 315-317; Alec Nove, Ann Am Acad Pol Soc Sci, 375 (Jan 1968), 241; Jan S. Prybyla, Russ R, XXVII, 1 (Jan 1968), 102; East Eur, XVI, 8 (Aug 1967), 56.

781. Gamarnikow, Michael. "The Reforms: A Survey." East Eur, XV, 1 (Jan), 13-23.

782. Grossman, Gregory. "Innovation and Information in the Soviet Economy." Am Econ R, LVI, 2 (May), 118-130.

783. Horowitz, Irving L. Three Worlds of Development. The Theory and Practice of International Stratification. Oxford: Oxford U Press, 475p. [paper] Reviews, Emory S. Bogardus, Sociology and Social Research, LI, 1 (Oct), 115-116; Remi Clignet, Am Soc R, XXXII, 2 (Apr 1967), 317; R.W. Gable, Am Pol Sci R, LXI, 2 (Jun 1967), 542; Asher Lans, Am Scholar, XXXV, 3 (Autumn), 785-788; Werner Levi, Ann Am Acad Pol Soc Sci, 368 (Nov), 230; E. F. Schumacher, Commentary, XLII (Oct), 137; Philip Van Slyck, Sat Rev, XLIX, Jun 11, p. 76; P. M. Worsley, Poli Sci Q, LXXXII, 1 (Mar 1967), 155; Christian Century, LXXXIII (May 4), 588; TLS, Aug 3, 1967, p. 702.

784. Inkeles, Alex. "Models in the Analysis of Soviet Society." Survey, no. 60 (Jul), 3-17.

785. Johansen, Leif. "Soviet Mathematical Economics." Econ J, LXXVI, no. 303 (Sept), 593-601.

786. Kantorovich, L. V. The Best Use of Economic Resources. P.F. Knightsfield, tr. [See ABREES, 1965, No. 1130] Review, Robert Dorfman, Am Econ R, LVI, 3 (Jun), 592-597.

787. Klatt, Werner. "The Twenty-third Congress of the CPSU: The Economic Perspective." Survey, no. 60 (Jul), 85-92.

788. Kutt, Aleksandr. "Soviet Industrial Planning and Management Reform." ACEN News, no. 121 (Jan-Feb), 18-23.

789. Majstrenko, I. "The Twenty-third Party Congress: The Economic Reform." Bull Inst St USSR, XIII, 5 (May), 13-15.

790. Neuberger, Egon. "Libermanism, Computopia, and Visible Hand: The Question of Informational Efficiency." Am Econ R, LVI, 2 (May), 131-144.

791. Obukhovich, A.P. "Participation by Workers' Organizations in Planned Social and Economic Development in Byelorussia." Int Lab R, XCIV, 5 (Nov), 449-464.

792. Posen, Gary S. "Recent Trends in Soviet Economic Reform." Int J, XXI, 4 (Autumn), 491-507.

793. Preobrazhensky, E. The New Economics. Brian Pearce, tr. Oxford: Oxford U Press, 310p. (1965) Reviews, Evsey D. Domar, Sov St, XVIII, 2 (Oct), 252-255; P.M. Sweezy, Am Econ R, LVI, 4, pt.1 (Sept), 921-924; Alfred Zauberman, Economica, XXXIII, no. 130 (May), 257-258.

794. Rosovsky, Henry, ed. Industrialization in Two Systems: Essays in Honor of Alexander Gerschenkron. NY: John Wiley & Sons, 289p. Reviews, Jerome B. Cohen, Am Hist R, LXXII, 4 (Jul 1967), 1347-1349; George G.S. Murphy, J Econ Hist, XXVII, 3 (Sept 1967), 420-423.

795. Schlesinger, Arthur, Jr. "A Muddling Evolution." Prob Comm, XV (Jul-Aug), 44-45.

796. Schlesinger, Rudolf. "On the Scope of Necessity and Error. Some Observations on Dr. Lewin's Article." [See ABREES, 1965, No.

783] Sov St, XVII, 3 (Jan), 353-367. [On early economic planning]

797. Segal, Gerald. "Automation, Cybernetics, and Party Control." Prob Comm, XV, 2 (Mar-Apr), 1-11.

798. Sharpe, Myron E. Planning, Profit, and Incentives in the U.S.S.R. Vol. I: The Liberman Discussion: A New Phase in Soviet Economic Thought. Vol. II: Reform of Soviet Economic Management. White Plains, N.Y.: International Arts and Sciences Press, vol. 1, 798p.; vol. II, 345p. Reviews, Robert W. Campbell, Slav R, XXVII, 4 (Dec 1968), 669-671; Ian M. Drummond, Can Slav St, III, 1 (Spring 1969), 143-144; I. Gordijew, Sov St, XIX, 3 (Jan 1968), 444-445.

799. Sherman, Howard J. "Marxist Economics and Soviet Planning." Sov St, XVIII, 2 (Oct), 169-188.

800. Sloan, Pat. "Soviet Plans: Post-Mortem and Project." Quart R, CCCIV, no. 650 (Oct), 402-403.

801. Sosnovy, Timothy. "The New Soviet Plan: Guns Still Before Butter." For Aff, XLIV, 4 (Jul), 620-632.

802. Tatu, Michel. "Economics and Politics. Soviet Reforms: The Debate Goes On." Prob Comm, XV, 1 (Jan-Feb), 28-34.

803. Thornton, Judith. "Factors in the Recent Decline in Soviet Growth." Slav R, XXV, 1 (Mar), 101-119.

804. van de Klundert, T., and H.J. Klok. "A Note on Strumilin's Model of Optimal Saving." Econ Plan, VI, 3, pp. 272-278.

805. Vvedensky, George. "The New Five-Year Plan." St Sov Un, VI, 1, pp. 20-25.

806. Wilber, Charles K. "A Non-monetary Index of Economic Development." Sov St, XVII, 4 (Apr), 408-416.

807. Wolfson, Murray. A Reappraisal of Marxian Economics. NY: Columbia U Press, 220p. Reviews,

D. F. Gordon, Am Econ R, LVII, 2
(Jun 1967), 627; Raymond Polin, Ann
Am Acad Pol Soc Sci, 370 (Mar 1967),
194; Joan Robinson, Poli Sci Q,
LXXXII, 4 (Dec 1967), 627-628; Ben
B. Seligman, Prob Comm, XVI, 3
(May-Jun 1967), 58-61; TLS, Nov 10,
p. 1018.

See also: 313, 967a, 1277

STATISTICS

808. Nemchinov, V. S., ed. The
Use of Mathematics in Economics
(Primenenie matematiki v ekonomi-
cheskikh issledovaniiakh; vol. 1,
1959). Alec Nove, tr. and ed. Cambridge, Mass.: MIT Press, 377p.
(1965) Reviews, Lawrence R. Klein,
Mo Lab R, LXXXIX, 7 (Jul), 788-789;
TLS, May 13, 1965, p. 374.

809. Nove, Alec. "Statistical
Puzzle Continues." Sov St, XVIII,
1 (Jul), 83-85.

See also: 322, 323, 426

AGRICULTURE

809a. Adams, Arthur E. "Edu-
cated Specialists and Change in Soviet
Agriculture," Agricultural History,
11, I, pp. 1-10.

810. Ballard, Allen B., Jr.
"Problems of State Farm Adminis-
tration." Sov St, XVII, 3 (Jan), 339-
352.

811. Bush, Keith. "Suggestions
for the Third Kolkhoz Congress."
Bull Inst St USSR, XIII, 11 (Nov),
41-51.

812. Domar, Evsey D. "The Soviet Collective Farm as a Producer
Cooperative." Am Econ R, LVI, 4,
pt. 1 (Sept), 735-757.

813. Dovring, Folke. "Soviet
Farm Mechanization in Perspective."
Slav R, XXV, 2 (Jun), 287-302.

814. Jackson, George D., Jr. "The
Krestintern and the Peasant as Revolutionary." Jahrb Gesch Osteur, XIV,
pp. 213-231.

815. Jasny, Naum. Khrushchev's
Crop Policy. [See ABREES, 1965, No.
1156] Reviews, Jeremy Anderson,
Slav R, XXVII, 1 (Mar 1968), 160-162;
Jerzy F. Karcz, Sou Econ J, XXXIII,
1 (Jul), 131-132; W(ilfred) K(napp),
Survey, no. 59 (Apr), 120-122.

816. Johnson, D. Gale. "The En-
vironment for Technological Change
in Soviet Agriculture." Am Econ R,
LVI, 2 (May), 145-153.

817. Kabysh, Simon. "Mechanization of Agriculture in the U.S.S.R."
Bull Inst St USSR, XIII, 8 (Aug), 28-32.

818. _____. "Mechanization of
Agriculture." St Sov Un, V, 3, pp.
72-78.

819. _____. "New Policy on Private Plots." St Sov Un, VI, 1, pp. 26-
34.

820. Laird, Roy D. "The New
'Zveno' Controversy: Forerunner of
Fundamental Change." Osteur Wirt,
XI, 4 (Dec), 254-261.

821. Lewin, M. "Who Was the
Soviet Kulak?" Sov St, XVIII, 2 (Oct),
189-212.

822. Miller, Robert F. "The Po-
litotdel: A Lesson from the Past."
Slav R, XXV, 3 (Sept), 475-496. [Mostly
MTS (Mashino-traktornye stantsii) po-
litotdely]

823. Nove, Alec. "Ideology and
Agriculture." Sov St, XVII, 4 (Apr),
397-407.

824. Ploss, Sidney I. Conflict
and Decision-Making in Soviet Russia:
A Case Study of Agricultural Policy,
1953-1963. [See ABREES, 1965, No.
1177] Reviews, Robert W. Campbell,
Am Hist R, LXXI, 2 (Jan), 629-630;
S. F. Cohen, Poli Sci Q, LXXXI, 2 (Jun),
320-321; Roy D. Laird, Russ R, XXV,
1 (Jan), 81-83; Peter Wiles, NY Rev
of Books, VI, Apr 28, p. 21.

825. Laird, Roy D., and Edward L. Crowley. Soviet Agriculture. [See ABREES, 1965, No. 1166] Review, Jan S. Prybyla, Russ R, XXV, 1 (Jan), 99-100.

826. Schwarz, Solomon. "Agriculture: The Curtain is Lifted." Prob Comm, XV, 2 (Mar-Apr), 12-20.

827. Wädekin, Karl-Eugen. "Internal Migration and the Flight From the Land in the U.S.S.R.: 1939-1959." Sov St, XVIII, 2 (Oct), 131-152.

828. Williams, D.S.M. "Russian Peasant Settlement in Semirech'ye." Cent Asian R, XIV, 2, pp.110-122.

829. "Country Reports: Soviet Union." Ag Abroad, XXI, 1 (Feb), 40-51; XXI, 4 (Aug), 23-26.

See also: 324, 673

INDUSTRY AND TRANSPORTATION

830. Azrael, Jeremy R. Managerial Power and Soviet Politics. Cambridge, Mass.: Harvard U Press, Russian Research Center Studies, 52, 161p. Reviews, John A. Armstrong, Slav R, XXVI, 2 (Jun 1967), 329-330; Joseph S. Berliner, Poli Sci Q, LXXXIII, 3 (Sept 1968), 446-447; J.P. Hardt, Sci, CCCLV (Mar 16, 1967), 1397; Barry M.Richman, Ann Am Acad Pol Soc Sci, 372 (Jul 1967), 156-158; Leonard Schapiro, Poli Q, XXXIX, 1 (Jan-Mar 1968), 105-106; Hugh Seton-Watson, Prob Comm, XVI, 4 (Jul-Aug 1967), 53-58; Peter Wiles, Slav East Eur R, XLVI, no. 106 (Jan 1968), 262-263; TLS, Jun 15, 1967, p.540.

831. Bush, Keith. "The Current Economic Reform: The Progress Made in Industry." Bull Inst St USSR, XIII, 10 (Oct), 33-43.

832. Davletshin, T. "The Legal Position of the State-Owned Industrial Enterprises in the U.S.S.R." Bull Inst St USSR, XIII, 5 (May), 3-9.

833. Guest, B. Roy. "The Growth of Soviet Air Cargo." J Geog, LXV, 7 (Oct), 323-327.

834. Kabaj, M. "Evolution of the Incentives System in U.S.S.R. Industry." Int Lab R, XCIV, 1 (Jul), 22-38.

835. Lovell, C.A. Knox. "Capital, Profit and Bonus in Soviet Industry: A Comment." Economica, XXXIII, 129 (Feb), 88-91.

836. Melnyk, Zinowij Lew. Soviet Capital Formation: Ukraine, 1928/29-1932. Munich: Ukrainian Free University Press, 182p. (1965) Review, Harry Hanak, Slav East Eur R, XLV, 105 (Jul 1967), 570-572.

837. Moorstein, Richard, and Raymond T. Powell. The Soviet Capital Stock, 1928-1962. Homewood, Ill.: Richard D. Irwin, 672p. [For the Economic Growth Center, Yale U.] Reviews, Earl J. Brubaker, J Econ Hist, XXVIII, 3 (Sept 1968), 479-482; Alfred Zauberman, Sov St, XIX, 4 (Apr 1968), 585-590.

838. Nutter, G. Warren. "The Relative Size of Soviet Industry: A Comment." J Pol Econ, LXXVI, 5 (Oct), 526-528. [Comment on an article by Judith Thornton; see ABREES, 1965, No. 1141]

839. Ryapolov, Gregory. "I Was a Soviet Manager." Harvard Bus R, XLIV, 1 (Jan-Feb), 117-125.

840. Richman, Barry M. Soviet Management. [See ABREES, 1965, No. 1198] Reviews, David Granick, Am Econ R, LVI, 1 (Mar), 263-265; Gerald B. Sperling, Sov St, XVIII, 7 (Jul), 108-110.

841. Swianiewicz, S. Forced Labor and Economic Development. An Enquiry into the Experience of Soviet Industrialization. [See ABREES, 1965, No. 1218] Reviews, Arthur E. Adams, Am Hist R, LXXI, 3 (Apr), 1022; Joseph S. Berliner, Am Econ R, LVI, 3 (Jun), 637-639; Naum Jasny,

Ann Am Acad Pol Soc Sci, 368 (Jan), 192; M.C. Kaser, Econ J, LXXVI, 304 (Dec), 890-893; Alfred Zauberman, Slav East Eur R, XLIV, no. 102 (Jan), 261-262.

842. Vvedensky, George A. "The Soviet Aluminum Industry." St Sov Un, V, 3, pp. 79-83.

843. _____. "The Uneven Development of the Soviet Oil and Gas Industry." Bull Inst St USSR, XIII, 2 (Feb), 32-35.

See also: 472, 518, 818, 829, 864

LABOR AND CONSUMER WELFARE

844. Brodersen, Arvid. The Soviet Worker: Labor and Government in Soviet Society. NY: Random House, 278p. Reviews, Jiri Kolaja, Am Soc R, XXXI, 6 (Dec), 888; Mary McAuley, Sov St, XIX, 2 (Oct 1967), 301-304; Peter J. Potichnyj, Slav R, XXVII, 4 (Dec 1967), 688-689.

845. Brown, Emily Clark. Soviet Trade Unions and Labor Organizations. Cambridge, Mass.: Harvard U Press, 394p. Reviews, Walter Galenson, Am Econ R, LVII, 2 (Jun 1967), 690; W. W. Kulski, Russ R, XXVI, 1 (Jan 1967), 80; Mary McAuley, Sov St, XIX, 2 (Oct 1967), 301-304; Peter J. Potichnyj, Slav R, XXVII, 4 (Dec 1967), 688-689; J.B. Sorenson, Am Pol Sci R, LXI, 1 (Mar 1967), 206; Peter Wiles, Prob Comm, XVI, 4 (Jul-Aug 1967), 62-64; J Pol Econ, LXXV, 1 (Feb 1967), 112.

846. Burck, Gilbert. "The Auspicious Rise of the Soviet Consumer." Fortune, LXXIV, 3, Aug, 130-133, 168-170, 172, 174.

847. Hajenko, F. "Manpower Utilization in the U.S.S.R." Bull Inst St USSR, XIII, 5 (May), 26-32.

848. Ivanov, S.A. "Industrial Labor Conventions in the U.S.S.R." Int Lab R, XCIII, 4 (Apr), 401-403.

849. Kutt, Aleksandr. "Con-sumer Goods in Soviet Industry." Bull Inst St USSR, XIII, 2 (Feb), 3-14.

850. Nash, Edmund. "U.S.S.R. Worktime Requirements for Consumer Purchases." Mo Lab R, LXXXIX, 7 (Jul), 772-773.

851. Schroeder, Gertrude. "Industrial Wage Differentials in the U.S.S.R." Sov St, XVII, 3 (Jan), 303-317.

852. "Significant Soviet Wage and Other Labor Data for 1965." Lab Dev Abroad, Apr, pp. 4-7.

See also: 320, 324, 432, 741, 790

MONEY AND FINANCE

853. Bush, Keith. "Soviet Gold Production and Reserves Reconsidered." Sov St, XVII, 4 (Apr), 490-493.

FOREIGN ECONOMIC RELATIONS

854. Adler-Karlsson, Gunnar. "The Semi-developed Soviet Economy — A Foreign Trade Illustration." Econ Plan, VI, 1, pp. 83-87.

855. Bush, Keith. "New Information on Soviet Foreign Trade." Bull Inst St USSR, XIII, 2 (Feb), 36-40.

856. Falkus, Malcolm E. "Russia and the International Wheat Trade, 1861-1914." Economica, XXXIII, no. 132 (Nov), 416-429.

857. Goldman, Marshall I. "Soviet Foreign Aid: Successes and Shortcomings." Osteur Wirt, XI, 3 (Sept), 193-208.

858. Nag, D.S. Foreign Economic Policy of Soviet Russia. Agra, India; 1964. Review, Charles Wegener, Ethics, LXXVII, 1 (Oct), 77-79.

859. Naleszkiewicz, Wladimir. "Technical Assistance of the American Enterprises to the Growth of the Soviet Union, 1929-1933." Russ R, XXV, 1 (Jan), 54-76.

860. Sharp, Mitchell. "Canada-U.S.S.R. Wheat Pact Renewed." Exter Aff, XVIII, 7 (Jul), 301-302.

REGIONAL ECONOMICS

861. Bott, Lydia. "Samarkand Initiative." Cent Asian R, XIV, 1, pp. 20-24.

862. Hajenko, F. "The Current Economic Reform: The General Significance and the Position of the Union Republics." Bull Inst St USSR, XIII, 10 (Oct), 21-33.

863. Mieczkowski, Z. "The Economic Regionalization of the Soviet Union in the Lenin and Stalin Period." Can Slav Pap, VII, 89-124.

864. Westwood, J. N. "The Vladikavkaz Railway: A Case of Enterprising Private Enterprise." Slav R, XXV, 4 (Dec), 669-675.

See also: 791

SOCIAL RELATIONS — GENERAL

865. Armytage, W. H. G. The Rise of the Technocrats. A Social History. London: Routledge & Kegan Paul, 448p. (1965) Review, TLS, Apr 7, 1968, p. 310. [Includes information on the Soviet Union]

866. _____. A Social History of Engineering. Cambridge, Mass.: MIT Press, 378p. Review, R. E. Carlson, Am Hist R, LXXII, 3 (Apr 1967), 927.

867. Bottomore, T. B. Classes in Modern Society. NY: Pantheon Books, 82p. Reviews, Christopher Lasch, NY Rev of Books, XI, Sept 12, 1968, p. 18; TLS, Apr 7, p. 311.

868. Green, Barbara B. "Soviet Politics and Interest Groups." Cur Hist, LI, no. 302 (Oct), 213-217.

869. "H. H." "Education and Social Mobility in the U.S.S.R." Sov St, XVIII, 1 (Jul), 57-65.

870. Hollander, Paul. "Leisure — An American and Soviet Value." Social Problems, XIV, 2 (Fall), 179-187.

871. _____. "The Uses of Leisure." Survey, no. 61 (Jul), 40-50.

872. Krylov, K. A. "Party Protection and Privileged Status in Soviet Society." Bull Inst St USSR, XIII, 3 (Mar), 26-31.

873. Levin, Alfred. "More on Social Stability, 1905-1917." Slav R, XXV, 1 (Mar), 149-154. [Refers to George L. Yaney, "A Critical Note," in Slav R, Sept 1965; see ABREES, 1965, No. 708]

874. Simirenko, Alex, ed. Soviet Sociology. Chicago: Quadrangle Books, 348p. Reviews, George Z. F. Bereday, Russ R, XXVII, 1 (Jan 1968), 91-94; W. Rex Crawford, Ann Am Acad Pol Soc Sci, 371 (May 1967), 265; R. A. Feldmesser, Sci, CLV, (Feb 17, 1967), 815; Mark G. Field, Am Soc R, XXXIII, 1 (Feb 1968), 158-159; Paul Hollander, Am Pol Sci R, LXII, 1 (Mar 1968), 252-253; Christian Century, LXXXIII, (Nov 30), 1474; East Eur, XVI, 6 (Jun 1967), 48.

875. "Soviet Youth: Nihilistic, Pessimistic, Critical." Prob Peop USSR, no. 26 (Winter), 60-62.

876. Voronitsyn, S. "An Insoluble Conflict." Bull Inst St USSR, XIII, 4 (Apr), 43-48. [Technicians versus intellectuals in Soviet society]

See also: 1277

WORK

877. Korsakov, R. "The System of Remuneration in the Soviet Merchant Marine." Int Lab R, XCIV, 4 (Oct), 398-414.

See also: 784

MARRIAGE, WOMEN, FAMILY AND YOUTH

878. Dodge, Norton T. Women in the Soviet Economy: Their Role in

Economic, Scientific and Technical Development. Baltimore: Johns Hopkins Press, 349p. Reviews, Sylvia Gilpin, Sov St, XIX, 1 (Jul 1967), 139-140; Judith Grunfeld, note on Gilpin review, Sov St, XIX, 4 (Apr 1968), 601-604; F. E. Ian Hamilton, Int Aff, XLIV, 10 (Jan 1968), 120-121; Holland Hunter, Ann Am Acad Pol Soc Sci, 373 (Sept 1967), 239-240; W. Phillips, Sci, CLIV, no. 3750 (Nov 11), 756-757; Judith Thornton, Russ R, XXVI, 2 (Apr 1967), 198-199; Peter Wiles, Prob Comm, XVI, 4 (Jul-Aug 1967), 62-64.

879. Heer, David M., and Judith G. Bryden. "Family Allowances and Fertility in the Soviet Union." Sov St, XVIII, 2 (Oct), 153-163.

880. _____. "Family Allowances and Population Policy in the U.S.S.R." J Marriage and Family, XXVIII, 4 (Nov), 514-519.

881. Juviler, Peter. "Soviet Families." Survey, no. 60 (Jul), 51-61.

882. Vlastovsky, V. G. "The Secular Trend in the Growth and Development of Children and Young Persons in the Soviet Union." Human Biology, XXXVIII, 3 (Sept), 219-230.

883. Waddington, Patrick. "Soviet Family Robinsons." Survey, no. 60 (Jul), 102-111.

See also: 591, 1229, 1233, 1279

HEALTH AND WELFARE

884. Amasoff, N. M. "Diary of a Russian Surgeon." George St. George, tr. Harpers, CCXXXIII, no. 1399 (Dec), 79-86.

885. Field, Mark G. "Health Personnel in the Soviet Union's Achievements and Problems." R Sov Med Sci, III, 1, pp. 1-20.

886. Korenevskaya, Elena. "Combatting Alcoholism in the U.S.S.R." Q J St Alcohol, XXVII, 1 (Mar), 97-101.

887. Kraus, Eva Maria. "The Use of Cadaver Blood in Soviet Medicine." R Sov Med Sci, III, 1, pp. 21-29.

888. _____. "The Use of Donor and Cadaver Bone Marrow in Soviet Medical Practice." R Sov Med Sci, III, 2, pp. 1-10.

889. Miklashevskaya, N. N. "Growth of the Head and Face in Boys of Various Ethnic Groups in the U.S.S.R." Human Biology, XXXVIII, 3 (Sept), 231-250.

890. Müller-Dietz, Heinz. "New Attacks on Homeopathy in the Soviet Union." R Sov Med Sci, III, 1, pp. 47-50.

891. Pavlenko, S. M. "Sanogenology — A Key Question in Medicine." R Sov Med Sci, III, 2, pp. 63-69.

892. Schulz, Heinrich. "Changes in Soviet Medical Ethics as an Example of Efforts to Find Stable Moral Values." St Sov Un, V, 4, pp. 49-61.

893. _____. "Historical Survey of Soviet Gerontology and Geriatrics." R Sov Med Sci, III, 2, pp. 11-32.

894. _____. "Soviet Military Medicine." Bull Inst St USSR, XIII, 6 (Jun), 14-20.

895. Volk, Sigmund. "Weightlessness as a Cause of Motion Sickness in Space." R Sov Med Sci, III, 1, pp. 30-40.

See also: 508

PSYCHOLOGY

896. Handbook of Soviet Psychology. Special Issue of Soviet Psychology and Psychiatry, Vol. IV, No. 3-4 (Spring-Summer). White Plains, N.Y.: International Arts and Sciences Press, 148p.

896a. Mead, Margaret. Soviet Attitudes toward Authority: An Interdisciplinary Approach to Problems of Soviet Character. NY: Schocken Books, 148p. [Orig. pub. in 1951]

See also Part I, Section VI (Philosophy), and: 236, 257, 259, 702, 1308, 1310, 1311, 1313

IX. THE INTELLECTUAL AND CULTURAL LIFE

RUSSIAN LANGUAGE

General description and grammar

897. Doljansky, Vera. Manual of the Russian Language for Adult Beginners. Jerusalem [Hebrew ed., 1964, 131p.]

898. Duff, C., and D. Makaroff. All-Purpose Russian for Adults. London: English Universities Press, 443p.

899. Jackson, E., and Elizabeth Bartlett Gordon. Russian Made Simple. NY: Doubleday, 209p. Review, Maurice I. Levin, Slav East Eur J, X, 1 (Spring), 95-96.

900. Khavronina, S. Russian as We Speak It. [2nd ed.] Moscow: Progress Publishers, 267p.

901. Maltzoff, Nicholas. Russian Reference Grammar. [See ABREES, 1965, No. 1294] Reviews, J. L. I. Fennell, Mod Lang R, LXI, 3 (Jul), 544; Anatole Flaume, Slav East Eur J, XI, 1 (Spring 1967), 108-110.

902. Potapova, Nina. Learning Russian I-IV. Moscow: Progress Publishers, 208; 171; 158; 152p. Review, Orrin Frink, Slav East Eur J, X, 1 (Spring), 96-98.

902a. Rocklyn, Eugene H., and Richard I. Moren. "A Feasibility Study of a Special Machine-Taught Oral-Aural Russian Language Course," pp. 73-77, in Stuart Margulies and Lewis D. Eigen, Applied Program Instruction. NY: John Wiley & Sons, 387p. (1962) Abstracted by H. L. Walton, Audio-Visual Communications Review, XIV, 1 (Spring), 147-148.

902b. Senn, Alfred E., and A. A. Rozhdestvensky. Cortina's Russian in Twenty Lessons. [5th ed.; originally pub. 1963] NY: Cortina, 444p.

903. Shaw, J. Thomas. The Transliteration of Modern Russian for English-Language Publications. Madison, Wis.: U Wisconsin Press, 15p. [paper]

904. Sokolsky, Anatole A. A History of the Russian Language. Tampa, Fla.: The author, 222p. Reviews, William W. Derbyshire, Slav East Eur J, XI, 2 (Summer 1967), 214-215; Serge A. Zenkovsky, Russ R, XXVI, 3 (Jul 1967), 314-315.

905. Ward, Dennis. The Russian Language Today. [See ABREES, 1965, No. 1299] Reviews, Walter A. Arndt, Russ R, XXVI, 2 (Apr 1967), 203-204; C. L. Drage, Slav East Eur R, XLIV, 102 (Jan), 200-203; Gilbert F. Holliday, Slav East Eur J, XI, 2 (Summer 1967), 215-217; Lang Q, IV, 3-4 (Spring-Summer), 14+.

906. Yakobson, Helen B. Conversational Russian: An Intermediate Course. [See ABREES, 1965, No. 1300] Review, David F. Robinson, Slav East Eur J, XI, 1 (Spring 1967), 107-108.

See also: Part I, Section VII, and 990

Readers (texts for language learning)

907. Aitken, Eleanor C., comp. and ed. Russian Poetry for Beginners. [2nd ed.] Chicago: Russian Language Specialties, 64p. (1965)

908. _____, comp. and ed. Russian Poetry for Intermediates from Pushkin to the Present Day. Chicago: Russian Language Specialties, 150p. (1965)

909. Anpilogova, B. G., E. Y. Vladimirsky, and E. Y. Sosenko, eds. Smile: Jokes, Anecdotes, Short Stories. Book One. V. N. Korotky, tr. Moscow: Progress, 102p. Review, Gilbert F.

Holliday, Slav East Eur J, X, 2 (Summer), 208-210.

910. Arzhak, Nikolai. Govorit Moskva. Washington, D.C.: Inter-Language Literary Association, 166p.

911. Babel', Isaac. Four Stories. A. B. Murphy, ed. [See ABREES, 1965, No. 1302] Review, Kenneth H. Ober, Slav East Eur J, X, 4 (Winter), 474-475.

912. Binyon, Timothy, ed. and tr. A Soviet Verse Reader. [See ABREES, 1965, No. 1303] Reviews, Evelyn Bristol, Slav East Eur J, X, 4 (Winter), 480; John E. Malmsted, Mod Lang J, L, 7 (Nov), 504-505.

913. Boronina, E. A Siberian Forest Adventure: Prikliuchenie v taige. G. A. Birkett, ed. NY: Appleton Century-Crofts, 33p. Review, Fan Parker, Slav East Eur J, XI, 2 (Summer 1967), 230-231.

914. Chekhov, A. P. The Seagull. [See ABREES, 1965, No. 1306] Review, Kenneth H. Ober, Slav East Eur J, X, 4 (Winter), 474-475.

915. Ehrenburg, I. The Actress: Aktërka, and Vsevolod Ivanov. Petya the Cock: Petja-petel. G. A. Birkett, ed. NY: Appleton Century-Crofts, 44p. Review, Fan Parker, Slav East Eur J, XI, 2 (Summer 1967), 230-231.

916. Fedin, K. Carp: Sazany. G. A. Birkett, ed. NY: Appleton Century-Crofts, 25p. Review, Fan Parker, Slav East Eur J, XI, 2 (Summer 1967), 230-231.

917. Fonvizin, Denis I. The Minor: Nedorosl'. W. Harrison, ed. [See ABREES, 1965, No. 1312] Review, C. L. Drage, Slav East Eur R, XLVI, 106 (Jan 1968), 228-229.

918. Fudel, N., ed. We Read Russian. Moscow: Foreign Languages Publishing House, 247p. Review, Orrin Frink, Slav East Eur J, X, 1 (Spring), 96-98.

919. Gibian, George, and Michael Samilov, eds. Modern Russian Short Stories. [See ABREES, 1965, No. 1313] Reviews, William W. Derbyshire, Mod Lang J, L, 3 (Mar), 236; Rebecca A. Domar, Slav East Eur J, X, 2 (Summer), 206-208; Robert L. Strong, Jr., Russ R, XXV, 3 (Jul), 319-320.

920. Gorky, M. Ilya's Childhood and Children. G. A. Birkett, ed. NY: Appleton Century-Crofts, 43p. Review, Fan Parker, Slav East Eur J, XI, 2 (Summer 1967), 230-231.

921. ____. The Lower Depths. Kurt Klein and Ira Goetz, eds. Letchworth, Herts.: Bradda, 137p. Review, Joachim T. Baer, Slav East Eur J, XII, 1 (Spring 1968), 98-99.

922. Il'f, Il'ia A., and Evgenii P. Petrov. Five Stories. M. J. F. Duncan, ed. Chicago: Russian Language Specialties, 116p. (1965) Review, Sigmund S. Birkenmayer, Slav East Eur J, XII, 1 (Spring 1968), 97-98.

923. Inber, Vera et al. Short Stories by Soviet Writers. [Parallel Russian-English texts] Moscow: Progress, 192p. Review, Gilbert F. Holliday, Slav East Eur J, X, 2 (Summer), 208-210.

924. Ivanov, Vsevolod. The Saga of the Sergeant: Byl' o serzhante. G. A. Birkett, ed. NY: Appleton Century-Crofts, 62p. Review, Fan Parker, Slav East Eur J, XI, 2 (Summer 1967), 230-231.

925. James, V. V Put'! Let's Go! London: British Broadcasting Corporation, 102p.

926. Johnson, E. L., and R. E. F. Smith. Russian Social Science Reader. NY: Pergamon Press, 206p. Review, Steven P. Hill, Slav East Eur J, XII, 2 (Summer 1968), 236-238.

927. Lavrenev, Boris A. The Forty-first: Sorok pervyi. Notes and vocabulary by S. Skipworth. [See ABREES, 1965, No. 1318] Review, Kenneth H. Ober, Slav East Eur J, X, 4 (Winter), 474-475.

927a. Lermontov, Mikhail Iu. A Hero of Our Time: Geroi nashego vremeni. D. J. Richards, ed. [See ABREES, 1965, No. 1319] Review, Rostislav D. Rozdestvensky, Slav East Eur J, X, 3 (Fall), 344-346.

928. Lewis, John Owen, and T. L. B. Wade. Russian Exercises for Language Laboratories. London: Methuen, 143p.

929. Maksim Gorky on Tolstoy. Intro. by F. M. Borras. Letchworth, Herts.: Bradda, 85p.

930. Panova, Vera F. Sputniki (The Traveling Companions). [See ABREES, 1965, No. 1324] Review, Robert L. Strong, Jr., Mod Lang J, L, 2 (Feb), 119.

931. Pargment, Lila. Conversational Reader of Russian Culture. [See ABREES, 1965, No. 1325] Reviews, Rostislav S. Rozdestvensky, Mod Lang J, L, 6 (Oct), 441-442; Valerie A. Tumins, Slav East Eur J, X, 2 (Summer), 214-215.

932. ____. Conversational Russian Reader. NY: Frederick Ungar, 174p.

933. Paustovsky, Konstantin. Zolotoi lin': The Golden Tench. Notes and vocab. by Lydia Saharova (20th Century Russian readers) Wellingborough, Northants.: Collets; NY: Ungar, 126p. Review, Joachim T. Baer, Slav East Eur J, XII, 1 (Spring 1968), 97-98.

934. Pitcher, H. J. Everyday Russian: A Reader. Chicago: Russian Language Specialties, 92p. Review, Sigmund S. Birkenmayer, Slav East Eur J, XII, 1 (Spring 1968), 97-98.

935. Pushkin, A. S. Boris Godunov. Victor Terras, ed. [See ABREES, 1965, No. 1326] Review, Sigmund S. Birkenmayer, Slav East Eur J, XI, 1 (Spring 1967), 101-102.

936. ____. Malen'kie tragedii. Little Tragedies. Notes and vocabu-

lary by Victor Terras. Letchworth, Herts.: Bradda, Chicago: Russian Language Specialties, 142p.

937. ____. Povesti pokoinogo Ivana Petrovicha Belkina. Norman Henley, ed. [See ABREES, 1965, No. 1327] Review, S. S. Birkenmayer, Slav East Eur J, XI, 1 (Spring 1967), 101-102.

938. Scriabine, Helene A., ed. Short Stories by Pushkin, Lermontov, and Dostoevsky. [See ABREES, 1965, No. 1329] Reviews, William W. Derbyshire, Mod Lang J, L, 3 (Mar), 240-241; Robert L. Strong, Jr., Slav East Eur J, X, 1 (Spring), 98-99.

939. Sholokhov, Mikhail A. Sud'ba cheloveka. Destiny of a Man. Patrick Waddington, ed. [See ABREES, 1965, No. 1330] Review, Gilbert F. Holliday, Slav East Eur J, X, 2 (Summer), 208-210.

940. Thompson, Lawrence C., Willis Konick and Vladimir Gross. Scenario of Ballad of a Soldier. Original screenplay by V. Yezhov and G. Chukrai. NY: Harcourt, Brace & World, 137p. Review, Ira Goetz, Slav East Eur J, XI, 3 (Fall 1967), 369-370.

941. Tolstoy, L. N. Smert' Ivana Il'icha. The death of Ivan Ilyich. M. Beresford, ed. Letchworth, Herts.: Bradda, 172p.

942. Turgenev, Ivan S. A Sportsman's Sketches: Zapiski okhotnika. W. Harrison, tr. [See ABREES, 1965, No. 1331] Review, Joachim T. Baer, Slav East Eur J, XI, 1 (Spring 1967), 101-102.

943. ____. Asya. F. G. Gregory, ed. [See ABREES, 1965, No. 1332] Review, J. T. Baer. [See No. 942]

944. ____. Fathers and Sons. E. R. Sands, ed. [See ABREES, 1965, No. 1333] Review, J. T. Baer. [See No. 942]

945. Vishnyakova, O., ed. Echo. Short Stories by A. Grin, K. Fedin, Y. Kuranov, V. Lidin, Y. Nagibin, L.

Panteleyev, E. Permyak, M. Prishvin, G. Skulsky. Vocabulary tr. by V. N. Korotky. Moscow: Progress, 88p. + 36p. vocabulary section. Review, Gilbert F. Holliday, Slav East Eur J, X, 2 (Summer), 208-210.

See also: 968

Phonetics, pronunciation and stress

946. Ward, Dennis. Russian Pronunciation Illustrated. Cambridge: Cambridge U Press, 101p. Review, Norman Luxenburg, Slav East Eur J, X, 4 (Winter), 482-483.

Morphology and syntax

947. Belevitskaya-Khalizeva, V. S., et al. Exercises in Russian Syntax. Moscow: Foreign Languages Publishing House, 250pp.; Workbook, 326pp. Review, Orrin Frink, Slav East Eur J, X, 1 (Spring), 96-98.

948. Jakobson, Jakov. "Grammatical Parallelism and its Russian Facet." Lang, XLII, 2 (Apr-Jun), 399-429.

949. Johnson, E. C. "Crimean Gothic Cognates." Lang Q, V, 1-2 (Fall-Winter), 33-38.

950. Matejka, Ladislav. Prerequisites to Syntactic Recognition in Russian: Clause Nuclei. [Research in Machine Translation] Detroit: Wayne State U, 127p. (1965) Review, Lew R. Micklesen, Slav East Eur J, XI, 2 (Summer 1967), 231-232.

951. Murphy, Arthur B. Aspectival Usage in Russian. [See ABREES, 1965, No. 1346] Review, Charles E. Bidwell, Slav East Eur J, XI, 2 (Summer 1967), 218-219.

952. Shapiro, Michael. "The Derivational Morphology of Russian Patrials." Lingua, XVI, 1 (Jan), 14-26; and XVI, 2 (Apr), 113-119.

953. Simmons, Robert W., Jr.

"Russian Past Passive Participles: Orthography and Stress." Slav East Eur J, X, 4 (Winter), 458-462.

954. Vilgelminina, A. A. The Russian Verb: Aspect and Voice. Moscow: Foreign Languages Publishing House, 143p. Review, Orrin Frink, Slav East Eur J, X, 1 (Spring), 96-98.

Dictionaries, studies of vocabulary and orthography

955. Benson, Morton, comp. Dictionary of Russian Personal Names, with a guide to stress and morphology. Philadelphia: U Pennsylvania Press, 175p. Review, Howard I. Aronson, Mod Lang J, L, 2 (Feb), 166-167.

956. Dmitrieff, A., comp. Russian-English Glossary of Library Terms. NY: Telberg Book Corporation, 161p. Review, Dmytro M. Shtohryn, Slav East Eur J, XI, 4 (Winter 1967), 490-491.

957. Gardiner, S. C. German Loanwords in Russian, 1550-1690. [See ABREES, 1965, No. 1352] Reviews, Herbert Galton, Slav East Eur J, X, 3 (Fall), 354-356; Valentin J. A. Kiparsky, Lingua, XX, 3 (Oct 1968), 323-327; H. Leeming, Slav East Eur R, XLV, 105 (Jul 1967), 537-539; Gerta Hüttl-Worth, Lang, XLIV, 1 (Spring), 141-144.

958. Hüttl-Worth, Gerta. Foreign Words in Russian: A Historical Sketch, 1550-1800. [See ABREES, 1965, No. 1355] Review, S. C. Gardiner, Slav East Eur R, XLV, 104 (Jan 1967), 216-217.

959. Katayen, Lelia, and Val Telberg. Russian-English Dictionary of Musical Terms. [See ABREES, 1965, No. 1358] Review, William W. Derbyshire, Slav East Eur J, X, 3 (Fall), 363-365.

960. Korn, David. The Russian Verb: A Reference Grammar with Dictionary. Washington, D.C.: Kamkin, 277p.

961. Paternost, Joseph. Russian-English Glossary of Linguistic Terms.

University Park, Pa.: Penn State U
Press, 230p. (1965) Review, Steven
P. Hill, Slav East Eur J, X, 1 (Spring),
93-95.

962. Pei, Mario. Glossary of
Linguistic Terminology. NY: Colum-
bia U Press, 299p. Review, Joseph
Paternost, Slav East Eur J, XII, 1
(Spring 1968), 116-118.

963. Sjöberg, Anders. "Two Unknown Translations of Meletij Smot-
rickij's Slavonic Grammar." Scando-
Slavica, XII (1966), 123-131.

964. Vakar, N. P. A Word Count
of Spoken Russian: The Soviet Usage.
Columbus: Ohio State U Press, 367p.
Reviews, Michael Klimenko, Can Slav
St, II, 3 (Fall 1968), 424-425; Joseph
Paternost, Slav East Eur J, XI, 1
(Spring 1967), 113-114.

Versification

965. Žirmunskij, V. Introduction
to Metrics: The Theory of Verse. C.
F. Brown, tr. The Hague: Mouton,
Slavistic Printings and Reprintings,
245p. Reviews, James Bailey, Russ
R, XXVI, 3 (Jul 1967), 317; letter
from Clarence F. Brown, Russ R,
ibid., 320-321; Morris Halle, Slav
East Eur J, XII, 2 (Summer 1968),
213-218; David G. Halliburton, J Aes
Art Crit, XXVII, 2 (Winter 1968), 231;
TLS, Nov 24, p. 1102.

Scientific Russian

966. Beresford, Michael. Complete Russian Course for Scientists
[See ABREES, 1965, No. 1371] Review, Maurice I. Levin, Slav East Eur
J, XI, 1 (Spring 1967), 105-107.

967. Kotz, Samuel. Russian-
English Dictionary and Reader in the
Cybernetical Sciences. NY: Aca-
demic Press, 214p.

967a. Kurakov, I. G. Science,
Technology and Communism: Some
Questions of Development. Carin
Dedijer, tr. Oxford: Pergamon, 126p.
Review, Stephan Lamed, Can Slav St,
II, 4 (Winter 1968), 588-589.

968. Magner, Thomas. Russian
Scientific and Technical Readings.
University Park, Pa. Penn State U,
200p. (1965) Review, Alex M. Shane,
Slav East Eur J, X, 2 (Summer), 213-
214.

Teaching of Russian

969. Aronson, Howard I. "Order
of Presentation of Grammatical Structures in the Teaching of Russian."
Slav East Eur J, X, 2 (Summer), 181-190.

970. Baker, Robert L. "Flexible
Scheduling for Individualized Instruction and Remedial Work in Russian."
Int J Am Ling, XXXII, 1, pt. 2 (Jan),
152-159.

971. Dewey, Horace W. "Person-
alized Exercises for Students of Ele-
mentary Russian." Mod Lang J, L, 1
(Jan), 12-15.

972. Liapunov, Marina Prochoroff.
"An Instructional Program in Russian
for Secondary Schools." Int J Am Ling,
XXXII, 1, pt. 2 (Jan), 147-151.

973. Rosen, Nathan. "All's Well
that Ends Badly." Slav East Eur J, X,
1 (Spring), 46-65.

974. Skarginsky, G. P. "Teacher
Training and Teachers of Russian."
Slav East Eur J, X, 4 (Winter), 498-
499.

975. Walker, Claire. "Russian
Teaching: It doesn't have to end badly."
Slav East Eur J, X, 3 (Fall), 316-326.

Onomastics

See: 955

LITERATURE

Survey studies, histories and
reference works

976. Adams, Robert Martin.
NIL: Episodes in the Literary Con-
quest of Void During the 19th Cen-
tury. NY: Oxford U Press, 249p.
Review, George P. Elliott, Book Week,
Nov 27, p. 24. [Discusses Goncharov,
Tolstoy, Dostoevskii]

977. Bowra, C. M. Poetry and
Politics, 1900-1960. Cambridge;
Cambridge U Press, 157p. Reviews,
Stanley Weintraub, Books Abr, XLI,
2 (Spring 1967), 214; NY Times Book
Rev, Oct 23, p. 40; TLS, Sept 8, p. 830.

978. Čiževska, Tatjana. Glossary
of the Igor Tale. The Hague: Mouton,
Slavistic Printings and Reprintings,
53, 405p. Review, Edward Stankiewicz,
Slav East Eur J, XI, 3 (Fall 1967),
345-346.

979. Gayev, A. "Socialist Realism Begins a New Offensive." Bull
Inst St USSR, XIII, 6 (Jun), 21-26.

980. Girard, René. Deceit, De-
sire and the Novel: Self and Other in
Literary Structure. Yvonne Freccero,
tr. Baltimore: Johns Hopkins Press,
318p. (1965) Review, Robert L. Bel-
knap, Slav East Eur J, XI, 4 (Winter
1967), 487-488. [Orig. pub. 1961;
Mensonge romantique et vérité ro-
manesque]

981. Heiman, Leo. "Nostalgia
and Nihilism." East Eur, XV, 8 (Aug),
55-56.

982. Hollander, Paul. "Models
of Behavior in Stalinist Literature: A
Case Study of Totalitarian Values and
Controls." Am Soc R, XXXI, 3 (Jun),
352-364.

983. Hollingsworth, Barry.
"Arzamas: Portrait of a Literary
Society." Slav East Eur R, XLIV,
103 (Jul), 306-326.

984. Ilarion, Metropolitan of Kiev.

Monk Chrabr on Slavic Writings. The
Oldest Cyrillic Version of 1348. I.
Ohienko, ed. (Readings in Slavic Lit-
erature, 4). Winnipeg: U Manitoba
Press, 28p. (1964) Review, Ladislav
Matejka, Slav East Eur J, X, 3 (Fall),
357-359.

985. Ivanov, Vyacheslav. "Sym-
bolism." Thomas E. Byrd, tr. Russ
R, XXV, 1 (Jan), 24-34.

986. Lathouwers, M. A. "The Idea
of the Fulfillment of History in Contemporary Soviet Literature." St Sov
Un, VI, 1, pp. 62-70.

987. Leighton, Lauren G. "The
Anecdote in Russia: Puškin, Vjazem-
skij, and Davydov." Slav East Eur J,
X, 2 (Summer), 155-156.

988. Lemon, Lee T., and Marion
J. Ries, eds. and trs. Russian Formalist Criticism. [See ABREES,
1965, No. 1395] Review, Robert P.
Hughes, Slav East Eur J, XII, 3 (Feb
1968), 367-369.

989. Lindstrom, Thaïs S. A Con-
cise History of Russian Literature.
Volume I: From the Beginnings to
Chekhov. NY: NY Univ Press, 233p.
Reviews, Sergei Kryzitski, Novyi
Zhurnal, no. 89 (1969), 290-291; Vadim
Liapunov, Slav East Eur J, XI, 3 (Fall
1967), 348-350; Philippe Radley, Slav
R, XXVII, 4 (Dec 1968), 689-690; Louis
J. Shein, Can Slav St, I, 1 (Spring 1967),
151-2.

990. Magner, Thomas F. Soviet
Dissertations for Advanced Degrees
in Russian Literature and Slavic Linguistics, 1934-1962. University Park,
Pa.: Penn State U Press, 100p.

991. Malof, Joseph. "Meter as
Organic Form." Mod Lang Q, XXVII,
1 (Mar), 3-17. [Russian Formalist
poetics]

992. Medish, Vadim. "The Soviet
Literary Scene." Russ R, XXV, 2 (Apr),
150-159.

993. Neuhauser, Rudolf. "Changing

Attitudes in Soviet-Russian Studies of Kievan and Old Russian Literature." Can Slav Pap, VII, pp. 182-197.

994. Nilsson, Nils Ake. "'Muzhaites' muzhi!' On the History of a Poetism." Scando-Slavica, XII, pp. 5-12.

995. Oulanoff, Hongor. The Serapion Brothers: Theory and Practice. The Hague: Mouton, 186p. Reviews, Gary Kern, Slav East Eur J, XII, 1 (Spring 1968), 90-91; Richard Sheldon, Russ R, XXVI, 2 (Apr 1967), 193-194; R. D. B. Thomson, Slav East Eur R, XLVI, 106 (Jan 1968), 234-235.

996. Reeve, F. D. The Russian Novel. NY: McGraw-Hill, 403p. Reviews, William E. Harkins, Slav East Eur J, XI, 3 (Fall 1967), 350-353; Oleg A. Maslenikov, Russ R, XXVI, 4 (Oct 1967), 419; R. W. Simmons, Books Abr, XLI, 4 (Fall 1967), 471; Virg Q R, XLII, 2 (Summer), 102.

997. Roberts, Spencer E. Soviet Historical Drama: Its Role in the Development of a National Mythology. [See ABREES, 1965, No. 1399] Reviews, Nadejda Gorodetzky, Mod Lang R, LXI, 4 (Oct), 736; Harold Swayze, Russ R, XXVI, 3 (Jul 1967), 306-307; R. D. B. Thomson, Slav East Eur R, XLIV, 103 (Jul), 496-497; Leon I. Twarog, Slav East Eur J, XII, 4 (Winter 1968), 467-470.

998. Schaarschmidt, G. "Interior Monologue and Soviet Literary Criticism." Can Slav Pap, VII, pp. 143-152.

999. Shakhovskaya, Zinaida. "The Significance of Religious Themes in Soviet Literature." St Sov Un, V, 4, pp. 119-129.

1000. Simmons, Ernest J. Introduction to Russian Realism: Pushkin, Gogol, Dostoevsky, Tolstoy, Chekhov, Sholokhov. [See ABREES, 1965, No. 1400] Reviews, John Fizer, Mod Lang J, L, 2 (Feb), 109-110; Nadejda Gorodetzky, Slav East Eur R, XLIV, 102 (Jan), 206-207; Nicholas Lee, Slav

East Eur J, X, 2 (Summer), 217-219; Oleg A. Maslenikov, Russ R, XXV, 3 (Jul), 321-322.

1001. Slonim, Marc. "News from Moscow." NY Times Book Rev, Oct 9, p. 60. [Publication of Katayev, "The Holy Well," and Boris Mozhayev, "From the Life of Kuzkin"]

1002. _____. "Russian Poets in Paris." NY Times Book Rev, Jan 9, p. 44.

1003. "The Soviet Myth of Cultural Freedom." Ukr Q, XXII, 2 (Summer), 101-106. [Deals with suppression of writers, especially Ukrainians, under the Soviet regime]

1004. Stone, Alan A., and Sue Smart Stone, eds. The Abnormal Personality through Literature. Englewood Cliffs, N.J.: Prentice-Hall, 423p. Review, American Imago, XXIII, 3 (Fall), 281. [Anthology of selections on abnormal personality from Chekhov, Gogol', Dostoevsky, Tolstoy, and European writers]

1005. Trensky, Paul I. "The Year 1812 in Russian Poetry." Slav East Eur J, X, 3 (Fall), 283-302.

1006. Weiss, Thomas. "The Guilt Complex in Communist Literature." East Eur, XV, 6 (Jun), 2-6; XV, 7 (Jul), 9-15.

See also: 244, 247, 248, 250, 251, 253, 492, 1253, 1719

Anthologies

1007. Friedberg, Maurice, and Robert A. Maguire, eds. and trs. A Bilingual Collection of Russian Short Stories, Vol. II. [See ABREES, 1965, No. 1406] Review, Xenia Gasiorowska, Slav East Eur J, X, 4 (Winter), 479-480.

1008. Gorodetsky, Nadejda, and Jesse S. Coulson. Russian Short Stories: 20th Century. [See ABREES, 1965, No. 1407] Review, Carl R. Proffer, Slav East Eur J, XI, 1 (Spring 1967), 104-105.

1009. Harper, Kenneth, Galina
Koulaeff, and Margarita Gisetti, eds.
New Voices: Contemporary Soviet
Short Stories. NY: Harcourt, Brace
& World, 201p. Review, Alex M.
Shane, Slav East Eur J, XI, 1 (Spring
1967), 102-104.

1010. Hayward, Max, and Edward
L. Crowley, eds. Soviet Literature in
the Sixties. [See ABREES, 1965, No.
1392] Review, R. D. B. Thomson, Slav
East Eur R, XLIV, 103 (Jul), 498-499.

1011. Markov, Vladimir, ed.
Modern Russian Poetry: An Anthol-
ogy with Verse Translations. NY:
Bobbs-Merrill, 842p. Merrill Sparks,
tr. Reviews, Helen Muchnic, Russ R,
XXVII, 2 (Apr 1968), 252-253; Victor
Terras, Slav East Eur J, XII, 3 (Fall
1968), 364-365.

1012. Ognyev, Vladimir, comp.
Vo ves golos. Soviet Poetry. Nina
Shulgina, notes; Bernard Meares, tr.
Moscow: Progress, 452p. Review,
Clarence F. Brown, Slav East Eur J,
XI, 2 (Summer 1967), 227-230.

1013. Reavey, George, ed. and
tr. The New Russian Poets 1953-
1966: An Anthology. NY: October
House, 319p. Review, R. W. Simmons,
Books Abr, XLI, 4 (Fall 1967), 504.

1014. Segel, Harold B., ed. and
tr. The Literature of Eighteenth Century Russia. NY: Dutton, 2 vols., 472
and 448p. [paper] Review, William B.
Edgerton, Slav East Eur J, XII, 1
(Spring 1968), 59-78.

1015. Steiner, George, ed. The
Penguin Book of Modern Verse Trans-
lation. Baltimore: Penguin, 332p.
Review, Victor Terras, Slav East Eur
J, XII, 3 (Fall 1968), 364-365.

1016. Stokes, A. D., ed. Khres-
tomatiya po drevnei russkoi literature. Letchworth, Herts.: Bradda,
336p. Review, William W. Derbyshire, Russ R, XXV, 3 (Jul), 322.

1017. Yarmolinsky, Avrahm.
Two Centuries of Russian Verse: An

Anthology. Babette Deutsch, tr. NY:
Random House, 322p. Review, NY
Times Book Rev, May 8, p. 26.

Translations of works of individ- ual authors and works about them

Akhmadulina, B.

1018. Akhmadulina, Bella. "Bride."
[poem] Stephan Stepanchev, tr. Harper's, CCXXXII, 1393, Jun, p. 50.

Akhmatova, A.

1019. Frank, Victor. "Anna
Akhmatova." Survey, no. 60 (Jul),
93-101.

1020. Gayev, A. "Anna Akhmatova:
An Example of Literary Integrity."
Bull Inst St USSR, XIII, 4 (Apr), 14-19.

Alyoshin, S.

1021. Revutsky, V. "A New View
of Don Juan: Samuel Alyoshin's Comedy 'At That Time in Seville'." Slav
East Eur R, XLIV, 102 (Jan), 88-97.

Annenkov, G.

1022. Annenkov, George. Dnevnik
moikh vstrech. Tragicheskiy tsikl. 2
vols. NY: Inter-Language Literary
Associates, 352 and 352p. Reviews,
Helen Muchnic, Russ R, XXVI, 1 (Jan
1967), 84, and XXVI, 2 (Apr 1967),
188-190; Fan Parker, Books Abr, XLI,
2 (Spring 1967), 235; R. D. B. Thomson,
Slav East Eur R, XLVI, 107 (Jul 1968),
510-511; Zoya Yurieff, Slav East Eur
J, XII, 3 (Fall 1968), 2; Viacheslav
Zavalishin, Novyi Zhurnal, no. 84, 271-
274, and no. 85, 285-6.

Artsybashev, M.

1023. Pachmuss, Temira. "Mik-
hail Artsybashev in the Criticism of
Zinaida Gippius." Slav East Eur R,
XLIV, 102 (Jan), 76-87.

Arzhak, N. [See Daniel, Iu]

Babel', I.

1024. Babel', Isaac. "Shabos Nahamu." Max Hayward, tr. Atlantic Monthly, CXVII, 3, Mar, pp. 79-81.

1025. Murphy, A. B. "The Style of Isaac Babel'." Slav East Eur R, XLIV, 103 (Jul), 361-380.

See: 911, 1383

Blok, A.

1026. Blok, Alexander. "On the Field of Kulikova." Jon Stallworthy and Peter France, trs. Crit Q, VIII, 1 (Spring), 30-34.

1027. Kemball, Robin. Alexander Blok: A Study in Rhythm and Metre. [See ABREES, 1965, No. 1418] Reviews, James Bailey, Slav East Eur J, XI, 1 (Spring 1967), 92-95; Richard F. Gustafson, Russ R, XXV, 4 (Oct), 421-423; R. D. B. Thomson, Slav East Eur R, XLVI, 106 (Jan 1968), 229-231; TLS, Aug 25, p. 761.

See: 977

Bondarev, Iu.

1028. Bondarev, Iurii. Silence. Elizaveta Fen, tr. [See ABREES, 1965, No. 1420] Review, NY Times Book Rev, Feb 20, 1967, p. 30.

Brodsky, J.

1029. "Three Poems." George L. Kline, tr. Russ R, XXV, 2 (Apr), 131-134.

Bulgakov, M.

1030. Slonim, Marc. "Moscow Art Theater Satirized." NY Times Book Rev, Mar 13, p. 42. [Note on Bulgakov's *Black Snow: A Theatrical Novel*]

Bunin, I.

1031. Pachmuss, Temira. "Ivan Bunin Through the Eyes of Zinaida Gippius." Slav East Eur R, XLIV, 103 (Jul), 337-350.

Bykov, V.

1032. Heiman, Leo. Review article on Vassili Bykov's novel, The Dead Don't Suffer Pain, published in 1966 in Novyi Mir. East Eur, XV, 8 (Aug), 55-56.

Chekhov, A.

1033. Bristow, Eugene K. "On Translating Chekhov." Q J Speech, LII, 3 (Oct), 290-294.

1034. Chekhov, Anton Pavlovich. The Cherry Orchard, Tyrone Guthrie, and Leonid Kipnis, trs. [See ABREES, 1965, No. 1425] See: 1033

1035. _____. The Cherry Orchard. Avrahm Yarmolinsky, tr. NY: Avon Books 191p. (1965) [paper] See: 1033]

1036. _____. Chekhov: The Major Plays. Ann Dunnigan, tr. NY: New American Library, 380p. (1964) Review, Thomas Winner, Slav East Eur J, X, 4 (Winter), 475-477. [Contains Ivanov, The Seagull, Uncle Vanya, The Three Sisters, The Cherry Orchard] [See: 1033]

1037. _____. The Early Plays by Chekhov. Alex Szogyi, tr. NY: Bantam Books, 314p. (1965) [See: 1033]

1038. _____. The Oxford Chekhov, Vol. III: Plays. Ronald Hingley, ed. and tr. Oxford: Oxford U Press, 343p. [Includes Uncle Vanya, The Three Sisters, The Cherry Orchard, The Wood-Demon] [See: 1033]

1039. _____. The Oxford Chekhov, Vol. VIII. Stories, 1895-1897. Ronald Hingley, ed. and tr. [See ABREES, 1965, No. 1427] Reviews, Robert L. Jackson, Slav R, XXVI, 2 (Jun 1967), 343-345; TLS, Jun 2, p. 496. [See 1033]

1040. _____. Platonov: A Play in Four Acts and Five Scenes. David

Magarshack, NY: Hill and Wang, 195p. Review, Helen Muchnic, NY Rev of Books, VII, 2, Sept 18, pp. 20-22. [See: 1033]

1041. ____. The Selected Letters of Anton Chekhov. Lillian Hellmann, ed. Sidonie K. Lederer, tr. NY: McGraw-Hill, 331p. (1965) Review, Rimvydas Silbajoris, Slav East Eur J, X, 4 (Winter), 477-478.

1042. ____. The Three Sisters. Tyrone Guthrie and Leonid Kipnis, trs. [See ABREES, 1965, No. 1429]. [See: 1033]

1043. ____. Ward Six and Other Stories. Ann Dunnigan, tr. NY: New American Library, 399p. (1965) Review, Karl D. Kramer, Slav East Eur J, X, 3 (Fall), 343-344.

1044. Conrad, Joseph L. "Čexov's The Man in a Shell: Freedom and Responsibility." Slav East Eur J, X, 4 (Winter), 400-410.

1045. Hagan, John. "Chekhov's Fiction and the Ideal of 'Objectivity'." PMLA, LXXXI, 5 (Oct), 409-417.

1046. Hingley, Ronald. Chekhov: A Biographical and Critical Study. NY: Barnes and Noble, 262p. Review, Helen Muchnic, NY Rev of Books, VII, 2, Sept 18, pp. 20-22.

1047. Moravcevich, Nicholas. "The Dark Side of the Chekhovian Smile." Drama Survey, V, 3 (Winter), 237-251.

1048. ____. "The Obligatory Scene in Chekhov." Drama Crit, IX, 2 (Spring), 97-103.

1049. Shestov, Leon. Chekhov and Other Essays. Intro. by Sidney Monas. Ann Arbor: U Michigan Press, 231p. Reviews, Helen Muchnic, NY Rev of Books, VII, 2, Sept 18, pp. 20-22; Temira Pachmuss, Slav East Eur J, XI, 3 (Fall 1967), 355-357; Peter Rossbacher, Russ R, XXVI, 1 (Jan 1967), 97.

1050. Smith, J. Oates. "Chekhov

and the Theater of the Absurd." Buck R, XIV, 3 (Dec), 44-58.

1051. States, Bert O. "Chekhov's Dramatic Strategy." Yale R, LVI, 2 (Dec), 212-223.

1052. Valency, Maurice. The Breaking String: The Plays of Anton Chekhov. NY: Oxford U Press, 324p. Reviews, Ronald Hingley, Russ R, XXVI, 3 (Jul 1967), 305-306; Nicholas Moravcevich, Drama Critique, IX, 3 (Fall), 163-164; NY Times Book Rev, Apr 2, 1967, p. 26; Virg Q R, XLIII (Spring 1967), 74; Thomas Winner, Slav East Eur J, XII, 1 (Spring 1968), 79-82.

1053. Winner, Thomas. Chekhov and His Prose. NY: Holt, Rinehart & Winston, 281p. Reviews, Donald Fanger, Nation, CCII (Jun 6), 684; Ronald Hingley, Russ R, XXVI, 3 (Jul 1967), 305-306; T. S. Lindstrom, Sat Rev, XLIX, Feb 19, p. 50; Ralph E. Matlaw, Slav East Eur J, XII, 2 (Summer 1968), 251-253; Helen Muchnic, NY Rev of Books, VII, 2, Sept 18, pp. 20-22; Virg Q R, XLII (Summer), 103; Robert L. Jackson, Slav R, XXVII, 2 (Jun 1968), 348-350.

Chukovskii, K.

1054. Chukovskii, Kornei. From Two to Five. Miriam Morton, ed. and tr. Berkeley, Los Angeles: U California Press, 170p.

1054a. Shneiderman, S. L. "Visit to Peredelkino." NY Times Book Rev, Jan 30, pp. 7, 36-38; correspondence: letter from Chukhovskii, Apr 17, p. 52.

Daniel, Iu.

See: 585, 910

Dostoevskii, F.

1055. Dostoevskii, Fedor. The Gambler; Bobok; A Nasty Story. Jessie Coulson, tr. Baltimore: Penguin, 238p.

1056. _____. Letters of Fyodor Michailovitch Dostoevsky. Ethel Colburn Mayne, tr. NY: McGraw-Hill, 344p. (1964) Review, Rimvydas Silbajoris, Slav East Eur J, X, 4 (Winter), 477-478.

1057. _____. Memoirs from the House of the Dead. Jessie Coulson, tr. [See ABREES, 1965, No. 1441] Review, Joseph Suhadolc, Slav East Eur J, X, 1 (Spring), 101-103.

1058. Dukas, Vytas, and Richard Lawson. "Goethe in Dostoevskij's Critical Works." Ger Q, XXXIX, 3 (May), 348-357.

1059. Fanger, Donald. Dostoevsky and Romantic Realism. A Study of Dostoevsky in Relation to Balzac, Dickens, and Gogol. [See ABREES, 1965, No. 1443] Reviews, Robert L. Strong, Jr., Slav East Eur J, X, 4 (Winter), 469-471; Gleb Struve, Russ R, XXV, 4 (Oct), 419-421; TLS, Mar 3, p. 165.

1060. Hunt, Joel. "Color Imagery in Dostoevskij and Balzac." Slav East Eur J, X, 4 (Winter), 411-423.

1061. Jackson, Robert Louis. "Chateaubriand and Dostoevskij: A Posing of the Problem." Scando-Slavica, XII, pp. 28-37.

1062. _____. Dostoevsky's Quest for Form: A Study of His Philosophy of Art. New Haven, Conn.: Yale U Press, 274p. (Yale Russian and East European Studies, 1). Reviews, Joseph Frank, Slav R, XXVI, 2 (Jun 1967), 339-343; Sven Linner, Slav East Eur J, XI, 1 (Spring 1967), 88-89; A. Nebol'skii, Novyi Zhurnal, no. 85, pp. 282-285; F. F. Seeley, Slav East Eur R, XLVI, 107 (Jul 1968), 503-505; Heinrich A. Stammler, Russ R, XXVI, 3 (Jul 1967), 301-302.

1063. Kuznetsov, Boris. "Einstein and Dostoevski." Paul Grigorieff, tr. Diogenes, no. 53 (Spring), 1-16.

1064. Lethcoe, James. "Self-

Deception in Dostoevskij's Notes from the Underground." Slav East Eur J, X, 1 (Spring), 9-21.

1065. Moravcevich, Nicholas. "Humor in Dostoyevsky." Buck R, XIV, 3 (Dec), 59-77.

1066. Mossman, Elliot D. "Dostoevskij's Early Works: The More than Rational Distortion." Slav East Eur J, X, 3 (Fall), 268-278.

1067. Seduro, Vladimir. "The Fate of Stavrogin's Confession." Russ R, XXV, 4 (Oct), 397-404.

1068. Steinberg, A. Dostoievsky. London: Bowes and Bowes, 126p. Reviews, TLS, Jun 2, p. 492.

1069. Trahan, Elizabeth. "Clamence vs. Dostoevsky: An Approach to La Chute." Comp Lit, XVIII, 4 (Fall), 337-350.

Esenin, S.

1070. de Graaff, Frances. Sergej Esenin: A Biographical Sketch. The Hague: Mouton, 178p. Reviews, Maurice Friedberg, Russ R, XXVII, 3 (Jul 1968), 363-368; R. D. B. Thomson, Slav East Eur R, XLVI, 106 (Jan 1968), 231-232.

Evtushenko, E.

1071. Evtushenko, Evgenii. "Do Russians Want Another War?" [poem] Mario Pei, tr. Columbia U Forum, IX, 1 (Winter), 41.

1072. _____. Poems. Peter Levi and Robin Milner-Guilland, trs. NY: Collins, 96p. [Text in English and Russian]

1073. _____. The Poetry of Yevgeny Yevtushenko 1953-1965. George Reavey, tr. [See ABREES, 1965, No. 1466] Reviews, Robert Conquest, NY Times Book Rev, Feb 13, p. 10; Andrew Field, Book Week, III, 18, Jan 9, p. 5+; Simon Karlinsky, Nation, CCIII (Nov 21), 549; Robert

Magidoff, Slav East Eur J, X, 2 (Summer), 210-211; Helen Muchnic, NY Rev of Books, VI, 4, Mar 17, pp. 3-4; F. D. Reeve, NY Times Book Rev, Mar 19, 1967, p. 26; Louis J. Shein, Russ R, XXV, 2 (Apr), 210; TLS, Nov 17, p. 1047.

1074. _____. Yevtushenko Poems. Authorized translation by Herbert Marshall. NY: Dutton, 190p. [Bilingual] Reviews, James M. Holquist, Slav East Eur J, XII, 4 (Winter 1968), 480-482; F. D. Reeve, NY Times Book Rev, Nov 13, p. 36; Edward Wasiolek, Book Week, IV, 4, Oct 2, p. 2+.

Fet, A.

1075. Gustafson, Richard F. The Imagination of Spring: The Poetry of Afanasy Fet. New Haven: Yale U Press, 278p. [Yale Russian and East European Studies, 2] Reviews, Anthony D. Briggs, Slav East Eur R, XLV, 105 (Jul 1967), 548-549; George Ivask, Novyi Zhurnal, no. 88, 292-294; Ralph E. Matlaw, Modern Philology, LXV (Aug 1967), 87; V. Setchkarev, Russ R, XXVI, 2 (Apr 1967), 187-188; Virg Q R, XLIII (Winter 1967), 22; Rimvydas Silbajoris, Slav East Eur J, XI, 3 (Fall 1967), 363-364.

Gippius, Z.

See: 1023, 1031

Gogol', N.

1076. Debreczeny, Paul. Nikolay Gogol and His Contemporary Critics. Philadelphia: American Philosophical Society, 68p. Reviews, G. Motolianets, Novyi Zhurnal, no. 90, 303-304; Carl R. Proffer, Slav East Eur J, XI, 3 (Fall 1967), 363-364; Peter Rossbacher, Russ R, XXVI, 4 (Oct 1967), 416.

1077. Driessen, Frederick C. Gogol as a Short-Story Writer: A Study of His Technique of Composi-

tion. Ian F. Finlay, tr. [See ABREES, 1965, No. 1470] Reviews, Donald Fanger, Slav East Eur J, X, 3 (Fall), 334-336; TLS, Jun 2, p. 496.

1078. Gogol', Nikolai. Dead Souls. Bernard G. Guerney, tr. [See ABREES, 1965, No. 1471] Review, Carl R. Proffer, Slav East Eur J, XI, 1 (Spring 1967), 115-116.

1079. Setchkareff, Vsevolod. Gogol: His Life and Works. Robert Kramer, tr. [See ABREES, 1965, No. 1474] Reviews, Carl R. Proffer, Russ R, XXV, 2 (Apr), 211; Robert L. Strong, Jr., Slav R, XXV, 2 (Jun), 358-359; NY Times Book Rev, Jan 2, p. 20.

Gor'kii, M.

1080. Gor'kii, Maksim. Letters. V. Dutt, tr. Moscow: Progress, 199p. Review, TLS, Oct 27, p. 3374.

1081. _____. My Childhood. Ronald Wilks, tr. Baltimore: Penguin, 234p.

1082. Levin, Dan. Stormy Petrel. [See ABREES, 1965, No. 1477] Reviews, Richard Freeborn, Sov St, XVIII, 2 (Oct 1967), 288; Simon Karlinsky, Russ R, XXV, 1 (Jan), 88-90.

1083. Weil, Irwin. Gorky: His Literary Development and Influence on Soviet Intellectual Life. NY: Random House, 240p. [paper] Reviews, Lydia W. Kesich, Slav R, XXVI, 2 (Jun 1967), 345-347; Z. Folejewski, Slav East Eur J, XI, 4 (Winter 1967), 477-478; Louis J. Shein, Russ R, XXVII, 1 (Jan 1968), 107-108; TLS, Oct 27, p. 3374.

Herzen, A.

1084. "Herzen and Kierkegaard." [Discussion] R. M. Davison, Slav R, XXV, 2 (Jun), 191-209 and 218-221; E. Lampert, ibid., 210-214; H. J. Blackham, ibid., 215-217.

Il'f, I., and E. Petrov.

See: 922

Ivanov-Razumnik, V.

1085. Ivanov-Razumnik, V. The Memoirs of Ivanov-Razumnik. P. S. Squire, tr. Oxford: Oxford U Press, 374p. (1965) Review, R. Beerman, Sov St, XVII, 4 (Apr), 509-511.

Karamzin, N. M.

1086. Cross, A. G. "N. M. Karamzin and Barthelemy's 'Voyage du Jeune Anacharsis'." Modern Language Review, LXI, 3 (Jul), 467-472.

Kaverin, V. A.

1087. Oulanoff, Hongor. "Kaverin's Xudožnik neizvesten: Structure and Motivation." Slav East Eur J, X, 4 (Winter), 389-399.

Kazakov, I.

1088. Kramer, Karl D. "Jurij Kazakov: The Pleasures of Isolation." Slav East Eur J, X, 1 (Spring), 22-31.

Korolenko, V.

1089. Shub, Vladimir. "Lenin and Vladimir Korolenko." Russ R, XXV, 1 (Jan), 46-53.

Lavrenev, B.

See: 927

Lermontov, M.

1090. Lermontov, Mikhail. The Demon and Other Poems. Eugene M. Kayden, tr. [See ABREES, 1484] Review, Orrin Frink, Slav East Eur J, XI, 2 (Summer 1967), 233-234.

1091. _____. The Demon. Dennis Ward, ed. [2nd rev. ed.] Letchworth, Herts.: Bradda, 81p. Review, Rostislav D. Roždestvensky, Slav East Eur J, X, 3 (Fall), 344-346.

1092. _____. A Hero of Our Time. Paul Foote, tr. Baltimore; Penguin, 185p.

1093. _____. A Lermontov Reader. Guy Daniels, tr. [See ABREES, 1965, No. 1485] Review, Tatiana Bobrinskoy, Slav East Eur J, X, 3 (Fall), 346-348.

1094. _____. Selected Poetry. C. E. L'Ami and Alexander Welikotny, tr. Winnipeg: U Manitoba Press (Readings in Slavic Literature, 6), 127p. (1965) Review, Rostislav D. Roždestvensky, Slav East Eur J, X, 3 (Fall), 344-346.

See also: 938

Leskov, N.

1095. Edgerton, William B. "Missing Letters to Leskov: An Unsolved Puzzle." Slav R, XXV, 1 (Mar), 120-132.

Maiakovskii, V.

1096. Humesky, Assya. Majakovskij and His Neologisms. NY: Rausen, 270p. (1964) Reviews, C. L. Drage, Slav East Eur R, XLIV, 103 (Jul), 497-498; Hugh McLean, Slav East Eur J, X, 2 (Summer), 225-227.

1097. Mayakovsky, Vladimir V. Mayakovsky. Poet in Red. Herbert Marshall, ed. and tr. [See ABREES, 1965, No. 1487] Reviews, Evelyn Bristol, Slav R, XXVII, 1 (Mar 1968), 164-165; Simon Karlinsky, Russ R, XXVI, 4 (Oct 1967), 413-415; Helen Muchnic, NY Rev of Books, VI, 4, Mar 17, p. 4; R. D. Spector, Sat Rev, XLIX (Feb 19), 42; Robert Conquest, NY Times Book Rev, Feb 13, p. 10.

1098. Moser, Charles A. "Mayakovsky and America." Russ R, XXV, 3 (Jul), 242-256.

1099. Stahlberger, Lawrence L. The Symbolic System of Mayakovsky. The Hague: Mouton, 151p. (Slavistic Printings and Reprintings, 14) (1964) Reviews, Evelyn Bristol, Slav R, XXVII, 1 (Mar 1968), 164-165; Oleg A. Maslenikov, Slav East Eur J, XII,

2 (Summer 1968), 249-251; Ella
Pacaluyko, Int J Slav Ling Poet, X,
pp. 191-194; R. D. B. Thomson, Slav
East Eur R, XLVI, 107 (Jul 1968),
507-508.

See also: 1383

Mandel'shtam, O.

1100. Mandel'shtam, Osip E.
The Prose of Osip Mandelstam: The
Noise of Time, Theodosia, The Egyp-
tian Stamp. Clarence Brown, tr.
[See ABREES, 1965, No. 1490] Re-
views, Olga Carlisle, Book Week, III,
18, Jan 9, p. 5+; George Ivask, Slav
East Eur J, X, 3 (Fall), 341-342;
Anita Norman, Russ R, XXV, 2 (Apr),
202.

1101. _____. "Tristia." [poem]
Stanley Kunitz, tr. Book Week, IV, 16,
Dec 25, p. 6.

1102. Nilsson, Nils Ake. "In-
somnia." Int J Slav Ling Poet, X,
pp. 148-154. [On Mandel'shtam's
poem]

1103. Terras, Victor. "Classical
Motives in the Poetry of Osip Mandel'-
štam." Slav East Eur J, X, 3 (Fall),
251-267.

Merezhkovskii, D.

1104. Stammler, Heinrich A.
"Julianus Apostata Redivivus. Dmit-
rij Merežkovskij: Predecessors and
Successors." Welt Slav, XI, 1/2, pp.
180-204.

Nabokov, V.

1105. Nabokov, Vladimir. De-
spair. NY: Putnam, 222p. Reviews,
Brigid Brophy, Book Week, III, 36,
May 15, p. 2; Andrew Field, NY Times
Book Rev, May 15, p. 5+; D. J. Enright,
NY Rev of Books, VII, 7, Nov 3, pp. 3-4.

1106. _____. The Eye. Dmitri
Nabokov and the author, trs. NY:
Phaedra, 114p. (1965) Reviews, D. J.
Enright [see No. 1105]; Julian Moyna-

han, NY Times Book Rev, Apr 3, p. 2;
TLS, Oct 6, p. 913.

1107. _____. Speak, Memory: An
Autobiography Revisited. NY: Putnam,
320p. Reviews, Nina Berberova, Russ
R, XXVI, 4 (Oct 1967), 405; D. J. Enright [see No. 1105]; correspondence,
ibid., VIII, 2 (Feb 9, 1967), 30-31.

1108. _____. The Waltz Invention:
A Play in Three Acts. Dmitri Nabokov,
tr. NY: Phaedra, 111p. Review, Brigid
Brophy, Book Week, III, 36, May 15, p. 2;
D. J. Enright [see No. 1105].

1109. Grosshans, Henry. "Vladi-
mir Nabokov and the Dream of Old
Russia." Texas St Lit Lang, VII, 4
(Winter), 401-410.

1110. Stegner, P. Escape into
Aesthetics. NY: Dial Press, 141p.
Review, D. J. Enright, NY Rev of Books,
VII, 7, Nov 3, pp. 3-4.

1111. Wilson, Edmund, and J.
Bronowski. Correspondence to Nabokov on the "dangerous animal" cou-
plets. NY Rev of Books, VI, 2, Feb
17, p. 29.

Nikolaeva, G.

1112. Sjöberg, Anders. "The Prose
Rhythm in Galina Nikolaeva's Tale
Rasskazi babki Vacilicy pro chudesa.
A Glosso-Dynamic Study." Scando-
Slavica, XII, pp. 49-56.

Odoevskii, V.

1113. Karlinsky, Simon. "A Hol-
low Shape: The Philosophical Tales
of Prince Vladimir Odoevsky." St
Romant, V, 3 (Spring), 169-182.

Olesha, I.

1114. Harkins, William E. "The
Theme of Sterility in Olesha's *Envy.*"
Slav R, XXV, 3 (Sept), 443-457.

Pasternak, B.

1115. Ivask, George. "A Note on

the Real Zhivagos." Russ R, XXV, 4 (Oct), 405-408.

1116. "Judgment on Pasternak. The All-Moscow Meeting of Writers, 31 Oct 1958: Stenographic Report." Survey, no. 60 (Jul), 134-163.

1117. Nag, Martin. "Ibsen and Pasternak." Scando-Slavica, XII, pp. 38-48.

1118. Pasternak, Boris. "Pasternak's Poems." Lydia Pasternak Slater, tr. Note, in TLS, Jan 20, p. 43.

1119. _____. The Poems of Dr. Zhivago. Donald Davie, tr. [See ABREES, 1965, No. 1503] Reviews, Babette Deutsch, NY Times Book Rev, Feb 20, p. 34; Peter Rossbacher, Russ R, XXV, 3 (Jul), 319.

1120. Plank, Dale L. Pasternak's Lyric: A Study of Sound and Imagery. The Hague: Mouton, 123p. [Slavistic Printings and Reprintings, 59] Reviews, R. D. B. Thomson, Slav East Eur R, XLVI, 107 (Jul 1968), 508-510; Z. Folejewski, Slav East Eur J, XII, 1 (Spring 1968), 94-95.

Patrikeev, V.

1121. Dewey, Horace W., and Mateja Matejic. "The Literary Arsenal of Vassian Patrikeev." Slav East Eur J, X, 4 (Winter), 440-452.

Pisemskij, A. F.

1122. Steussy, R. E. "The Bitter Fate of A. F. Pisemsky." Russ R, XXV, 2 (Apr), 170-183.

Pushkin, A.

1123. Gregg, Richard A. "Balzac and the Women in The Queen of Spades." Slav East Eur J, X, 3 (Fall), 279-282.

1124. Mitchell, S. "The Digressions of Yevgeny Onegin: Apropos of Some Essays by Ettore Lo Gatto." Slav East Eur R, XLIV, 102 (Jan), 51-65.

1125. Pushkin, Aleksandr. The Complete Prose Tales of Alexander Sergeyevitch Pushkin. Gillon R. Aitken, tr. NY: W. W. Norton, 495p. Review, Clarence Brown, Slav East Eur J, XII, 4 (Winter 1968), 485-486.

1126. _____. Eugene Onegin: A Novel in Verse. Vladimir Nabokov, tr. [See ABREES, 1964, No. 1960] Review, Alexander Gerschenkron, Modern Philology, LXIII, 4 (May), 336-347.

1127. _____. Little Tragedies. Eugene M. Kayden, tr. [See ABREES, 1965, No. 1514] Review, Victor Terras, Slav East Eur J, X, 1 (Spring), 100-101.

1128. Shaw, J. Thomas. "Recent Soviet Scholarly Books on Puškin: A Review Article." Slav East Eur J, X, 1 (Spring), 66-84.

See also: 935-938, 987, 1000

Sękowski, J.

1129. Pedrotti, Louis. "Józef-Julian Sękowski; The Genesis of a Literary Alien. [See ABREES, 1965, No. 1522] Review, H. B. Segel, Slav East Eur J, X, 1 (Spring), 110-111.

Shevyrev, S. P.

1130. Gronicka, Andre von. "The Russian Poet-Critic S. P. Shevyrëv, on Goethe." Comp Lit, XVIII, 2 (Spring), 145-161.

Sholokhov, M.

1131. James, Carl. "Soviet Press Reception of Sholokhov's Designation as 1965 Nobel Prize Winner." Mod Lang J, L, 1 (Jan), 18-20.

1132. Moravia, Alberto. "Open Letter to Sholokhov." Raymond Rosenthal, tr. Dissent, XIII, 4 (Jul-Aug), 401-404.

See also: 939

Siniavskii, A.

1133. Bailey, George. "The Trial of Two Soviet Writers — A Special Report." Reporter, XXXIV, 4 (Feb. 24), 34-37.

1134. Brown, Deming. "Moscow: The Defense Does Not Rest." Reporter, XXXV, 4 (Sept 22), 43-45.

1135. Hayward, Max. "The Case of Tertz-Sinyavski." Dissent, XIII, 1 (Jan-Feb), 88-91.

1136. ____. "The Moscow Trial." Part R, XXXIII, 2 (Spring), 227-239.

1137. Labedz, Leopold, and Max Hayward. "Writers in Prison: The Arrests." Prob Comm, XV, 2 (Mar-Apr), 65-70.

1138. On Trial: The Soviet State versus "Abram Tertz" and "Nikolai Arzhak." Max Hayward, ed. and tr. NY: Harper & Row, 183p. Reviews, Joseph J. Darby, Slav R, XXVII, 1 (Mar 1968), 157-158; Andrew Field, NY Times Book Rev, Sept 18, pp. 48-50; Theodore Frankel, Book Week, III, 48, Aug 7, p. 2+; Michael Glenny, Survey, no. 66 (Jan 1968), 144-147; Marshall MacDuffie, Sat Rev, XLIX, Aug 6, p. 25; Helen Muchnic, NY Rev of Books, VII, 9, Dec 1, pp. 26-28; Walter Odajnyk, Ukr Q, XXII, 4 (Winter), 371-372; Louis J. Shein, Russ R, XXVI, 2 (Apr 1967), 199-200; Vernon C. Warren, Jr., West Poli Q, XX, 1 (Mar 1967), 221-222; East Eur, XV, 11 (Nov), 54-55; Book Week, Aug 7, p. 1. [An unofficial transcript of the Sinyavsky-Daniel trial]

1139. Tertz, Abram. On Socialist Realism [with] The Trial Begins. George Dennis and Max Hayward, trs. [See ABREES, 1965, No. 1401] Review, Philip Rahv, Book Week, III, 34, May 1, p. 1+.

Solzhenitsyn, A.

1140. Lukacs, Georg. "Solzhenit-

syn and the New Realism." The Socialist Register, 1965, 197-215. [See item 12]

Tarsis, V.

1141. Tarsis, Valeriy. Ward 7: An Autobiographical Novel. Katya Brown, tr. NY: Dutton, 159p. (1965) Reviews, Robert Coles, Dissent, XIII, 3 (May-Jun), 320-323; Glendy Culligan, Book Week, III, 18, Jan 9, p. 17; Walter Dushnyck, Ukr Q, XXII, 1 (Spring), 76-79; Willis Konick, Slav East Eur J, X, 3 (Fall), 342-343; Robert Somner, Contemp Psych, XI, 9 (Sept), 446.

1142. Stetzko, Slava. "Valeriy Tarsis and his Ideological Outlook: The Author of *Ward 7.*" Ukr R, XIII, 1 (Spring), 42-44.

Tertz, A. (Pseud) [See Siniavskii]

Tiutchev, F.

1143. Gregg, Richard A. Feodor Tiutchev: The Evolution of a Poet. [See ABREES, 1965, No. 1540] Reviews, Clarence A. Manning, Ukr Q, XXII, 1 (Spring), 89-90; Ralph E. Matlaw, Slav East Eur J, X, 1 (Spring), 112-114; Peter Rossbacher, Russ R, XXV, 1 (Jan), 92-94.

Tolstoi, L.

1144. Jones, W. Gareth. "George Eliot's 'Adam Bede' and Tolstoy's Conception of 'Anna Karenina'." Mod Lang R, LXI, 3 (Jul), 473-481.

1145. Lampert, Evgenii. "On Tolstoi, Prophet and Teacher." Slav R, XXV, 4 (Dec), 604-614.

1146. Lednicki, Wacław. Tolstoy Between War and Peace. [See ABREES, 1965, No. 1546] Reviews, R. F. Christian, Slav East Eur R, XLIV, 103 (Jul), 493-494; D. H. Stewart, Slav East Eur J, X, 4 (Winter), 490-492; Edward Wasiolek, Russ R, XXV, 2 (Apr), 208.

1147. Tolstoi, Lev N. Anna

Karenina. Leonard J. Kent and Nina Berberova, eds. NY: Modern Library, 851p. (1965)

1148. ____. Darkness and Light: Three Short Works by Tolstoy. Peter Rudy, ed. NY: Holt, Rinehart & Winston, 266p. [The Death of Ivan Ilyich, The Power of Darkness, The Fruits of Enlightenment] Review, Daniel Bures, Slav East Eur J, XI, 1 (Spring 1967), 114-115.

1149. ____. Hadji Murat: A Tale of the Caucasus. W. G. Carey, tr. NY: McGraw-Hill, 196p.

1150. ____. Resurrection. Rosemary Edmonds, tr. Baltimore: Penguin, 568p. Review, Frank Mocha, Slav East Eur J, XII, 2 (Summer 1968), 242.

1151. ____. War and Peace. Constance Garnett, tr. NY: Modern Library, 1136p.

1152. ____. War and Peace. The Maude Translation. George Gibian, ed. NY: W.W. Norton, 1484p.

Tsvetaeva, M.

1153. Karlinsky, Simon. "Cvetaeva in English: A Review Article." Slav East Eur J, X, 2 (Summer), 191-196.

1154. ____. Marina Cvetaeva: Her Art and Life. Berkeley: U California Press, 317p. Reviews, Nina Berberova, NY Rev of Books, VIII (Mar 9, 1967), p. 24; Richard Gustafson, Slav R, XXVI, 3 (Sept 1967), 514-515; George Ivask, Russ R, XXVI, 2 (Apr 1967), 185-187; J. Daniel Le Van, Books Abr, XLI, 2 (Spring 1967), 217; Hugh MacLean, Novyi Zhurnal, no. 88, 268-269; F. D. Reeve, Slav East Eur J, XI, 3 (Fall 1967), 360-363; R. D. B. Thomson, Slav East Eur R, XLVI, 106 (Jan 1968), 232-234; TLS, Feb 23, 1967, p. 149; Virg Q R, XLIII (Summer 1967), 122.

Turgenev, I.

1155. Turgenev, Ivan. Fathers and Sons. Ralph E. Matlaw, ed. and tr. NY: W.W. Norton, 342p. Review, Nicholas Lee, Slav East Eur J, XII, 2 (Summer 1968), 242.

Volodin, A.

1156. Volodin, Aleksandr. Five Evenings. Ariadne Nicolaeff, tr. Minneapolis: U Minnesota Press, 101p. Reviews, Joachim T. Baer, Slav East Eur J, XII, 1 (Spring 1968), 98-99; Nicholas Moravcevich, Drama Critique, IX, 3 (Fall), 164-165.

Voznesenskii, A.

1157. Auden, W.H. "The Poetry of Andrei Voznesensky." NY Rev of Books, VII, 6, Apr 14, p. 3+.

1158. Voznesensky, Andrei. Antiworlds (Antimiry). Patricia Blake and Max Hayward, eds. W. H. Auden and others, tr. NY: Basic Books, 120p. Reviews, Thomas E. Bird, Russ R, XXVI, 2 (Apr 1967), 194-195; E. J. Simmons, NY Times Book Rev, Jun 19, pp. 6-7; Edward Wasiolek, Book Week, III, 37, May 23, p. 2.

1159. ____. Antiworlds and the Fifth Ace. Patricia Blake and Max Hayward, eds. W. H. Auden et al., trs. [Bilingual edition] NY: Basic Books, 296p. Review, Daniel Bures, Slav East Eur J, XII, 3 (Fall 1968), 366-367. [See also: Reviews, 1158]

1160. ____. "Autumn in Sigulda." [poem] Edwin Morgan, tr. TLS, Jan 6, p. 5.

1161. ____. "Five Poems by Andrei Voznesensky." W. H. Auden, tr. of: "The Cashier," "My Achilles Heart," "The Nose," "Hunting a Hare"; Richard Wilbur, tr. of "Dead Still." NY rev of Books, VI, 6, Apr 14, pp. 6-7.

1162. ____. "Leaves and Roots." Stanley Kunitz, tr. Book Week, III, 35, May 8, p. 6. [poem from 'Antiworlds']

1163. ____. "Poems." Patricia Blake, Stanley Kunitz, Stanley Moss, and William Jay Smith, trs. Col U Forum, IX, 2 (Spring), 13-15.

1164. ____. "A Talk with Andrei Voznesensky." Atlantic Monthly, CCXVIII, 7, Jul, pp. 49, 51-52.

1165. ____. Selected Poems. Anselm Hollo, tr. NY: Grove Press, 107p.

1166. ____. Selected Poems. Authorized translation. Herbert Marshall, tr. NY: Hill & Wang, 129p. Reviews, Thomas E. Bird, Russ R, XXVI, 2 (Apr 1967), 194-195; E. J. Simmons, NY Times Book Rev, Jun 19, pp. 6-7; Edward Wasiolek, Book Week, III, 37, May 23, p. 2+.

1166a. ____. "Two Poems." Stanley Kunitz, tr. Atlantic Monthly, CCXVIII, 7, Jul, p. 50.

Yurasov, V.

1167. Yurasov, Vladimir. Parallax. Tatiana Balkoff Drowne, tr. NY: W.W. Norton, 628p. Reviews, Igor Chinnov, Slav East Eur J, XII, 1 (Spring 1968), 92-94; East Eur, XVI, 7 (Jul 1967), 59.

Zamiatin, E.

1168. Collins, Christopher. "Zamjatin's 'We' as Myth." Slav East Eur J, X, 2 (Summer), 125-133.

1169. ____. "Zamyatin, Wells and the Utopian Literary Tradition." Slav East Eur R, XLIV, 103 (Jul), 351-360.

1170. White, John J. "Mathematical Imagery in Musil's 'Young Törless and Zamyatin's 'We'." Comp Lit, XVIII, 1 (Winter), 71-78.

1171. Zamiatin, Yevgeny. The Dragon: Fifteen Stories. Mirra

Ginsburg, tr. and ed. NY: Random House, 291p. Reviews, Patricia Blake, NY Times Book Rev, Feb 26, 1967, p. 1; Helen Muchnic, NY Rev of Books, VIII, Jun 15, 1967, p. 4; Alex M. Shane, Slav East Eur J, XII, 2 (Summer 1968), 240-241; Ivar Spector, Sat Rev, L (Apr 1, 1967), 36; Virg Q R, XLIII (Summer 1967), 110. [See also: 1383]

Zhukovskii, V.

1172. Ober, Kenneth H., and Warren U. Ober. "Žukovskij's First Translation of [Thomas] Gray's 'Elegy'." Slav East Eur J, X, 2 (Summer), 167-172.

FOLKLORE

1173. Sokolov, Y. M. Russian Folklore. Catherine Ruth Smith, tr. Felix J. Oinas, "Introduction and Bibliography," v-xxix. Hatboro, Pa.: Folklore Associates, 760p. Review, Michael Klimenko, Slav East Eur J, XII, 3 (Fall 1968), 381-382.

HISTORY OF THOUGHT AND CULTURE

1174. Avrich, Paul. "Anarchism and Anti-Intellectualism in Russia." J Hist Ideas, XXVII, 3 (Jul-Sept), 381-390.

1175. Bill, Valentine T. The Russian People: A Reader on their History and Culture. [See ABREES, 1965, No. 1575] Review, Michael Klimenko, Slav East Eur J, XI, 2 (Summer 1967), 231-232.

1176. Billington, James H. The Icon and the Axe: An Interpretive History of Russian Culture. NY: Alfred A. Knopf, 837p. Reviews, Michael Cherniavsky, Poli Sci Q, LXXXII, 1 (Mar 1967), 88-93; Andrew Field, NY Times Book Rev, Aug 21, p. 5; Z. Folejewski, Slav East Eur J, XI, 2 (Summer 1967), 237-238; George D.

Jackson, Jr., Slav R, XXVI, 1 (Mar 1967), 119-127; correspondence, XXVI, 3 (Sept 1967), and XXVII, 1 (Mar 1968), 179-180; Lionel Kochan, Eng Hist R, LXXXIII, 327 (Apr 1968), 387-388; Woodford D. McClellan, Virg Q R, XLII, 4 (Fall), 632-636; Richard Pipes, Am Hist R, LXXII, 4 (Apr 1967), 1039-1041; Nicholas V. Riasanovsky, Russ R, XXVI, 1 (Jan 1967), 74-76; Thomas Riha, Sov St, XIX, 4 (Apr 1968), 581-585; TLS, Dec 29, p.1202; Avrahm Yarmolinsky, Book Week, III, 41, Jun 19, p.9+.

1177. Brandes, Georg. Impressions of Russia. Reprinted from the edition of 1889. Intro. by R. Pipes. Samuel C. Eastman, tr. NY: Thomas Y. Crowell, 276p.

1178. Brown, Edward J. Stankevich and His Moscow Circle, 1830-1840. Stanford: Stanford U Press, 149p. Reviews, Richard F. Gustafson, Slav East Eur J, XI, 3 (Fall 1967), 357-358; Sidney Monas, Am Hist R, LXXIII, 1 (Oct 1967), 181-182; Nicholas V. Riasanovsky, Slav R, XXVI, 2 (Jun 1967), 338-339; Edward C. Thaden, Russ R, XXVI, 1 (Jan 1967), 76-78; TLS, Jan 12, 1967, p.30; Virg Q R, XLIII (Winter 1967), 28.

1179. Elkin, B. "Attempts to Revive Freemasonry in Russia." Slav East Eur R, XLIV, 103 (Jul), 454-472.

1180. Fülop-Miller, René. The Mind and Face of Bolshevism. [See ABREES, 1965, No. 1259] Review, Maurice Friedberg, Russ R, XXV, 2 (Apr), 203-204.

1180a. Hertzen, Aleksander Ivanovich. From the Other Shore. Moura Budberg, tr., and The Russian People and Socialism, tr. from the French by Richard Wollheim. Intro. by Isaiah Berlin. NY: Humanities Press, 208p. [Orig. pub. 1956]

1181. Johnson, Priscilla, and Leopold Labedz, eds. Khrushchev and the Arts. [See ABREES, 1965, No. 1581] Reviews, Frederick C.

Barghoorn, Pub Opin Q, XXX, 2 (Summer), 332-335; Herbert J. Ellison, West Poli Q, XIX, 3 (Sept), 555-556; Victor S. Frank, Prob Comm, XV, 3 (May-Jun), 46-49; Peter Juviler, Int J, XXI, 2 (Spring), 260-261; Edward B. Richards, J Poli, XXVIII, 1 (Feb), 214-216.

1182. Lampert, E. Sons against Fathers. [See ABREES, 1965, No. 1584] Review, Joseph Frank, Russ R, XXV, 1 (Jan), 77-78.

1183. Lavrin, Janko. "Bakunin, the Slav and the Rebel." Russ R, XXV, 2 (Apr), 135-149.

1184. McNally, Raymond T. "Chaadaev vs. Xomjakov in the Late 1830's and the 1840's." J Hist Ideas, XXVII, 1 (Jan-Mar), 73-91.

1185. ____. "The Books in Pĕtr Ja. Čaadaev's Libraries." Jahrb Gesch Osteur, XIV, 4, pp. 495-512.

1186. Raeff, Marc. Russian Intellectual History: An Anthology. NY: Harcourt, Brace & World, 404p. Reviews, George W. Simmonds, Slav R, XXVII, 2 (Jun 1968), 317-318; Joseph L. Wieczynski, Russ R, XXVI, 2 (Apr 1968), 201-202.

1187. Seth, Ronald. The Russian Terrorists. London: Barrie and Rockliff, 303p. Review, Paul Avrich, Sov St, XIX, 2 (Oct 1967), 305-306.

1188. Spector, Ivar. An Introduction to Russian History and Culture. [See ABREES, 1965, No. 687] Review, Lionel Kochan, Slav East Eur R, XLIV, 102 (Jan), 274-275.

1189. Venturi, Franco. Roots of Revolution: A History of the Populist and Socialist Movements in Nineteenth Century Russia. Francis Haskell, tr. NY: Grosset & Dunlap, 886p.

1190. Vernadsky, George. "The Prijutino Brotherhood," pp. 857-863, in Orbis Scriptus: Festschrift fur Dmitri Tschiževskij. Dietrich Gerhardt, ed. Munich: Wilhelm Fink, 972p.

1191. Viereck, Peter, et al. Creativity in the Soviet Union. (Special issue of Tri-Quarterly, Northwestern University, Spring 1965). Review, Victor S. Frank, Prob Comm, XV, 3 (May-Jun), 46-49.

1192. Walker, Franklin A. "P. A. Lavrov's Concept of the Party." West Poli Q, XIX, 2 (Jun), 235-250.

See also: 534, 876

RUSSIAN AND SOVIET PHILOSOPHY

1193. Addis, Laird. "Freedom and the Marxist Philosophy of History." Philosophy of Science, XXXIII, 2, pp. 101-117. [Includes brief discussion of Plekhanov's views of history]

1193a. Birjukov, B. V. Two Soviet Studies on [Gottlob] Frege. Ignacio Angelelli, ed. and tr. Dordrecht: Reidel, 101p. (1964) Review, R. H. Stoothoff, Philosophical Quarterly, XVI, 3 (Fall), 396.

1194. Blakeley, Thomas J. "Soviet Philosophic Method: The Case of B. M. Kedrov." St Sov Thought, VI, 1, pp. 1-24.

1195. _____. "Open Questions in Contemporary Soviet Epistemology." St Sov Thought, VI, 3, pp. 185-189.

1196. Blanshard, Brand. "Reflections on Economic Determinism." J Philosophy, LXIII, 7 (Mar), 169-178.

1196a. Boeselager, W. F. "Soviet Dialectical Methodology." St Sov Thought, VI, 2, pp. 135-144.

1197. Bornstein, Morris. "Ideology and the Soviet Economy." Sov St, XVIII, 1 (Jul), 74-80. [See also: 1200, 1205, 1213, 1214]

1198. Calian, Carnegie S. The Significance of Eschatology in the Thoughts of Nicholas Berdyaev. [See ABREES, 1965, No. 1594] Reviews, Nikolai P. Poltoratzky, Russ R, XXV, 3 (Jul), 316-317; Alexander Schme-

mann, St Vladimir's Sem Q, X, 3, pp. 213-214.

1199. Comey, David Dinsmore. "Current Trends in Soviet Logic." Inquiry (Oslo), IX, 1, pp. 94-108.

1200. Daniels, Robert V. "The Ideological Vector." Sov St, XVIII, 1 (Jul), 71-73. [See also: 1197, 1205, 1213, 1214]

1201. Edie, J. M., J. P. Scanlan, and M. Zeldin with G. Kline, eds., Russian Philosophy. [3 vols.] [See ABREES, 1965, No. 1597] Reviews, George Florovsky, Russ R, XXV, 4 (Oct), 409-411; M. Isenberg, Ethics, LXXVI, 3 (Apr), 229; Robert W. Simmons, Jr., Slav East Eur J, XI, 4 (Winter 1967), 490.

1202. Fleischer, Helmut. "Open Questions in Contemporary Soviet Ontology." St Sov Thought, VI, 3, pp. 168-184.

1203. Fock, V. A. "Quantum Mechanics and Dialectical Materialism: Comments." Slav R, XXV, 3 (Sept), 411-413. [See also: 1204]

1204. Graham, Loren R. "Quantum Mechanics and Dialectical Materialism." Slav R, XXV, 3 (Sept), 381-410; reply to V. A. Fock, ibid., 418-420. [See also: 1203, 1292]

1205. Joravsky, David. "Soviet Ideology." Sov St, XVIII, 1 (Jul), 2-19. [See also: 1197, 1200, 1213, 1214]

1206. Kopnin, P. V. "Dialectical Materialism and Metaphysics." Int Phil Q, VI, pp. 33-44.

1207. Laszlo, Ervin. "The Second Sovietology." St Sov Thought, VI, 4, pp. 274-290.

1208. Lobkowicz, N. "Is the Soviet Notion of Practice Marxian?" St Sov Thought, VI, 1, pp. 25-36.

1209. McNeal, Robert H. "The Study of Bolshevism: Sources and Methods. A Review Article." Int J, XXI, 4 (Autumn), 521-526.

1210. Mendel, Arthur P. "The Rise and Fall of 'Scientific Socialism'." For Aff, XLV, 1 (Oct), 98-111.

1211. ____. "Current Soviet Theory of History: New Trends or Old?" Am Hist R, LXXII, 1 (Oct), 50-73.

1212. Malaniuk, Evhen. "To the Problem of Bolshevism." Ukr R, XIII, 1 (Spring), 17-33; XIII, 2 (Summer), 32-46; XIII, 3 (Autumn), 40-54.

1213. Meyer, Alfred G. "The Functions of Ideology in the Soviet Political System. A Speculative Essay Designed to Provoke Discussion." Sov St, XVII, 3 (Jan), 273-285. [See also: 1197, 1200, 1205, 1214]

1214. Reddaway, Peter B. "Aspects of Ideological Belief in the Soviet Union: Comments on Professor Meyer's Article." Sov St, XVII, 4 (Apr), 473-483. [See also: 1197, 1200, 1205, 1213]

1215. ____. "The Search for New Ideals in the U.S.S.R.: Some First-Hand Impressions." St Sov Un, V, 4, pp. 83-90.

1216. Schiebel, J. "National-Liberation Movements, Historical Materialism, and Soviet Philosophy." St Sov Thought, VI, 2 (Jun), pp. 105-123.

1217. Stackelberg, Georg A. von. "The Soviet Concept of the Revolutionary Democratic State and its Political Significance." Bull Inst St USSR, XIII, 4 (Apr), 3-13.

See also Part 1, Section VI-Philosophy, Marxism-Leninism, and 1184, 1185, 1192, 1292, 1297, 1303, 1307, 1318

RELIGION — GENERAL

1217a. "Appeals for Religious Freedom: Documents." St. Vladimir's Sem Q, X, 1, pp. 1, 67-76, 77-108, 108-111.

1218. Anderson, Paul B. "The Problem of Alienation: Life Without Spiritual or Religious Ideals." St Sov Un, V, 4, pp. 13-23.

1219. Bociurkiw, Bohdan R. "Religion and Soviet Society." Survey, no. 60 (Jul), 62-71.

1220. Bogolepov, A. A. "A. A. Bogolepov, A Bibliography." St Vladimir's Sem Q, X, 1-2, pp. 9-11.

1221. ____. "Church Reforms in Russia 1905-1918." A. E. Morrhouse, tr. St Vladimir's Sem Q, X, 1-2, pp. 12-66.

1222. Bourdeaux, Michael. Opium of the People: The Christian Religion in the USSR. [See ABREES, 1965, No. 1610] Reviews, Robert A. Feldmesser, Prob Comm, XVI, 5 (Sept-Oct 1967), 137-138; D. Pospielovsky, Sov St, XVII, 4 (Apr), 514-515; TLS, Jul 22, 1967, p. 616.

1223. Cherniavsky, Michael. "The Old Believers and the New Religion." Slav R, XXV, 1 (Mar), 1-39.

1224. Dunn, Ethel. "A Slavophile Looks at the Raskol and the Sects." Slav East Eur R, XLIV, 102 (Jan), 167-179. [Ivan Aksakov, 1823-1886]

1225. Fedotov, George P. The Russian Religious Mind. Vol. 1: Kievan Christianity: The 10th to the 13th Centuries. Vol. II: The Middle Ages: The 13th to the 15th Centuries. John Meyendorff, ed., Vol. II. Thomas E. Bird, compiler of Fedotov bibliography, Vol. II. Cambridge, Mass.: Harvard U Press, 431 and 423pp. Reviews, James H. Billington, Slav R, XXVII, 4 (Dec 1968), 638-639; Ludvik Nemec, Slav East Eur J, XI, 3 (Fall 1967), 373-374; Serge A. Zenkovsky, Russ R, XXVI, 3 (Jul 1967), 296-298; N. Zernov, Eng Hist R, no. 328, p. 646.

1226. Fine, John V. A., Jr. "Fedor Kuritsyn's 'Laodikijskoe Poslanie' and the Heresy of the Judaisers." Spec, XLI, 3 (Jul), 500-504.

1227. Fletcher, William C. "Protestant Influences on the Outlook of the Soviet Citizen Today." St Sov Un, V, 4, pp. 62-82.

1228. _____. A Study in Survival: The Church in Russia, 1927-1943. [See ABREES, 1965, No. 1612] Reviews, Edward M. Bennett, Russ R, XXV, 4 (Oct), 425-426; John Meyendorff, St Vladimir's Sem Q, X, 1-2, pp. 114-116; Judith Cohen Zacek, Church Hist, XXXV, 2 (Jun), 249-250; TLS, Feb 10, p. 106.

1229. Gardner, Johann von. "The Attraction of Church Ritual among Soviet Youth." St Sov Un, V, 4, pp. 57-61.

1230. Hayward, Max. "Religion and the Changing Intellectual Outlook in the USSR: Summary." St Sov Un, V, 4, pp. 130-135.

1231. Holt, Simma. Terror in the Name of God: The Story of the Freedom Doukhobors. NY: Crown Publishers, 312p. (1965) TLS, Jan 27, pp. 53-54.

1232. Konstantinow, Dimitry. "The Philosophical and Psychological Foundations of Soviet Atheism." Bull Inst St USSR, XIII, 2 (Feb), 26-31.

1233. _____. "Orthodoxy and the Younger Generation in the USSR." St Sov Un, V, 4, pp. 24-34.

1234. Meyendorff, John. "The Church in Russia, an Editorial." St Vladimir's Sem Q, X, 1-2, pp. 3-6.

1235. Miller, D. A. "The Pečerskij Assumption and its Influence on Medieval Russian Orthodoxy." Jahrb Gesch Osteur, XIV, 3, pp. 321-326.

1236. Nelson, J. Robert. "Orthodoxy in Russia." Christian Century, LXXXIII, 39 (Sept 28), 1170-1171.

1237. Struve, Nikita. "Pseudo-Religious Rites Introduced by the Party Apparatus." St Sov Un, V, 4, pp. 44-48.

1238. Teodorovich, Nadezhda.

"The Rejuvenation of the Russian Orthodox Clergy." St Sov Un, V, 4, pp. 35-43.

1239. _____. "Monasteries of the Russian Orthodox Church." Bull Inst St USSR, XIII, 9 (Sept), 3-12.

1240. _____. "Recent Developments in the Moscow Patriarchate." Bull Inst St USSR, XIII, 12 (Dec), 17-28.

1241. Zatko, James J. Descent into Darkness: The Destruction of the Roman Catholic Church in Russia, 1917-1923. [See ABREES, 1965, No. 1626] Reviews, Warren B. Walsh, Am Hist R, LXXI, 2 (Jan), 628-629; Judith Cohen Zacek, Church Hist, XXXV, 4 (Dec), 478.

See also: 438, 473, 517, 999

RELIGION — JUDAISM
(INCLUDING ANTI-SEMITISM)

1242. "Atheism and the Jewish Religion: More Publications." Jews in Eastern Europe, III, 4 (Jun), 21-30.

1243. Baron, Salo W. The Russian Jew Under Tsars and Soviets. [See ABREES, 1964, No. 189] Reviews, Stephen P. Dunn, Slav R, XXIV, 4 (Dec 1965), 702-705; corr., XXVI, 1 (Mar 1967), 155-159; Alfred A. Greenbaum, Sov St, XVII, 3 (Jan), 385-386; Sidney Monas, Am Hist R, LXXI, 2 (Jan), 626-628; Robert M. Seltzer, Slav East Eur J, X, 1 (Spring), 114-5. [See also: 1262]

1244. Brumberg, Joseph, and Abraham Brumberg. Sovyetish Heymland. An Analysis. NY: Anti-Defamation League of B'nai Brith. [paper] 56p. [See also: 1252]

1245. "Criticism from the Left." Jews in Eastern Europe, III, 4 (Jun), 50-56.

1246. "Deteriorating Position Reported." Jews in Eastern Europe, III, 4 (Jun), 12-21.

1247. Frumkin, J., G. Aronson, and A. Goldenweiser, eds. Russian

Jewry (1860-1917). NY: Thomas Yoseloff, 492p. Reviews, J. Miller, Sov St, XIX, 1 (Jul 1967), 145-146; I. Levitan, Novyi Zhurnal, no. 84, 281-284; Albert Parry, Russ R, XXVI, 1 (Jan 1967), 91.

1248. Greenberg, Louis. The Jews in Russia: The Struggle for Emancipation. New Haven: Yale U Press, 213p. (1965) Review, Harold Shukman, Sov St, XIX, 1 (Jul 1967), 146.

1249. "Intervention." Jews in Eastern Europe, III, 4 (Jun), 72-100.

1250. "Is There a Change? The Jewish Problem Since Khrushchev." Jews in Eastern Europe, III, 4 (Jun), 3-11.

1251. "Israel: The Cold Wind from Moscow." Jews in Eastern Europe, III, 5 (Oct), 39-46.

1252. "Jewish Culture: Assessments of Sovietish Heimland." Jews in Eastern Europe, III, 4 (Jun), 31-39. [On Yiddish-language magazine published in Moscow] [See also: 1244]

1253. "The Jewish Writer in the Soviet Union." Jews in Eastern Europe, III, 4 (Jun), 39-49.

1254. Lamm, Hans. "Jews and Judaism in the Soviet Union." St Sov Un, V, 4, pp. 102-118.

1255. "More About Re-Emigrants." Jews in Eastern Europe, III, 5 (Oct), 46-50. [Soviet accounts of Jews who returned to the USSR from Israel]

1256. "Promises in London Puzzle Moscow." Jews in Eastern Europe, III, 5 (Oct), 23-33. [On problems of Jewish culture in the Soviet Union]

1257. Rogger, Hans. "The Beilis Case: Anti-Semitism and Politics in the Reign of Nicholas II." Slav R, XXV, 4 (Dec), 615-629.

1258. Samuel, Maurice. Blood Accusation: The Strange History of the Beilis Case. NY: Alfred A.

Knopf, 286p. Reviews, John S. Curtiss, Russ R, XXVI, 1 (Jan 1967), 96; corr., ibid., 3 (Jul 1967), 320; Sidney Harcave, NY Times Book Rev, Sept 18, p. 10; Granville Hicks, Sat Rev, XLIX, Sept 10, p. 37; Martin Hindus, Book Week, Sept 18, p. 14; K. G. Jackson, Harper's, CCXXXIII, Oct, 128; Virgilia Peterson, Reporter, XXXV (Oct 20), 57; Leonard Schapiro, NY Rev of Books, VIII, Jun 1, 1967, p. 32; TLS, Apr 6, 1967, p. 286.

1259. Shvarts, Solomon M. Evrei v Sovetskom Soiuze s nachala vtoroi Mirovoi voiny (1939-1965). NY: American Jewish Workers' Committee, 425p. Reviews, D. Anin, Novyi Zhurnal, no. 87, 348-352; S. Ettinger, Slav R, XXVII, 3 (Sept 1968), 494-496; Joshua Rothenberg, Russ R, XXVII, 3 (Jul 1967), 314.

1260. Shapiro, Leon. "Yiddish Books in the Soviet Union after Stalin." Jewish Book Annual, XXIV, pp. 5-13.

1261. "Some Recent Publications." Jews in Eastern Europe, III, 5 (Oct), 34-38. [Anti-religious aspects of Soviet anti-Semitism]

1262. Weinryb, Bernard D. "A Note on Anti-Semitism in Soviet Russia (Post-Stalin Period)." Slav R, XXV, 3 (Sept), 523-527. [See: 1243]

1263. Weiss, David W. "The Plight of the Jews in the Soviet Union." Dissent, XIII, 4 (Jul-Aug), 447-464.

1264. "Western Communists: British Party Executive's Appeal." Jews in Eastern Europe, III, 5 (Oct), 51-58.

1265. Wiesel, Elie. The Jews of Silence — A Personal Report on Soviet Jewry. NY: Holt, Rinehart & Winston, 143p. Reviews, Abraham Brumberg, Reporter, XXXVI, Mar 9, 1967, 60; Oscar Handlin, Atlantic Monthly, CCXVIII, Dec, p. 147; Max Hayward, Commentary, XLIII (Mar 1967), 91; Neal Kozodoy, East Eur, XVI, 8 (Aug 1967), 55; Herbert Kupferberg, Book Week, May 7, 1967, p. 13; Walter Laqueur, NY Rev of Books, VIII, Mar 23,

1967, p. 23; Harry Schwartz, Sat Rev, XLIX, Nov 26, p. 42; I. B. Singer, NY Times Book Rev, Jan 8, 1967, p. 16.

1266. Woodhouse, Charles E., and Henry J. Tobias. "Primordial Ties and Political Process in Pre-Revolutionary Russia: The Case of the Jewish Bund." Comp St Soc Hist, VIII, 3 (Apr), 331-360.

1267. "World Opinion." Jews in Eastern Europe, III, 5 (Oct), 61-68.

See also: 445, 446, 530, 1319

EDUCATION

1268. Bailey, George. "Cultural Exchange as the Soviets Use It." Reporter, XXXIV, 7 (Apr 7), 20-25.

1269. Bakalo, Ivan. "Post-graduate Research in the Soviet Union." St Sov Un, V, 3, pp. 84-92.

1270. Benton, William. The Teachers and the Taught in the U.S.S.R. NY: Atheneum, 174p.

1271. Binnington, John P. "Soviet Information Experts Tour United States Information Facilities." Spec Lib, LVII, 3 (Mar), 194-196.

1272. Dewey, Horace W. "Some Current Soviet Views on Foreign Language Methodology." For Lang Courier, XXVII, (Dec), 16-18.

1273. Dexter, Paul. "The Life of African Students in the Soviet Union." R Sov Med Sci, III, 2, pp. 45-58.

1274. Kreusler, Abraham. "The Soviet School at the Crossroads." Slav East Eur J, X, 3 (Fall), 377-381.

1275. Lawrov, V. V. "Socialist System of Financing Education — Major Factor of Social Progress of the National Republics of the Soviet Union: A Comment." Pub Fin, XXI, 1-2 (Summer), 170-183.

1276. Menchinskaya, Natalie. "Learning Research Carried Out at the Institute of Pedagogy at the Acad-emy of Pedagogical Sciences of the U.S.S.R." Int R Educ, XII, 1, pp. 16-23.

1277. Noah, Harold J. Financing Soviet Schools. NY: Columbia U Teachers College Press, 294p. Review, Michael Kaser, Sov St, XX, 3 (Jan 1969), 386-387; Frederic Lilge, Slav R, XXVII, 3 (Sept 1968), 504-505.

1278. Pei, Mario. "Russia's Secret Weapon." Mod Age, X, 4 (Fall), 364-5. [The "secret weapon" is education]

1279. Satina, Sophie. The Education of Women in Pre-Revolutionary Russia. NY: The author, 153p. Reviews, E. Grot, Russ R, XXVI, 2 (Apr 1968), 202; Roman Gul', Novyi Zhurnal, no. 87, 352-354.

1280. Saxena, K. N. "Edifices of Extramural Education in the Soviet Union." Science and Culture, XXXII, 8 (Aug), 403-404.

1281. Sokolsky, Anatole A. "Foreign-Language Teaching in the U.S.S.R." Lang Q, IV, 3-4 (Spring-Summer), 33-34.

1282. Tarnawsky, Marta. "Book-burning a la Soviet." Ukr Q, XXII, 1 (Spring), 53-62. [The library's role in withholding books]

1283. Troufanoff, I. P. "The Museum of Anthropology and Ethnology of the Academy of Sciences of the U.S.S.R." Cur Anthro, VII, 2 (Apr), 231-233.

1284. Voronitsyn, S. S. "Education and Science under the Party's Control." Bull Inst St USSR, XIII, 8 (Aug), 33-37.

1285. _____. "Education Problems in the U.S.S.R." Bull Inst St USSR, XIII, 9 (Sept), 21-23.

1286. Wheeler, Geoffrey. "Asian Studies in the Soviet Union." Cent Asian R, XIV, 3, pp. 232-240.

See also: 98, 511, 809a, 869, 1340

SCIENCE

1287. Bakalo, Ivan. "Disruption in Science Research Organization." St Sov Un, VI, 1, pp. 40-48.

1288. Brožek, Josef. "Russian Contributions on Brain and Behavior." Sci, CLII, 3724 (May 13), 930-933.

1289. Dobrov, G. M. "Predicting the Development of Science." Minerva, IV, 2 (Winter), 218-230. [Translated from Voprosy filosofii]

1290. Dorozynski, Alexander. The Man They Wouldn't Let Die. [See ABREES, 1965, No. 1689] Reviews, Joseph D. Harris, Russ R, XXV, 1 (Jan), 98-99; TLS, Apr 21, p. 345.

1291. Esper, Thomas. Review of F. N. Zagorsky, Vladimir Sergeevich Knabbe (Moscow, 1965), 87p. Technology and Culture, VII, 1 (Winter), 93-94. [Knabbe's role in developing mechanical engineering in Russia]

1292. Feyerabend, Paul K. "Dialectical Materialism and the Quantum Theory." Slav R, XXV, 3 (Sept), 414-417. [See: 1203, 1204]

1293. Gagarin, Grigori. "The Crisis in the Field of Biology." St Sov Un, V, 3, pp. 56-71.

1294. Galton, D. "Iosif Khristianovich Hamel' (1788-1861)." Slav East Eur R, XLIV, 103 (Jul), 473-474. [Scientist-inventor]

1295. Kapitza, Peter L. "Problems of Soviet Scientific Policy." Minerva, IV, 3 (Spring), 391-397.

1296. ____. "The Scientist and the Plans." Minerva, IV, 4 (Summer), 555-560. [Translated from Literaturnaia Gazeta]

1297. Kerschner, Lee R. "Cybernetics and Soviet Philosophy." Int Phil Q, VI, 2 (Jun), 270-285.

1298. Korol, Alexander. Soviet Research and Development. [See ABREES, 1965, No. 1698] Reviews, Richard C. Gripp, West Poli Q, XIX,

1 (Mar), 177-178; Jan S. Prybyla, Russ R, XXV, 2 (Apr), 198-199.

1299. Langer, Elinor. "Peace Questionnaire: Soviets Seek Views of U.S. Scientists." Sci, CLIII, 3733 (Jul 15), 276-277.

1300. Manheim, F. T. "Soviet Books on Oceanography." Sci, CLIV, 3752 (Nov 25), 995-998. [Review article]

1301. McElheny, Victor K. "Science Center in Siberia." Sci, CLII, 3725 (May 20), 1047. [Akademgorodok]

1302. ____. "Franco-Russian Collaboration in Science: DeGaulle's Visit." Sci, CLIII, 3731 (Jul 1), 43-45.

1303. Müller-Markus, S. "Niels Bohr in the Darkness and Light of Soviet Philosophy." Inquiry (Oslo), IX, 1, pp. 73-93.

1304. Murray, B. C., and M. E. Davies. "A Comparison of U.S. and Soviet Efforts to Explore Mars." Sci, CLI, 3713 (Feb 25), 945-954.

1305. Olby, Robert C. Origins of Mendelism. London: Constable, 204p. Review, TLS, Apr 7, p. 310.

1306. Olgin, C. "Speculative Cybernetics." Bull Inst St USSR, XIII, 8 (Aug), 3-17.

1307. Payne, T. R. "On the Theoretical Foundations of Soviet Psychology." St Sov Thought, VI, 2, pp. 124-134.

1308. Parry, Albert. "Science and Technology versus Communism." Russ R, XXV, 3 (Jul), 227-241.

1309. Ryzl, Milan. "Pioneer of Soviet Science — L. L. Vasiliev." Journal of Parapsychology, XXX, 2 (Jun), 114-117.

1310. Schäfer, Georg. "In Defiance of the Ideologists: Parapsychology in the Soviet Union." Journal of Parapsychology, XXX, 1 (Mar), 48-52.

1311. Shelton, William. "The Russians Mean to win the Space Race."

Fortune, LXXIII, 2, Feb, pp. 140-143, 174-180, 185

1313. "Some Problems of Scientific Policy in the Soviet Union." Minerva, IV, 2 (Winter), 215-218.

1314. Tokarev, S. A. "The Problem of Totemism as seen by Soviet Scholars." Cur Anthro, VII, 2 (Apr), 185-188.

1315. Turkevich, John. "Soviet Science Appraised." For Aff, XLIV, 3 (Apr), 489-500.

1316. _____. "The Soviet Space Effort." Cur Hist, LI, 302 (Oct), 226-232.

1317. Volk, Sigmund. "Soviet Research on Artificial Foods." R Sov Med Sci, III, 1, pp. 55-62.

1318. Voronitsyn, S. "Science as a Philosophy of Life in the U.S.S.R." Bull Inst St USSR, XIII, 11 (Nov), 51-55.

See also: 127, 967, 1203, 1204

FINE ARTS

1319. Abramsky, Chimen. "El Lissitzky as Jewish Artist and Typographer." Studio International CLXXII, 882, pp. 182-185.

1320. Bower, Anthony. "The Splendid Frivolity of Fabergé." Art in America, LIV, 2 (Mar-Apr), 92-95.

1321. Carlisle, Olga. "A Soviet Sculptor, Ernst Neizvestnii." Art in America, LIV, 1 (Jan-Feb), 104-107.

1322. Catteau, Jacques. "Soviet Painting." Survey, no. 59 (Apr), 73-87.

1323. Ernest, John. "Constructivism and Content." Studio International, CLXXI, 876 (Apr), 148-156.

1324. Gabo, Naum, and Nicholas Pevsner. "The Realist Manifesto." Studio International, CLXXI, 876 (Apr), 126.

1325. Gabo, N. "Naum Gabo Talks about his Work." Studio International, CLXXI, 876 (Apr), 127-131.

1326. Gayev, A. "The Fate of Russian Historical Relics under the Communist System." Bull Inst St USSR, XIII, 5 (May), 41-47. [Preservation of ancient Russian historical treasures]

1327. Gosling, Nigel. Leningrad. [See ABREES, 1965, No. 1711] Review, Dmitri von Mohrenschildt, Russ R, XXV, 2 (Apr), 204-205.

1328. Gray, Cleve. "Naum Gabo Talks about Constructivism." Art in America, LIV, 6 (Nov-Dec), 48-55.

1329. Hare, Richard. The Art and Artists of Russia. [See ABREES, 1965, No. 1712] Reviews, Ralph Berry, Brit J Aesth, VI, 1 (Jan), 95-96; Vera K. Ostoia, Slav R, XXVI, 3 (Sept 1967), 519-520.

1330. The Hermitage, Leningrad: Baroque and Rococo Masters. Introduction and notes by V. F. Levinson-Lessing and the staff of the State Hermitage. Intro. tr. by A. Denesova. London: Paul Hamlyn, 95p. Review, TLS, Jun 23, p. 546.

1331. Hill, Anthony. "Constructivism — The European Phenomenon." Studio International, CLXXI, 876 (Apr), 140-147.

1332. Konechny, Dusan, and Lev Nisberg. "Moscow Kineticists." Studio International, CLXXII, 880 (Aug), 90-92.

1333. Lazarev, Viktor. Old Russian Murals and Mosaics: From the XI to the XVI Century. Boris Roniger, tr.; revised by Nancy Dunn. London: Phaidon, 291p. Review, TLS, Oct 13, p. 932.

1334. Mead, Igor, and Paul Sjeklocha. "The Varvaristy: Soviet Unofficial Art." Russ R, XXV, 2 (Apr), 115-130.

1335. Thompson, David. "Outline for a Public Art." Studio International, CLXXI, 876(Apr), 132-139.

See also: 1181, 1235

MUSIC HISTORY AND CRITICISM

1336. Austerlitz, Robert. "Text and Melody in Mansi Songs." Current Musicology, Spring 1966, pp. 37-57.

1337. Austin, William W. Music in the Twentieth Century from Debussy through Stravinsky. NY: W.W. Norton, 708p.

1338. Bakst, James. A History of Russian-Soviet Music. NY: Dodd, Mead, 416p. Reviews, R. Sterling Beckwith, Notes of the Music Library Association, XXII, 2 (Dec), 268-269; Stanley Krebs, Slav R, XXVI, 3 (Sept 1967), 522-523; Boris Schwarz, Prob Comm, XVI, 4 (Jul-Aug), 69-70; Gerald Seaman, Russ R, XXVI, 1 (Jan 1967), 87-88; Virg Q R, XLIII (Winter 1967), 54.

1339. Fuchs, J. "They Do It Themselves: 'Goskontsert'." Music Journal, XXIV, 5 (May), 17+.

1340. Nikolayev, Alexander. "The Training of Soviet Musicians." Music Journal, XXIV, 12 (Dec), 40+.

1341. Seaman, Gerald. "Amateur Music-Making in Russia." Music and Letters, XLVII, 3 (Jul), 249-259. [18th and 19th Centuries]

1342. _____. "The Rise of Russian Piano Music." The Music Review, XXVII, 3 (Aug), 177-193. [From the music of Trutovskii (c.1740-1810) to that of Genishta (1795-1853)]

1343. Tcherepnin, Alexander. Russische Musik-Anthologie. Anthology of Russian Music. German tr., Guido Waldmann; English tr., Alfred Swan. Bonn: M.P. Belaieff, 77p. [Russian music, 17th through 19th centuries]

1344. Vikharieff, Yuri. "Answers from the Soviet Union." Jazz, V, 2 (Feb), 22-23.

1345. _____. "Jazz Festivals in Russia: 1966." Jazz, V, 9 (Sept), 10-12.

1346. Whistler, Harvey, and Georgeanna Whistler. "Nikolaus Ferder Kittel: The Russian [François] Tourte." Music Journal, XXIV, 5 (May), 26-28+; 6 (Jun), 31-32+. [Russian craftsman and bow-maker]

See also: 959, 1392, 1492

MUSIC — BIOGRAPHY

Chaikovskii, P.

1347. Evans, Edwin. Tchaikovsky. (Master Musicians Series) Rev. ed. NY: Farrar and Strauss, 226p. Review, David Lloyd-Jones, The Musical Times, CVII (Jul), 605.

1348. Hanson, Lawrence, and Elisabeth Hanson. Tchaikovsky: The Man Behind the Music. NY: Dodd, Mead, 385p. Review, Boris Schwarz, Slav R, XXVII, 1 (Mar 1968), 167-169. [This is the American edition of the work; see ABREES, 1965, No. 1737]

1349. James, Burnett. "The Symphonies of Tchaikovsky." Audio Record Review, V, 6 (Feb), 15-18.

1350. Roslavleva, Natalia. "The Birth of the Sleeping Beauty." The Dancing Times, LVII, 674 (Nov), 74-76.

Glazunov, A.

1351. Seaman, Gerald. "The Symphonies of Glazunov." Musical Opinion, LXXXIX, (Mar), 336-337.

Malko, N.

1352. Malko, Nicolai. A Certain Art. Berthe Malko, comp., tr. and ed. NY: Morrow, 235p. Review, Ainslee Cox, Music Journal (1966 annual), 78. [Malko is a Russian conductor]

Muradeli, V.

1353. Muradeli, Vano. "A Soviet Composer Speaks: Thoughts on Modern Music." Music Journal, XXIV, 1 (Jan), 51+.

Prokofiev, S.

1354. Hanson, Lawrence, and Elisabeth Hanson. Prokofiev: A Biography. [See ABREES, 1964, No. 76] Review, Malcolm Brown, Notes of the Music Library Association, XXII, 2 (Winter 1965-66), 879-881.

1355. Pugliese, Giuseppe. "The Unknown World of Prokofiev's Operas." High Fidelity, XVI, 6 (Jun), 44-50.

Rachmaninoff, S.

1356. Bertensson, Sergei, and Jay Leyda, with the assistance of Sophia Satina. Sergei Rachmaninoff: A Lifetime in Music. [See ABREES, 1965, No. 1733] Reviews, Howard Ferguson, Music and Letters, XLVII, 2 (Apr), 164-165; Anthony Payne, Music and Musicians, XIV, 6 (Feb), 64; TLS, Feb 24, p. 136.

Richter, S.

1357. Neygauz, Genrikh Gustavovich. "More about Richter." Soviet Life, CXII, 1 (Jan), 22-23

Shostakovich, D. D.

1358. Hopkins, G.W. "Review of a First Performance." Tempo, no. 75 (Winter 1965-66), 23-25. [Shostakovich's 9th String Quartet]

1359. Layton, Robert. "Shostakovich and the Symphony." Making Music, No. 62 (Autumn), 10-12.

1360. Shostakovich, Dmitri, and V. Vinogradov. "Modernists are antisocial acrobats." Music Journal, XXIV, 3 (Mar), 55+. [Condemnation

of avant-garde musical attitudes in composition]

1361. Slonimsky, Sergei. "Stenka Razin's Victory." Musical Events, XXI, 9 (Sept), 10-12.

1362. Souster, Tim. "Shostakovich at the Crossroads." Tempo, no. 78 (Autumn), 2-9. [On Shostakovich's Fourth and Fifth Symphonies]

See also: 252, 1392

Shostakovich, M.

1363. Ivanov, Ivan. "Shostakovich Junior is Applauded." Music Journal, XXIV, 2 (Feb), 62+. [Discusses the career of Maxim Shostakovich, son of the composer and conductor]

Skriabin, A. N.

1364. Hughes, Matt Cordell. Tonal Orientation in Skriabin's Preludes: An Analysis on the Basis of Information Theory. [Unpublished Master's thesis, University of Texas] Review, Michael Kassler, Current Musicology (Spring), 82-86.

1365. Sabaneeff, Leonid. "A. N. Scriabin — A Memoir." Russ R, XXV, 3 (Jul), 257-267.

Solovchuk, G. A.

1366. Ustinov, Peter. "Gennady Afanasievitch Solovchuk." Music and Musicians, XIV, 5 (Jan), 35. [Solovchuk is a contemporary Soviet composer]

Stravinsky, I.

1367. Craft, Robert. "The 'Rite of Spring': Genesis of a Masterpiece." Perspectives of New Music (Fall-Winter), 20-36.

1368. _____. "With Stravinsky in Warsaw." Harper's, CCXXXII, 1389 (Feb), 66-75.

1369. Goodwin, Noel. "Stravinsky

at the Crossroads." Music and Musicians, XIV, 11 (Jul), 16. [Stravinsky's 'Oedipus Rex']

1370. Hopkins, G. W. "Stravinsky's Chords." Tempo, no. 76 (Spring), 6-12; and no. 77 (Autumn), 2-9.

1371. Lanchbery, John. "Stravinsky Peasants and Pianos." About the House, II, 2 (Jun), 40-42. [Discusses "Les Noces"]

1372. Lerner, Gerald. "Stravinsky's Italian Comedy." Records and Recording, IX, 10 (Jul), 22+. ["Pulcinella"]

1373. Siohan, Robert. Stravinsky. [See ABREES, 1965, No. 1742] Review, John Westcombe, Music in Education, XXX, 322 (Nov-Dec), 306.

1374. Stravinsky, Igor. "Stravinsky on the Musical Scene and Other Matters." NY Rev of Books, VI, 8, May 12, pp. 10-12.

1375. _____, and Robert Craft. Stravinsky: Themes and Episodes. NY: Alfred A. Knopf, 352p. Reviews, Clive Barnes, NY Times Book Rev, Sept 18, p. 6; Simon Karlinsky, Slav R, XXVII, 3 (Sept 1968), 452-458; Martin Mayer, Book Week, Oct 9, p. 3+; Harvey Sollberger, Perspectives of New Music (Fall-Winter), 148-152; Virgil Thomson, NY Rev of Books, VII, Dec 15, 3-4; Atlantic Monthly, CCXVIII, Oct, p. 218.

1376. White, Eric Walter. Stravinsky: The Composer and his Works. Berkeley and Los Angeles: U California Press, 608p. Reviews, Benjamin Boretz, Harper's, CCXXXIV, Feb 1967, p. 108; Peter A. Evans, Music and Letters, XLVIII, 2 (Apr), 142-145; Simon Karlinsky, Slav R, XXVII, 3 (Sept 1968), 452-458; Lawrence Morton, Musical Quarterly, LIII, 4 (Oct 1967), 589; Eric Salzman, NY Times Book Rev, Dec 11, p. 7; Virgil Thomson, NY Rev of Books, VII, Dec 15, pp. 3-4; TLS, Feb 16, 1967, p. 120.

1377. Whitwell, David. "Stravinsky — His Music for Winds." The Instrumentalist, XX, 11 (Jun), 50-53.

MUSIC AND POLITICS

1378. Bakst, James. "The Soviet View of Art." Music Journal, XXIV, 10 (Dec), 58-59.

1379. Peterson, Floyd. "Musical Aesthetics in Soviet Russia." Music Journal, XXIV, 1 (Jan), 54-56+. [On repercussions of the 1948 Central Committee Decree on Music]

THEATER ARTS

1380. Barnes, Clive. "The Only Five Great Ballet Companies." Harper's, CCXXXII, 1392, May, pp. 62-68. [Moscow's Bolshoi, Leningrad's Kirov]

1381. Brustein, Robert. The Theater of Revolt: Studies in Modern Drama from Ibsen to Genet. NY: Little, Brown and Co., 435p. Review, Geraldine Hammond, Modern Drama, IX, 2 (Sept), 231-234. [Includes discussion of Chekhov]

1382. Edwards, Christine. The Stanislavsky Heritage: Its Contribution to the Russian and American Theaters. NY: NYU Press, 345p. (1965) Review, TLS, May 29, p. 472.

1383. Glenny, Michael, ed. Three Soviet Plays. Baltimore: Penguin, 218p. Review, James M. Holquist, Slav East Eur J, XI, 2 (Summer 1967), 232-233. [The Bedbug, by Vladimir Mayakovsky, Max Hayward, tr.; Marya, by Isaac Babel', Michael Glenny and Harold Shukhman, trs.; The Dragon, by Yevgeny Schwartz, Max Hayward and Harold Shukhman, trs.]

1383a. Hayward, Max. "A Note on Recent Developments in the Soviet Theater." Cahiers du Monde Russe et Soviétique, VII, 3 (Jul-Sept), 408-413.

1384. Jonas, Klaus W. "Rainer Maria Rilke and the Sacharoffs." Yale U Lib Gaz, XL, 3 (Jan), 168-178. [Rilke and the Russian dancers]

1385. Karsavina, Tamara. "Origins of the Russian Ballet." The Dancing Times, LVI, 672 (Sept), 622-624+.

1386. Keefer, Lubov. "The Operetta Librettos of Ivan Turgenev." Slav East Eur J, X, 2 (Summer), 134-154.

1387. Lawson, Joan, ed. More Soviet Dances. London: Imperial Society of Teachers of Dancing. Review, "C. R.," English Dance and Song, XXVIII, 4 (Autumn), 98.

1388. Roslavleva, Nataliya. Era of the Russian Ballet. NY: Dutton, 320p. Reviews, S. J. Cohen, J Aes Art Crit, XXVI, 3 (Fall 1967), 137; Mary Grace Swift, Can Slav St, I, 1 (Spring 1967), 138-140; TLS, Jul 27, 1967, p. 660.

1389. Toporkov, V. "Stanislavsky Works with Tartuffe." James B. Woodward, tr. Drama Survey, V, 1 (Spring), 73-77.

1390. Voznesensky, Andrei. "Plisetskaya: A Sketch for a Portrait." Max Hayward, tr. NY Rev of Books, VII, 8 (Nov 17), pp. 14-15.

1391. Welsh, David J. Russian Comedy, 1765-1823. The Hague: Mouton, 133p. Reviews, C. L. Drage, Slav East Eur R, XLVI, 106 (Jan 1968), 224-225; J. G. Garrard, Russ R, XXVII, 1 (Jan 1968), 108; Robert W. Simmons, Jr., Slav East Eur J, XII, 4 (Winter 1968), 470.

See also: 997, 1030, 1034-1038, 1040, 1048, 1050, 1052

CINEMA

1392. "Shostakovich's Film Music: New Hamlet Released." Music Journal, XXIV, 3 (Mar), 54+. [The music for the film "Hamlet" directed by Kozintsev] [See also: 252]

See also: 940

COMPETITION

1393. Richards, D. J. Soviet Chess: Chess and Communism in the U.S.S.R. Oxford: Clarendon Press, 201p. (1965) Reviews, Geir Kjetsaa, Slav East Eur R, XLV, 105 (Jul 1967), 574-576; H. G. Schenk, Sov St, XVIII, 1 (Jul), 115-116.

Three. East Europe

GENERAL

1394. Carlton, Robert G., ed. Newspapers of East Central and Southeastern Europe in the Library of Congress. [See ABREES, 1965, No. 1778] Review, A. Helliwell, Slav East Eur R, XLV, 105 (Jul 1967), 577.

1395. "Doctoral Dissertations in the United States." Austrian H Yearb, II, pp. 240-241.

1396. Fischer-Galati, Stephen. "East Central Europe: Continuity and Change." J Int Aff, XX, 1, pp. 1-8.

1397. Glaser, Kurt. "Chances for Freedom in East Central Europe." Cent Eur J, XIV, 11 (Nov), 342-352.

1398. Hanak, Lubomir. "New Tasks for Central Europe's Exiles." Cent Eur J, XIV, 4 (Apr), 114-116.

1399. Horniker, Arthur Leon. "Ottoman-Turkish Diplomatics. A Guide to the Literature." Balk St, VII, 1, pp. 135-154.

1400. Legters, Lyman H. "The Government Stake in East European Studies." Russ R, XXV, 4 (Oct), 383-396.

1401. "Nineteen Sixty-Five MLA International Bibliography: East European." PMLA, LXXXI, 2 (May), 350-385.

1402. "Present Research Projects in the United States and Canada." Austrian H Yearb, II, pp. 224-233.

1403. Rudnyckyj, Jaroslav B. Slavica Canadiana A. D. 1964. Winnipeg: Canadian Association of Slavists; Polish Research Institute in Canada; Ukrainian Free Academy of Sciences, 64p. (1965) Review, W. T. Žyla, Slav East Eur J, XI, 1 (Spring 1967), 116-

117. [J. B. Rudnyckyj, compiler of Ukrainian items; J. M. Kirschbaum, of Slovakian; and T. W. Krychowski, of Polish items in a bibliography of writings by Slavs in Canada]

1404. Schroeder, Paul W. "American Books on Austria-Hungary." Austrian H Yearb, II, pp. 172-194. [See comments by Arthur J. May, p. 195, and Schroeder's reply, pp. 196-7]

1405. Štědrý, Vladimír. "The Escapees, Allies of the West." Cent Eur J, XIV, 12 (Dec), 381-386.

1406. Singleton, F. B. Background to Eastern Europe. [See ABREES, 1965, No. 1804] Review, R. V. Burks, Balk St, VII, 2, pp. 465-467.

1407. "United States Publications on Austria-Hungary." Austrian H Yearb, II, pp. 234-239.

HISTORY

1408. Bárány, George. "Wilsonian Central Europe: Lansing's Contribution." Hist, XXVIII, 2 (Feb), 224-251.

1409. Bass, Robert. "East European Communist Elites: Their Character and History." J Int Aff, XX, 1, pp. 106-117.

1410. Brown, J. F. The New Eastern Europe. The Khrushchev Era and After. NY: Praeger, 313p. Reviews, Robert Bass, East Eur, XV, 4 (Apr), 51-53; Yaroslav Bilinsky, Ann Am Acad Pol Soc Sci, CCLXVIII (Sept), 184-5; R. V. Burks, Slav R, XXVI, 2 (Jun 1967), 326-328; J. A. Boucek, Int J, XXII, 1 (Autumn), 141-142; Stephen Fischer-Galati, Balk St, VII, 2, pp. 470-471; Joseph Rothschild, Pol R, XI, 3 (Summer), 81-82; Joseph S.

Roucek, Cent Eur J, XIV, 10 (Oct), 323-324; J. S. Roucek, West Poli Q, XIX, 3 (Sept), 543-544; George A. Schöpflin, Survey, no. 65 (Oct 1967), 113-115; TLS, Sept 8, p. 836.

1411. Bushkoff, Leonard. "Images and Attitudes: East European History at the American Historical Association Meeting." Balk St, VII, 1, pp. 166-171.

1412. Fichtner, Paula Sutter. "An Absence Explained: Archduke Ferdinand of Austria and the Battle of Mohács." Austrian H Yearb, II, 11-16. [See comments by S. Fischer-Galati: 17, 18]

1413. Holzner, Lutz. "The Rhine-Main-Danube Waterhighway." J Geog, LXV, 6 (Sept), 270-281.

1414. Jelavich, Barbara. "The Philorthodox Conspiracy of 1839. A Report to Metternich." Balk St, VII, 1, pp. 89-102.

1415. Kienitz-Garza, Ernesto. "Magdeburg, Mediator Between East and West." Cent Eur J, XIV, 7-8 (Jul-Aug), 236-240.

1416. Macartney, C. A. Independent Eastern Europe: A History. NY: St. Martin's Press, 499p. [paper] [Reprint of the 1st edition, 1962]

1417. Raditsa, Bogdan. "The Disunity of the Slavs." Orbis, X, 4 (Winter), 1082-1090.

1417a. Saks, Edgar V. Esto-Europa: A Treatise on the Finno-Ugric Primary Civilization in Europe. Montreal & Lund, 239p. [Distributed by Verlag Võitleja, Heidelberg.) Review, Demitri B. Shimkin, Slav R, XXVII, 4 (Dec 1968), 640.

1418. Stone, Norman. "Moltke — Conrad: Relations between Austro-Hungarian and German General Staffs, 1909-1914." Hist J, IX, 2, pp. 201-228.

1419. Tomiak, Janusz J. "A British Poet's Account of the Raising of the Siege of Vienna in 1683." Pol R, XI, 4 (Autumn), 66-74. [On a poem of Alexander Tyler, (? - 1689)]

See also: 1464

INTERNATIONAL RELATIONS

1420. Auer, Paul. "A Western Policy for Eastern Europe." Cent Eur J, XIV, 1 (Jan), 11-13.

1421. "Bonn's Dialogue with East Europe." East Eur, XV, 5 (May), 2-9.

1422. Bregman, Alexander. "Germany's Search for an Eastern Policy." East Eur, XV, 3 (Mar), 2-7.

1423. Burks, R. V. The Dynamics of Communism in Eastern Europe. Princeton: Princeton U Press, 244p. [paper] [First published 1961]

1424. Brzezinski, Zbigniew. Alternative to Partition: For a Broader Conception of America's Role in Europe. [See ABREES, 1965, No. 1809] Reviews, Max Beloff, Prob Comm, XV, 4 (Jul-Aug), 46-50; Adam Bromke, Int J, XXI, 2 (Spring), 211-217; John C. Farrell, J Int Aff, XX, 1, pp. 172-173; Elke Frank, J Poli, XXVIII, 2 (May), 451-453; Jacques Freymond, Survey, no. 58 (Jan), 128-133; Jerzy Hauptmann, Ukr Q, XXII, 1 (Spring), 86-88; Josef Korbel, W Poli, XVIII, 4 (Jul), 749-760; TLS, Feb 10, p. 98.

1425. Campbell, John C. American Policy Toward Communist Eastern Europe. The Choices Ahead. [See ABREES, 1965, No. 1810] Reviews, Adam Bromke, Int J, XXI, 2 (Spring), 211-217; Elke Frank, J Poli, XXVIII, 2 (May), 451-453; Jerzy Hauptmann, Cent Eur J, XIV, 3 (Mar), 106-107; Leonas Sabaliunas, Litua, XII, 1 (Spring), 92-93.

1426. Canada and Eastern Europe. Canadian Slavonic Papers, Vol. VIII. Adam Bromke, ed. H. Gordon Skilling, "Canada and Eastern Europe," 3-15, 46-52. [Discussion, 16-45]

1427. Collier, D. S., and K. Gla-
ser, eds. Western Policy and East-
ern Europe. Chicago: Regnery, 245p.
Reviews, L. A. D. Dellin, East Eur,
XV, 11 (Nov), 55-56; Joseph S. Roucek,
Int R Hist Poli Sci, III, 2 (Dec), 164-166.

1428. Czechanowski, S. "New
Course in German Policy." Pol Ger,
X, 36 (Apr-Jun), 12-17.

1429. _____. "West Germany's
Eastern Policy Moves." Pol Ger, X,
37 (Jun-Sept), 3-6.

1430. Dobriansky, Lev E. "A
U.S. Policy of Unfinished Liberation."
Ukr Q, XXII, 4 (Winter), 300-321.

1431. Görgey, Laszlo. "Emerging
Patterns in West German-East European Relations." Orbis, X, 3 (Fall),
911-929.

1432. Gradl, Johann B. "German-
Polish Reconciliation and Expellee
Claims." Cent Eur J, XIV, 4 (Apr),
111-113

1433. Hassner, Pierre. "German
and European Reunification: Two
Problems or One?" Survey, no. 61
(Oct), 14-37.

1434. Hinterhoff, E. "The Problem of German Reunification." Pol
Ger, X, 37 (Jul-Sept), 18-26.

1435. Ionescu, Ghita. The Break-
up of the Soviet Empire. [See ABREES,
1965, No. 1817] Reviews, Josef Korbel, Slav R, XXV, 3 (Sept), 547-548;
Arpad von Lazar, Am Pol Sci R, LX,
2 (Jun), 459-460.

1436. Kudlicki, S. "West Germany's Eastern European Policy."
Pol Ger, X, 38 (Oct-Dec), 3-9.

1437. London, Kurt, ed. Eastern
Europe in Transition. Baltimore:
Johns Hopkins Press, 364p. Reviews,
Alfred J. Bannan, Hist, XXX, 1 (Nov
1967), 98-99; Carl Beck, Am Pol Sci
R, LXII, 1 (Mar 1968), 289-290; Vac-
lav Beneš, East Eur Q, I, 4 (Jan 1968),
416-419; John C. Campbell, Slav R,
XXVI, 3 (Sept 1967), 497-498; George

Gömöri, Sov St, XX, 1 (Jul 1968), 144-
146; Harry Hanak, Int Aff, XLIV, 1
(Jan 1968), 117-118; Viktor Meier,
Prob Comm, XVI, 4 (Jul-Aug 1967),
58-61; Wayne S. Vucinich, Am Hist R,
LXXIII, 2 (Dec 1967), 539-540; Joseph
F. Zacek, J Dev Areas, I, 3 (Apr 1967),
411.

1438. Mares, Vaclav E. "Aid
Avenues in East Europe." Cur Hist,
LI, 299 (Jul), 36-44.

1439. Richthofen, Bolko von.
"Germany's Eastern Frontier as Dis-
cussed in Recent Publications." Cent
Eur J, XIV, 4 (Apr), 117-119.

1440. Štědrý, Vladimir. "RFE:
A Wasted Weapon." Cent Eur J, XIV,
4 (Apr), 120-127. [On the role of
Radio Free Europe]

1441. Speier, Hans. "The Hall-
stein Doctrine." Survey, no. 61 (Oct),
93-104.

1442. Stehle, Hansjakob. "The
Federal Republic and Eastern Europe." Survey, no. 61 (Oct), 70-79.

1443. Sylvester, Anthony. "East
Europeans in the Maghreb." East Eur,
XV, 7 (Jul), 2-8. [On technical assis-
tance to Tunisia, Algeria, and Morocco]

1444. Tudyka, Kurt, P. "The
Foreign Policy of the German Democratic Republic." Survey, no. 61 (Oct),
56-69.

1445. Visoianu, Constantin.
"'Europe to the Urals' and the Captive
Nations." ACEN News, 125 (Sept-
Oct), 28-30.

See also: 48, 50, 53

PUBLIC AFFAIRS,
LAW AND GOVERNMENT

1446. Beneš, Vaclav, Andrew
Gyorgy, and George Stambuk. Eastern European Governments and Politics. NY: Harper & Row, 247p. Reviews, Carl Beck, Am Pol Sci R,
LXII, 1 (Mar 1968), 289-290; Philip

W. Buck, West Poli Q, XX, 2, pt. 1 (Jun 1967), 459-460; Viktor Meier, Prob Comm, XVI, 4 (Jul-Aug 1967), 58-61.

1447. Ionescu, Ghita. The Politics of the European Communist States. NY: Praeger, 312p. (1967) Reviews, Harry Hanak, Int Aff, XLIV, 1 (Jan 1968), 117-118; Robert A. Rupen, Am Pol Sci R, LXII, 2 (Jun 1968), 663-4; TLS, Sept 21, 1967, p. 831.

1448. Karol, K.S. "Reflections on the People's Democracies." The Socialist Register, 1965, 30-44. [See item 12]

1449. Skilling, H. Gordon. The Governments of Communist East Europe. NY: Thomas Y. Crowell, 256p. Reviews, Robert Bass, East Eur, XV, 9 (Sept), 69-71; Ghita Ionescu, Sov St, XVIII, 4 (Apr 1967), 530-532; Jaroslaw Piekalkiewicz, Review of Politics, XXX, 1 (Jan 1968), 90-93; George Schöpflin, Survey, No. 65 (Oct 1967), 113-115; R.V. Burks, Slav R, XXVI, 2 (Jun 1967), 326-328.

1450. Taylor, Pauline B., and Michael Csizmas. "Two Aspects of Pre-Trial Procedure in Eastern Europe." J Int Commis Jur, VII, 1 (Summer), 20-54.

1451. "Television in Eastern Europe." East Eur, XV, 4 (Apr), 12-15.

1452. "Writers and Journalists: A Pressure Group in East European Politics." Jour Q, XLIII, 1 (Spring), 95-106.

ECONOMICS

1453. "Advertising in Eastern Europe." East Eur, XV, 1 (Jan), 2-12.

1454. "Agricultural Reforms in Eastern Europe." Bull Int Commis Jur, no. 28 (Dec), 44.

1455. Developing the East European Market. Geneva: Business International S.A., Research Report 66-4, 86p. [Prepared by the editors of Business Europe]

1456. Gamarnikow, Michael. "Can they Decentralize?" East Eur, XV, 7 (Jul), 16-23.

1457. ____. "The Cost of Reform." ibid., 8 (Aug), 15-21.

1458. ____. "The Meaning of Economic Revisionism." Prob Peop USSR, no. 26 (Winter), 39-46.

1459. ____. "Prices and the Market." East Eur, XV, 5 (May), 10-15.

1460. ____. "Reform in Agriculture." ibid., 11 (Nov), 17-24.

1461. Garvy, George. Money, Banking and Credit in Eastern Europe. NY: Federal Reserve Bank of New York, 167p. [paper]

1462. Grossman, Gregory. "Economic Reforms: A Balance Sheet." Prob Comm, XV, 6 (Nov-Dec), 43-55.

1463. Hayenko, Fedor. "The 'Communist Labour' Movement." St Sov Un, V, 3, pp. 46-55.

1464. Jackson, George D, Jr. Comintern and Peasant in East Europe 1919-1930. NY: Columbia U Press, 351p. Reviews, R.V. Burks, Am Hist R, LXXII, 2 (Jan 1967), 643-644; R.V. Daniels, Prob Comm, XVI, 4 (Jul-Aug 1967), 71-2; L.A.D.Dellin, East Eur Q, I, 4 (Jan 1968), 406-8; M. K. Dziewanowski, Cent Eur Fed, XIV, 1 (Jul), 44-45; Charles Gati, Slav R, XXVII, 1 (Mar 1968), 155-157; Andrzej Korbonski, Pol R, XI, 2 (Summer), 82-84; H. Malcolm Macdonald, Sou Soc Sci Q, XLVII, 3 (Dec), 339-340; Frank Munk, West Poli Q, XX, 1 (Mar 1967), 223-224; Jaroslaw Piekalkiewicz, Am Pol Sci R, LXI, 2 (Jun 1967), 538-9; Joseph S. Roucek, Russ R, XXV, 4 (Oct), 426; R.E.F. Smith, Sov St, XVIII, 4 (Apr 1967), 536; Troian Stoianovich, Ann Am Acad Pol Soc Sci, CCCLXIX, (Jan 1967), 198; TLS, Nov 10, p. 1024; Virg Q R, XLII (Autumn) 152.

1465. Kaser, Michael. Comecon: Integration Problems of the Planned Economies. [See ABREES, 1965, No. 106] Review, Frederic L. Pryor, Econ of Planning, VI, 1, pp. 95-96.

1466. Korbonski, A. "The Agricultural Problems in East Central Europe." J Int Aff, XX, 1, pp. 72-88.

1467. Montias, John Michael. "Economic Nationalism in Eastern Europe: Forty Years of Continuity and Change." J Int Aff, XX, 1, pp. 45-71.

1468. Pinder, John. "EEC and Comecon." Survey, no. 58 (Jan), 101-117.

1469. Pommer, Hans Jörg. "Reforms in Eastern Europe: Report on a Conference." Prob Comm, XV, 9-10 (Sept-Oct), 77-80.

1470. Pryor, Frederic L., and George F. Staller. "The Dollar Values of the Gross National Products in Eastern Europe." Econ Planning, VI, 1, pp. 1-26.

1471. Pryor, F. L. "Trade Barriers of Capitalist and Communist Nations against Foodstuffs exported by Tropical Underdeveloped Nations." R Econ Stat, XLVIII, 406-412.

1472. Schaefer, Henry. "An East European Payments Union?" East Eur, XV, 3 (Mar), 14-21.

1473. Spulber, Nicolas. The State and Economic Development in Eastern Europe. NY: Random House, 179p. Reviews, Leonard Bushkoff, Balk St, IX, 1 (1968), 260-264; John C. Campbell, Slav R, XXVI, 3 (Sept 1967), 497-498; L. A. D. Dellin, East Eur, XVI, 7 (Jul 1967), 58.

1474. Vaughn, Ralph. "Doing Business with the East." East Eur, XV, 11 (Nov), 25-27.

1475. Zauberman, Alfred. "A Few Remarks on [Michael] Kalecki's Theory of Economic Growth under Socialism." Kyklos, XIX, 3, pp. 411-424.

See also: 1413

SOCIAL RELATIONS

1476. Hammond, Thomas T. "Nationalism and National Minorities in Eastern Europe." J Int Aff, XX, 1, pp. 9-31.

1477. Heltai, George G. "Changes in the Social Structure of the East Central European Countries." J Int Aff, XX, 1, pp. 165-171.

1478. Roucek, Joseph S. "Communism and Intelligentsia in the East Bloc States." Cent Eur J, XIV, 2 (Feb), 39-46.

1479. Zaporowski, Bogdan. "The Young Generation of Post-Stalin East Europe." Cent Eur Fed, XIV, 2 (Dec), 21-25.

IDEOLOGY, PHILOSOPHY AND RELIGION

1480. Babić, Ivan. "Blanshard's Reduction of Marxism." Branko Ožbolt and Ante Starčević, trs. J Philosophy, LXIII, No. 23, 745-756.

1481. "The Decline of the Churches." East Eur, XV, 6 (Jun), 7-12.

1482. DeGeorge, Richard T. "Morality, Ethics and East-European Marxism." Inquiry (Oslo), IX, 1, pp. 11-29.

1483. "Focus on Religion in East Europe." ACEN News, no. 123, (May-Jun), 20-25.

1484. Laszlo, Ervin. "Philosophy in Eastern Europe: An Introduction." Inquiry (Oslo), IX, 1, pp. 1-10.

1485. _____. "Dynamics of Ideological Change in Eastern Europe." Inquiry (Oslo), IX, 1, pp. 47-72.

1486. Lemberg, Eugen. "The Intellectual Shift in East-Central European Marxism-Leninism." Mod Age, XI, 2 (Spring), 131-143.

LITERATURE AND THE ARTS

1487. Alvarez, A. Under Pressure. The Writer in Society: Eastern Europe and the U.S.A. Baltimore: Pelican, 189p. Review, Edmund Zawacki, Slav East Eur J, XI, 2 (Summer 1967), 238-241.

1488. Conover, W. "Jazz Today in Prague, Warsaw, and Budapest." Downbeat, XXXIII (Jan 27), 26-7.

1489. Mond, Jerzy, and Robert Richter. "Writers and Journalists as a Pressure Group in Eastern Europe." Pol R, XI, 1 (Winter), 92-108. [Po-

land, Hungary and Chechoslovakia, 1954-1964]

1490. Petrus, Earl P. "The Golem: Significance of the Legend." Psych R, LIII, 1 (Spring), 63-68.

1491. Svitak, Ivan. "Kafka as Philosopher." Survey, no. 59 (Apr), 36-40.

1492. Wellesz, Egon, and Miloš Velimirovič, eds. Studies in the Eastern Chant, Vol. I. Oxford: Oxford U Press, 134p. Reviews, David Wulstan, Music and Letters, XLVIII, 3 (Jul), 270-271; TLS, Dec 22, p.1184.

II. EAST CENTRAL EUROPE

CZECHOSLOVAKIA

General

1493. Bondy, François. "The Empty Pedestal." Enc, XXVII, 1 (Jul), 73-82.

1494. Heymann, Frederick G. Poland and Czechoslovakia. Englewood Cliffs, N.J.: Prentice-Hall, 181p. Reviews, Otakar Odložilik, Am Hist R, LXXII, 4 (Jul 1967), 1444; Joseph F. Zacek, J Mod Hist, XL, 3 (Sept 1968), 413-414; East Eur, XVI, 9 (Sept 1967), 56.

1495. Rechcigl, Miloslav, Jr. "Czechoslovak Contributions to American Science and Scholarship." Abstracts of Papers, Third Congress of the Czechoslovak Society of Arts and Sciences in America. NY: Czechoslovak Society of Arts and Sciences in America, 64p.

1496. ____. The Czechoslovak Contribution to World Culture. [See ABREES, 1964, No. 459] Reviews, Z. R. Dittrich, Slav East Eur R, XLIV, 103 (Jul), 499; Paul I. Trensky, Slav East Eur J, X, 2 (Summer), 221-224.

1497. ____. "The Czechoslovak Society of Arts and Sciences in America and its Activities in the Field of History of Science." Archives internationales d'Histoire des Sciences, XIX, pp.282-283.

History

1498. [George, King of Bohemia] The Universal Peace Organization of King George of Bohemia. A Fifteenth Century Plan for World Peace, 1462-1464. London: Merlin Press, (1964) Review, A. N. E. D. Schofield, Slav East Eur R, XLV, 104 (Jan 1967), 238-241.

1499. Heymann, Frederick G. George of Bohemia: King of Heretics. [See ABREES, 1965, No. 1868] Reviews, Howard Kaminsky, Spec, XLI, 3 (Jul), 543-546; Otakar Odložilik, Ren News, XIX, 1 (Spring), 31-32; Cecil Parrott, Hist Today, XVI, 1 (Jan), 64; Gunther E. Rothenberg, Historian, XXVIII, 2 (Feb), 320-321; A. N. E. D. Schofield, Slav East Eur R, XLV, 104 (Jan 1967), 238-241.

1500. Holotík, L'udovít, ed.

Studia Historica Slovaca. Vols. I, II, and III. Bratislava: Vydavateľstvo Slovenskej Akadémie Vied, 1963, 1964, 1965; 252, 287, 347pp. Review, Stanley B. Kimball, Slav East Eur J, XI, 1 (Spring 1967), 117-119. [Contributions in English, French, and German from the Historical Institute of the Slovak Academy of Sciences]

1501. Koči, Josef, and Jiří Kořalka. "The History of the Habsburg Monarchy (1576-1918) in Czechoslovak Historiography Since 1945." Austrian H Yearb, II, pp. 198-223.

1502. Nemec, Ludvik. "The Czech Role in the Christianization of Poland." Cent Eur Fed, XIV, 1 (Jul), 6-11.

1503. Odložilik, Otakar. The Hussite King: Bohemia in European Affairs, 1440-1471. [See ABREES, 1965, No. 1874] Review, Howard Kaminsky, Spec, XLI, 3 (Jul), 543-546; A. N. E. D. Schofield, Slav East Eur R, XLV, 104 (Jan 1967), 238-241.

1504. Parrott, Cecil. "Otakar Přemysl, King of Bohemia." Hist Today, XVI, 11 (Nov), 765-772.

1505. _____. "St. Wenceslas of Bohemia." ibid., 4 (Apr), 225-233.

1506. Seebohm, Hans-Christoph. "Political Aspects of the Munich Agreement." Cent Eur J, XIV, 10 (Oct), 295-300.

1507. Středrý, Vladimir. "A Czech Commentary on the Sudeten German Question." Cent Eur J, XIV, 7-8 (Jul-Aug), 233-235.

1508. Spinka, Matthew. John Hus' Concept of the Church. Princeton: Princeton U Press, 451p. Reviews, Otakar Odložilik, Am Hist R, LXXII, 1 (Oct), 165-166; G. R. Potter, English Historical Review, LXXXII, 325 (Oct 1967), 828-829; A. N. E. D. Schofield, Slav East Eur R, XLV, 105 (Jul 1967), 556-558.

1509. _____, ed. and tr. John

Hus at the Council of Constance. [See ABREES, 1965, No. 1876] Review, A. N. E. D. Schofield, Slav East Eur R, XLV, 5 (Jun 1967), 556-558.

1510. Ulc, Otto. "How the Czechs Fell in 1956." Cent Eur Fed, XIV, 1 (Jul), 23-28.

1511. Vital, David. "Czechoslovakia and the Powers, September 1938." J Contemp Hist, I, 4, pp. 37-67.

1512. Watt, D. C. "The May Crisis of 1938: A Rejoinder to Mr. Wallace." Slav East Eur R, XLIV, 103 (Jul), 475-480. [See W. V. Wallace, "The Making of the May Crisis of 1938," ibid., XLI, 97 (Jun 1963), 368-390; and "A Reply to Mr. Watt," ibid., XLIV, 103 (Jul 1966), 481-485]

1513. Wright, William E. Serf, Seigneur, and Sovereign: Agrarian Reform in Eighteenth-Century Bohemia. Minneapolis: U Minnesota Press, 217p. Reviews, Frederick G. Heymann, Am Hist R, LXXIII, 1 (Oct 1967), 174-175; Emile Karafiol, Slav R, XXVII, 4 (Dec 1967), 679-680; Doris G. Phillips, J Econ Hist, XXVII, 3 (Sept 1967), 431-433; Joseph Zacek, J Mod Hist, XL, 4 (Dec 1968), 673-4.

Public affairs, law and government

1514. Brown, A. H. "Pluralistic Trends in Czechoslovakia." Sov St, XVII, 4 (Apr), 453-472.

1515. "Freedom of Worship and the Czechoslovak Regime." ACEN News, 123 (May-Jun), 17-19.

1516. Kuhn, Heinrich. "Czechoslovakia's National Minorities." Cent Eur J, XIV, 6 (Jun), 190-196.

1517. _____. "Czechoslovakia's National Minorities." ibid., 10 (Oct), 305-308.

1518. Meier, Viktor. "Politics in Prague." Survey, no. 59 (Apr), 4-11.

1519. "New Czechoslovak Labour

Code." Int Lab R, XCIII, 1 (Jan), 80-89.

1520. Polach, J. G. "Nuclear R & D Organization in Poland and Czechoslovakia." Cent Eur Fed, XIV, 2 (Dec), 26-41. [Research and development]

1521. Skilling, H. Gordon. "Communism and Czechoslovak Traditions." J Int Aff, XX, 1, pp. 118-136.

1522. Tyl, Rudolf. "Disabled Persons' Co-operatives in the Czechoslovak Socialist Republic." Int Lab R, XCIII, 2 (Feb), 143-148.

1523. Velímsky, Vítezslav. "The Stimulation of Administrative Decisions: A New Instrument for the Training of Directors of Social Security Funds." Bull Int Soc Sec Assoc, XIX, 9-10 (Sept-Oct), 380-384.

1524. "Visit of Czech Parliamentarians to Canada." Exter Aff, XVIII, 8 (Aug), 331-332.

See also: 1489

Economics

1525. Goldman, J., and J. Flek. "Economic Growth in Czechoslovakia." Econ Plan, VI, 2, pp. 125-137.

1526. Hanak, Harry. "Recent Trends in Czechoslovakia: I. Economic Reforms; II. Slovak Nationalism." W Today, XXII, 2 (Feb), 78-88.

1526a. _____. "Recent Trends in Czechoslovakia: The Writer's Campaign of Criticism." ibid., 3 (Mar), 130-134.

1527. Michal, Jan. "The New Economic Model." Survey, no. 59 (Apr), 61-72.

1528. Montias, J. M. "Economic Reform in Perspective." Survey, no. 59 (Apr), 48-60.

1529. Nekola, Jirí, and Ladislav Rîha. "Country Case Studies of Research, Development and Economic

Growth: Czechoslovakia." Int Soc Sci J, XVIII, 3, pp. 377-387.

1530. Pesek, Boris P. Gross National Product of Czechoslovakia. [See ABREES, 1965, No. 1902] Reviews, Jan M. Michal, J Pol Econ, LXXVI, 1 (Feb), 97-99; Alfred Zauberman, Int Aff, XLII, 2 (Apr), 313-314.

Science

1531. de Beer, Gavin. "What Mendel Knew." New York Rev of Books, VII, 2 (Aug 18), 18-20. [Review article on Fundamenta Genetica: The Revised Edition of Mendel's Classic Paper with a Collection of Twenty-seven Original Papers Published During the Rediscovery Era. Selection and Commentary by Jaroslav Krizenecky. Prague: Czechoslovak Academy of Sciences; and Oosterhout, Netherlands: Moravian Museum, 400p.

1532. Cox, Frank. "A Visit to Leipzig and Prague Psychological Institutes." Am Psych, XXI, 11 (Nov), 1076.

1533. Rechcigl, Miloslav, Jr. "Czechoslovak Science." Sci, CLIV, 924-926.

Sociology and education

1534. Kolaja, Jiri. "Demography in Poland and Czechoslovakia." Survey, no. 59 (Apr), 122-124.

1535. Sadler, J. E. J[ohann] A[mos] Comenius and the Concept of Universal Education. NY: Barnes & Noble, 318p.

1536. Tosch, Berta. "Czechoslovak Tourism." Cent Eur J/Sud Bull, XIV, 1 (Jan), 24-27.

Language

1537. Wojatsek, Charles, comp. Česke Četby. Denver: Czechoslovak Society of America, 325p. (1964) Review, Beatrice M. Nosco, Slav East

Eur J, X, 1 (Spring), 99-100. [Intermediate reader of Czech literature for English speaking people].

1538. Vachek, Josef. The Linguistic School of Prague: An Introduction to its Theory and Practice. Bloomington, Ind.: Indiana U Press, 184p.

1539. _____, ed. Travaux linguistiques de Prague, Vol. II. Les problèmes du centre et de la périphérie du système de la langue. University, Ala.: U Alabama Press, 287p. Review, Francis Salter, Can Slav St, II, 4 (Winter 1968), 591-593.

Literature and the arts

1540. Andic, V.E. "Third Congress of the Czechoslovak Society of Arts and Sciences." Cent Eur Fed, XIV, 2 (Dec), 10-13.

1541. Bezruč, Petr. Silesian Songs. Ian Milner, tr. Brno: Artia, 91p.

1542. Blackwell, Vera. "Literature and the Drama." Survey, no. 59 (Apr), 41-47.

1543. Bradbrook, B.R. "František Langer (1888-1965): An Appreciation." Slav East Eur R, XLIV, 103 (Jul), 486-490.

1544. Clapham, John. Antonin Dvořák, Musician and Craftsman. NY: St. Martin's Press, 359p. Reviews, Richard Gorer, The Musical Times, CVII (Dec), 1062; Alec Robertson, Music and Letters, XLVII, 2 (Apr), 140-142.

1545. _____. "Dvořák and the American Indian." The Musical Times, CVII (Oct), 863-867. [Influence of the American Indian on Dvorak's music]

1546. Elschek, Oskar. "Methodological Problems in Slovak Ethnomusicology." Ethnomusicology, X, 2 (May), 191-198.

1547. Elshekova, A. "Methods of Classification of Folk-tunes." Journal of the International Folk Music Council, XVIII, pp. 56-76. [Discusses classification of Czechoslovakian folk music]

1548. Gardavsky, Čeněk, ed. Contemporary Czechoslovak Composers. Prague: Panton, 562p. (1965)

1549. "Happenings in Prague." Studio International, CLXXII, 882, 210-211. [An artistic 'manifestation' by Czech artists and writers]

1550. Kirschbaum, J.M. Pan-Slavism in Slovak Literature: Jan Kollár — Slovak Poet of Pan-Slavism. NY: Slovak Institute, 47p. Review, Paul I. Trensky, Slav East Eur J, XI, 2 (Summer 1967), 227.

1551. Krenek, Ernst. Exploring Music. Essays. Margaret Shenfield and Geoffrey Skelton, trs. NY: October House, 245p. Review, Michael Tilmouth, Music and Letters, XLVIII, 1 (Jan 1967), 75.

1552. Lederer, Jiri. "Television Lights and Shadows." Survey, no. 59 (Apr), 30-35.

1553. Liehm, A.J. "Success on the Screen." Survey, no. 59 (Apr), 12-20.

1554. Matuska, Alexander. Karel Čapek. Man Against Destruction. London: Allen & Unwin, 425p. Review, B.R. Bradbrook, Slav East Eur R, XLV, 104 (Jan 1967), 230-231.

1555. Michna, Adam Vaclav. Missa Sancti Wenceslai. Prague: Artia, text 19p. in Czech, German and English; 120p. music. Jan Racek, ed.

1556. Nolte, Ewald V. "Choral Music in the Moravian Archives." American Choral Review, IX, 1 (Fall), 6.

1557. Slonim, Marc. "European Notebook: the Czech poet Vladimir Holan." NY Times Book Rev, Oct 9, p. 60.

1558. Stribrny, Zdeněk, ed. Charles University on Shakespeare. Prague: Charles University, 176p. [Essays on Shakespeare]

1559. Vinton, John. Review of: Štepánek, Vladimir, and Bohumil Karásek. An Outline of Czech and Slovak Music. Part I: Czech Music. Prague: Orbis, 1964; in Notes of the Music Library Association, XXII, 2, p.919.

See also: 1403, 1448, 1489

HUNGARY

General

1560. "Hungary Revisited." East Eur, XV, 10 (Oct), 2-9.

1561. Pesthy, Peter. "Budapest, a Danube Pearl." Cent Eur J, XIV, 5 (May), 164-172.

History

1562. Aczél, Tamás, ed. Ten Years After: The Hungarian Revolution in the Perspective of History. NY: Holt, Rinehart & Winston, 253p. Reviews, Jerzy Hauptmann, Cent Eur J, XVI, 1 (Jan 1968), 33-34; Viktor Meier, Prob Comm, XVI, 4 (Jul-Aug 1967), 58-61; TLS, Jan 12, 1967, p.30.

1563. Auer, Paul. "Hungary Ten Years Ago." Cent Eur J, XIV, 10 (Oct), 301-304.

1564. Bárány, George. "The Awakening of Magyar Nationalism Before 1848." Austrian H Yearb, II, pp. 19-49. [See comment by Keith Hitchins, 50-51, and reply by Bárány, 52-54]

1565. Braham, Randolph L., ed. Hungarian-Jewish Studies. NY: World Federation of Hungarian Jews, 359p. Review, Keith Hitchins, Am Hist R, LXXIII, 2 (Dec 1967), 535-536.

1566. Fellner, Fritz. Review of: Alfred D. Low, The Soviet Hungarian Republic and the Paris Peace Conference. Transactions of the American Philosophical Society, new series, vol. LIII, pt. 10, 1963, 91p.; in Austrian H Yearb, II, pp.313-315.

1567. Gosztony, Peter I. "General Maleter: A Memoir." Prob Comm, XV, 3-4 (Mar-Apr), 54-61.

1568. Heltai, George. "November 1956: The End in Budapest." East Eur, XV, 10 (Oct), 10-15.

1569. Karolyi, Countess Catherine [Andrassy]. A Life Together. The Memoirs of Catherine Karolyi. London: Allen & Unwin, 343p. Reviews, F. L. Carsten, Slav East Eur R, XLV, 105 (Jul 1967), 565-566; TLS, Dec 1, p. 1119.

1570. Kiraly, Bela K. "The Organization of National Defense During the Hungarian Revolution." Cent Eur Fed, XIV, 1 (Jul), 12-22.

1571. ____. "From Death to Revolution. A Memoir of the Hungarian Revolution." Dissent, XIII, 6 (Nov-Dec), 709-724.

1572. Moravcsik, Gy. "Hungary and Byzantium in the Middle Ages," in the Cambridge Medieval History, Vol. IV, pt. 1, 566-591. [See item 26a]

1573. Pach, Z. P. "The Development of Feudal Rent in Hungary in the Fifteenth Century." Econ Hist R, XIX, 1 (Apr), 1-14.

1574. Polanyi, Michael. "The Message of the Hungarian Revolution." Am Scholar, XXXV, 4 (Autumn), 661-676.

1575. Stolte, Stefan C. "The Hungarian Revolution: Ten Years After." Bull Inst St USSR, XIII, 12 (Dec), 28-37.

1576. Stone, Norman. "Hungary and the Crisis of July, 1914." J Contemp Hist, I, 3, pp.147-164.

1577. Szilassy, S. "America and the Hungarian Revolution of 1848-1849."

Slav East Eur R, XLIV, 102 (Jan), 180-196.

1578. Váli, Ferenc A. "Transylvania and the Hungarian Minority." J Int Aff, XX, 1, 32-44.

See also: 30

Public affairs, law and government

1579. Fabian, Bela. "Hungary Remains a Prison." ACEN News, 122 (Mar-Apr), 2-6.

1580. Laszlo, Ervin. The Communist Ideology in Hungary. Dordrecht: D. Reidel, 351p. Review, George G. Heltai, Slav R, XXVI, 3 (Sept 1967), 499.

1581. Lazar, A. J. von. "Class Struggle and Socialist Construction: The Hungarian Paradox." Slav R, XXV, 2 (Jun), 303-313.

1582. Maller, Sandor. "The Hungarian National Commission for UNESCO." Int R Ed, XII, 3, pp. 259-270.

1583. Mariska, C. L. "Social Insurance in Hungary." Bull Int Soc Sec Assoc, XIX, 3-4 (Mar-Apr), 91-110.

1584. Nagy, Karoly. "Hungary's Alienated Workers." Prob Comm, XV, 4 (Jul-Aug), 72-77.

1585. Pfeiffer, Zoltan. "Hungary's Dwindling Birth Rate." ACEN News, 122 (Mar-Apr), 25-27.

1586. Savarius, Vincent. "Janos Kadar: Man and Politician." East Eur, XV, 10 (Oct), 16-21.

1587. Schöpflin, George A. "Hungary Today: The Balance-Sheet of Kadar's Ten Years in Power." W Today, XXII, 11 (Nov), 455-459.

See also: 1489

Economics

1588. Asztalos, I., G. Enyedi, B. Sarfalvi, and L. Simon. Geographical Types of Hungarian Agriculture. Review, Geog, LI, 4(Nov), 417-418.

1589. Balaszy, Sandor. "Payroll and Employment Taxation and the Economics of Employment in Hungary." Int Lab R, XCIII, 5 (May), 509-520.

1590. Bod, Peter. "A Decision Problem of Long-term Economic Planning. Suboptimizing the Expansion of the Raw Material Base." Econ Plan, VI, 2, pp. 179-189.

1591. Faluvegi, Lajos. "The Planning of Budgetary Expenditure on Education on the Basis of a Mathematical Model — The Method Employed in Hungary." Pub Fin, XXI, 1-2 (Summer), 206-229; comment by Alan T. Peacock, ibid., 230-235.

1592. Held, Joseph. "Hungary: Iron out of Wood." Prob Comm, XV, 6 (Nov-Dec), 37-43.

1593. Kondor, György. "Elaboration of an Optimum Transportation and Processing Program for Sugar-Beet." Econ Plan, VI, 1, pp. 43-52.

1594. Timár, János. Planning the Labor Force in Hungary. Lynn Turgeon, tr. White Plains, NY: International Arts and Sciences Press, 155p. (Eastern European Economies, IV, No. 2-3, Winter-Spring) Review, Paul Marer and George Pall, East Eur, XVI, 2 (Feb 1967), 55-56.

1595. Vajda, Imre. "Brakes and Bottlenecks in Hungary's Economic Growth." Econ Plan, VI, 3, pp. 228-240.

Language

1596. Bánhidi, Z., Z. Jókay, and D. Szabó. A Textbook of the Hungarian Language. London: Collett's, 530p. Reviews, Laszlo Tikos, Slav East Eur J, X, 3 (Fall), 350-351; TLS, Feb 10, p. 105.

1597. Budenz, Jozsef. A Comparative Dictionary of the Finno-Ugric Elements in the Hungarian

Vocabulary. Bloomington, Ind.: Indiana U Press, 994p.

1598. Fishman, Joshua A. Hungarian Language Maintenance in the
United States. Bloomington, In.: Indiana U Press, 58p. Reviews, B.
Kálmán, Lingua, XX, 1 (Jun 1968),
109-111; Laszlo Tikos, Slav East
Eur J, XI, 3 (Fall 1967), 346-347.

1599. Laziczius, Gyula. Selected
Writings of Gyula Laziczius. Thomas
A. Sebeok, ed. The Hague: Mouton,
226p. Review, K. J. Kohler, Lingua,
XX, 3 (Oct 1968), 313-318.

Literature and the Arts

1600. Attila, Jozsef. Poems.
Thomas Kabdebo, ed. Michael Beevor,
Michael Hamburger, Thomas Kabdebo,
John Szekely, and Vernon Watkins, trs.
London: Danebo Book Company. Re-
view, TLS, Jul 21, p. 636.

1601. Christian Art in Hungary.
Collections from the Esztergom
Christian Museum. Budapest: Hun-
garian Academy of Sciences; Cam-
bridge: Cambridge U Press, 162p.
Review, TLS, Aug 11, p. 720.

1602. DeMan, Paul. "Georg
Lukacs's Theory of the Novel."
Mod Lang Notes, LXXXI, 5 (Dec),
527-534.

1603. Gömöri, George. Polish
and Hungarian Poetry, 1945 to 1956.
Oxford: Clarendon Press, 277p. Reviews, Victor Contoski, Poetry, CX
(Apr 1967), 54; Laszlo Tikos, Slav
East Eur J, XI, 4 (Winter 1967), 484-
486; TLS, Jul 21, p. 636.

1604. _____. "Social Conflicts in
Hungarian Literature, 1920-1965." J
Int Aff, XX, 1, pp. 151-164.

1605. Ignotus, Paul. "Radical
Writers in Hungary." J Contemp
Hist, I, 2, pp. 149-168.

1606. Jones, D. Mervyn. Five
Hungarian Writers. Oxford: Oxford
U Press, 333p. Review, George

Gömöri, Slav R, XXVI, 2 (Jun 1967),
348-349; TLS, Oct 6, p. 921. [Dis-
cusses Miklós Zrínyi; Kelemen Mikes;
Mihály Vörösmarty, József Eötvös,
Sándor Petöfi]

1607. Kampis, Anatol. The History of Art in Hungary. Lili Hálápy,
tr. Budapest: Corvina, 399p.

1608. Lengyel, Jozseph. From
Beginning to End. Ilona Duczynska,
tr. London: Peter Owen, 175p. Review, TLS, Dec 1, p. 1113. [Short
stories based on experiences in a
prison camp]

1609. Németh, László. Revulsion.
NY: Grove Press, 542p. Reviews,
Maggie Rennert, Book Week, Apr 17,
p. 18; R. L. Stillwell, Sat Rev, XLIX
(Mar 12), p. 36; Paul Tabori, East
Eur, XV, 9 (Sept), 67-69; correspon-
dence from Sandor Kiss, with Tabori's
reply, ibid., 11 (Nov), 53-54; TLS,
Aug 19, 1965, p. 709.

1610. Ray, David. From the
Hungarian Revolution: A Collection
of Poems. Ithaca, N.Y.: Cornell U
Press, 210p. Reviews, Paul-Thomas
Szabadsag, Cent Eur Fed, XIV, 2
(Dec), 43-45; East Eur, XV, 7 (Jul),
56.

1611. Tezla, A. An Introductory
Bibliography to the Study of Hungar-
ian Literature. [See ABREES, 1964,
No. 2157] Reviews, Lorant Czigany,
Slav East Eur R, XLIV, 103 (Jul),
500; Paul-Thomas Szabadsag, Cent
Eur Fed, XIV, 2 (Dec), 43-45.

1612. Tabori, Paul. "The Poet's
Plight and the Poet's Power." East
Eur, XV, 9 (Sept), 11-17.

See also: 1489

Music

Bartók, B.

1613. Harrison, Max. "Bartók's
String Quartets." Audio Record Review, VII, 3 (Nov), 9-10.

1614. Ringer, Alexander L. "The Art of the Third Guess: Beethoven to [Reinhold] Becker to Bartók." Musical Quarterly, LII, 3 (Jul), 304-312.

1615. Stevens, Halsey. Review of: Meyer, Peter, Béla Bartók's Ady-Lieder, Opus 16 (Diss., Zürich Univ., 1965); in Current Musicology, Fall-Winter, 189-191.

1616. _____. "Bartók - Heretic Absolved." Pavilion, III, 1, p. 16+.

1617. _____. The Life and Music of Béla Bartók. NY: Oxford U Press. (1964) Review, John Vinton, Notes of the Music Library Association, XXII, 4 (Jun), 1220-1222.

1618. _____. "Some 'Unknown' Works of Bartók." Mus Q, LII, 1 (Jan), 37-55.

1619. Trützschler, Heinz. "The Chamber Music of Bartók." Music Journal, XXIV, 5 (May), 25+.

1620. Veress, Sandor. "Some Notes on Béla Bartók." Peabody Notes, XIX, 3 (Spring), 3-6. [Bartók's interest in folk music]

1621. Vinton, John. "Bartók on his own Music." Journal of the American Musicological Society, XIX, 2 (Summer), 232-243.

1622. _____. "Toward a Chronology of the 'Mikrokosmos'." Studia Musicologica, VIII, 41-69.

Kodály, Z.

1623. Darazs, Arpad. "The Kodály Method for Choral Training." American Choral Review, VIII, 3 (Mar), 8-13.

1624. di Bonaventura, Mario. "Zoltan Kodály: Man and Mountain." Pan Piper of Sigma Alpha Iota (Menasha, Wis.), LVIII, 3 (Mar), 15-16.

1625. Helm, Everett. "Kodály Education in Action." Hi Fi/Musical America, XVI, (Jul), 30-31.

1626. Szönyi, E. "Zoltan Kodály's Pedagogic Activities: His Musical Creations for Youth." International Music Educator, no. 13 (Mar), 418-425.

1627. McLean, Ursula. "Hungary's Prizewinners." Opera, XVII, 8 (Aug), 621-626. [On Hungarian opera]

1628. Szabolcsi, Bence. A Concise History of Hungarian Music. Sára Karig, tr. London: Barrie & Rockcliff. Review, John S. Weissman, Tempo, no. 75, 37-38.

1629. _____. A History of Melody. Cynthia Jolly and Sára Karig, trs. NY: St Martin's Press, 312p.

See also: 1488

POLAND

General

1630. "The Alfred Jurzykowski Foundation Prizes." Pol R, XI, 1 (Winter), 121-128.

1631. Heydenkorn, B. "Poland in 1965: Personal Observations." Can Slav Pap, VII, 132-142.

1632. Jazdżewski, Konrad. Poland. [See ABREES, 1965, No. 2061] Review, V. Koressar, Slav East Eur J, XI, 4 (Winter 1967), 502-504.

1633. Krzyżanowski, Ludwik, Claire A. Stachelek, and Joseph Wieczerzak. "Bibliography of Materials Written in English on Poland, and Items by Polish Authors (1964-1965)." Pol R, XI, 2 (Spring), 110-128; for 1965-1966, ibid. 3 (Summer), 104-110.

1634. Niemcewicz, Julian U. Under Their Vine and Fig Tree: Travels through America in 1797-1799. [See ABREES, 1965, No. 2059] Review, Jerzy Pietrkiewicz, Slav East Eur R, XLIV, 103 (Jul), 509-510.

1635. Nitecki, André. "Polish

Books in America and the Farming-
ton Plan." College and Research Libraries, XXVII, 6 (Nov), 439-449.

1636. Stehle, Hansjakob. The
Independent Satellite. [See ABREES,
1965, No. 2102] Reviews, Stephen
Fischer-Galati, Ann Am Acad Pol Soc
Sci, CCCLXV (May), 184; Leopold B.
Koziebrodski, J Poli, XXVIII, 3 (Aug),
689-691; W. W. Kulski, Russ R, XXV,
3 (Jul), 312-314.

1637. Symmons-Symonolewicz,
Konstantin. "The Polish-American
Community — Half a Century after
'The Polish Peasant'." Pol R, XI, 3
(Summer), 67-73. [Refers to William
Thomas and Florian Znaniecki, The
Polish Peasant in Europe and Amer-
ica]

1638. Ziffer, Bernard, and Frank
Mocha. "Poland in 1965: Chronicle
of Events." Pol R, XI, 2 (Spring), 89-
109; [From July 1, 1965, to December 31, 1965]

1638a. ____. "Chronicle of
Events." Pol R, XI, 3 (Summer), 85-
103. [From January 1, 1966, to June
30, 1966]

See also: 1494

History

1639. Brock, P. "Daniel Ernst
Jablonski and Education in Lower
Lusatia." Slav East Eur R, XLIV,
103 (Jul), 444-453.

1640. Brock, Peter, and Wiktor
Weintraub. "Marek Wajsblum (1903-
1962): Historian of Polish Culture."
Pol R, XI, 2 (Spring), 3-10.

1641. Brozek, A. "The German
Census of 1939 and the Polish Minor-
ity in the Reich." Pol Ger, X, 38 (Oct-
Dec), 15-23.

1642. Buczek, Daniel S. "Church,
State and Holy See in Medieval Poland." Pol R, XI, 3 (Summer), 62-66.

1643. Coleman, Marion Moore,

tr. Mazeppa Polish and American: A
Translation of Słowacki's Mazeppa,
Together with a Brief Survey of Ma-
zeppa in the United States. Cheshire,
Conn.: Cherry Hill Books, 81p. Re-
view, Irene Nagurski, Slav East Eur
J, XII, 1 (Spring 1968), 96-97.

1644. Eissner, Albin. "Poland's
'Drang nach Osten'." Cent Eur J,
XIV, 12 (Dec), 374-380.

1645. "Galli Anonymi Chronicon."
Francis B. Lazenby, tr. Pol R, XI, 4
(Autumn), 5-9.

1646. Gorski, K. "The Origins
of the Polish Sejm." Slav East Eur
R, XLIV, 102 (Jan), 122-138.

1646a. Hoskins, Janina W.
"Printing in Poland's Golden Age."
Q J Lib Cong, XXIII, 3 (Jul), 204-218.

1647. Jędrzejewicz, Wacław.
"The Polish Plan for a 'Preventive
War' against Germany in 1933." Pol
R, XI, 1 (Winter), 62-91.

1648. Koczy, Leon, comp. University of Cracow: Documents Con-
cerning Its Origins. Millenium Polo-
niae Christianae Scotia, 95p.

1649. Korbonski, Stefan. "Polish Millennium." ACEN News, 121
(Jan-Feb), 3-7.

1650. ____. Warsaw in Exile.
David J. Welsh, tr. NY: Praeger,
325p. Reviews, Roman Smal-Stocki,
Ukr Q, XXII, 4 (Winter), 366-368;
Anthony Sylvester, East Eur, XV, 10
(Oct), 47-48; Pol Ger, X, 2 (Apr-Jun),
51-2.

1651. Kujawski, Marian. "The
Battle of Kirchholm: A Masterpiece
of Early Seventeenth Century Military
Tactics." Pol R, XI, 1 (Winter), 40-
61. [On battle between Poles and
Swedes on September 27, 1605]

1652. Kukiel, Marian. "Polish
Historians Abroad." East Eur, XV,
8 (Aug), 22-24.

1653. Kutolowski, John F.

"English Radicals and the Polish Insurrection of 1863-1864." Pol R, XI, 3 (Summer), 3-28. [On David Urquhart and W. E. Adams]

1654. Piszczkowski, T. "Poland and France." Pol Ger, X, 2 (Apr-Jun), 18-24. [Information based on the papers of Jan Szembek, Under-Secretary of State in the Polish Foreign Ministry in the 1930's]

1655. Roos, Hans. A History of Modern Poland: From the Foundation of the State in the First World War to the Present Day. (Geschichte der Polnischen Nation, 1916-1960.) J. R. Foster, tr. London: Eyre & Spottiswoode, 303p. Reviews, Sov St, XVIII, 4 (Apr 1967), 535-536; TLS, Aug 18, p. 739.

1656. Rothschild, Joseph. Pilsudski's Coup d'Etat. NY: Columbia U Press, 447p. [East Central European Studies of Columbia University] Reviews, Lucjan Blit, Slav East Eur R, XLVI, 106 (Jan 1968), 256-258; M. K. Dziewanowski, East Eur Q, I, 4 (Jan 1968), 409-410; Stephen Fischer-Galati, Historian, XXX, 1 (Nov 1967), 978; Zygmunt J. Gasiorowski, Slav R, XXVII, 1 (Mar 1968), 143-145; Thaddeus V. Gromada, Pol R, XIII, 3 (Summer 1968), 82-84; Joseph Korbel, Poli Sci Q, LXXXIII, 2 (Jun 1968), 313-314; S. Fischer-Galati, Ann Am Acad Pol Soc Sci, CCCLXXI (May 1967), 219.

1656a. Siekanowicz, Peter. "Christianity and Law in Poland: A Thousand Years." Q J Lib Cong, XXIII, 4 (Oct), 321-331

1657. Wajsblum, Marek. "Quakers and Poland, 1661-1919." Pol R, XI, 2 (Spring), 11-22.

1658. Wasiutynski, W. "Poland's Christian Millennium." Pol Ger, X, 2 (Apr-Jun), 3-11.

1659. Zakrzewska, Barbara. "Poland's Millennium and the Seven-Hundredth Anniversary of the Found-

ing of Warsaw." Prof Geog, XVIII, 1 (Jan), 42-44.

See also: 36, 551, 556, 1494, 1502, 1664, 1718

International Relations

1660. Briggs, Herbert W. "Institut de Droit International: The Warsaw Session, 1965." Am J Int Law, LX, 3 (Jul), 517-525.

1661. Bromke, Adam. "Poland and France: The Sentimental Friendship." East Eur, XV, 2 (Feb), 9-15.

1662. Brozek, A. "The Concept of 'Ostflucht' in Germany." Pol Ger, X, 2 (Apr-Jun), 29-34. [Migrations from east of the Oder-Neisse area]

1663. Drobnik, J. "Thoughts on Polish-German Relations." Pol Ger, X, 3 (Jul-Sept), 7-17.

1664. Drzewieniecki, Walter M. "Poland and the League of Nations." Pol R, XI, 1 (Winter), 109-120.

1665. Gamarnikow, Michael. "Poland's Plan for the 'Northern Tier' — An Interview with Władislaw Tykociński." East Eur, XV, 11 (Nov), 9-16. [Tykociński was Polish Minister in West Berlin from 1952 to 1965]

1666. Krippendorff, Ekkehart. "Beyond the Oder-Neisse: A Critique of Bonn's Ostpolitik." Survey, no. 61 (Oct), 47-55.

1667. Kudlicki, S. "First Attempts at Reconciliation." Pol Ger, X, 1 (Jan-Mar), 3-11.

1668. Lubomirski, S. "Is There a German Frontier of 1937?" Pol Ger, X, 2 (Apr-Jun), 25-28.

1669. Watt, Donald Cameron. "British Opinion and the Oder-Neisse Line." Survey, no. 61 (Oct), 118-128.

See also: 1679

Public affairs, law and government

1670. Bregman, Alexander. "The Polish Question." Survey, no. 58 (Jan), 159-167.

1671. _____. "The Strange Case of Kuron and Modzelewski." East Eur, XV, 12 (Dec), 7-12. [On the Polish Communist Party.]

1672. Bromke, Adam. "Communism and Political Realism in Poland." J Int Aff, XX, 1, pp. 137-150.

1673. _____. "History and Politics in Poland." Prob Comm, XV, 9-10. (Sept-Oct), 65-71.

1674. Chrypinski, Vincent C. "Legislative Committees in Polish Lawmaking." Slav R, XXV, 2 (Jun), 247-258.

1675. Fisher, Jack C. City and Regional Planning in Poland. Ithaca, N.Y.: Cornell U Press, 507p. Reviews, Curtis J. Berger, Poli Sci Q, LXXXIII, 3 (Sept 1968), 484-485; John W. Dykstra, Pol R, XIII, 3 (Summer 1968), 84-85; Joseph Velikonja, Slav R, XXVII, 2 (Jun 1968), 343-345; Barbara Zakrzewska, J Dev Areas, I, 1 (Oct), 97-99.

1676. Hauptmann, Jerzy. "Ideology in Poland." Cent Eur J, XIV, 1 (Jan), 14-16.

See also: 1489, 1520

Religious affairs

1677. Bregman, Alexander. "Gomulka's Long Hot Spring." East Eur, XV, 8 (Aug), 2-5, 12-14. [On church-state relations in Poland]

1678. Dinka, Frank. "Sources of Conflict Between Church and State in Poland." R Poli, XXVIII, 3 (Jul), 322-349.

1679. "Exchanges of Letters between the Catholic Hierarchy of Poland and of Germany." Pol Ger, X, 1 (Jan-Mar), 28-44.

1680. Hauptmann, Jerzy. "Reflections from Lindenfels. A Seminar on the Churches in Contemporary Poland." Cent Eur J/Sud Bull, XIV, 7-8 (Jul-Aug), 223-228.

1681. Monticone, Ronald C. "The Catholic Church in Poland, 1945-1966." Pol R, XI, 4 (Autumn), 75-100.

1682. Schöpflin, George. "Church and State in Poland." W Today, XXII, 4 (Apr), 177-180.

1683. Wyszyński, Stefan, Cardinal. The Deeds of Faith. Alexander T. Jordan, tr. NY: Harper & Row, 187p. Review, East Eur, XVI, 7 (Jul 1967), 60. [Selected letters, addresses and essays]

See also: 1642, 1649, 1658, 1659

Economics

1684. Alton, Thad P. "Polish Economic Planning." J Int Aff, XX, 1, pp. 89-105.

1685. _____, et al. Polish National Income. [See ABREES, 1965, No. 2122] Review, George R. Feiwel, Am Econ R, LVI, 5 (Dec), 1300-1302.

1686. "Facts and Figures." Pol Ger, X, 4 (Jul-Sept), 37-40.

1687. Feiwel, George R. The Economics of a Socialist Enterprise: A Case Study of the Polish Firm. NY: Praeger, 414p. Reviews, Jerzy Hauptmann, Cent Eur J, XIV, 9 (Sept), 291-292; Alfred Zauberman, Econ J, LXXVI, 304 (Dec), 888-889.

1688. Gamarnikow, Michael. "Economic Reforms in Poland." Pol Ger, X, 1 (Jan-Mar), 12-27.

1689. Jaska, E., and R. Choquette. "Poland." Ag Abroad, XXI, 3 (Jun), 22-24.

1690. Korbonski, Andrzej. The Politics of Socialist Agriculture in Poland, 1945-1960. [See ABREES, 1965, No. 2110] Reviews, Jerzy F. Karcz, J Poli Econ, LXXVI, 1 (Feb),

96-97; Z.A. Pelczynski, Poli St, XIV,
2 (Jun), 243-244; Jan S. Prybyla, Am
Hist R, LXXI, 2 (Jan), 624-625.

1691. Mieczkowski, Bogdan.
"Poland: More Workers Than Jobs?"
East Eur, XV, 3 (Mar), 22-25.

1692. Smolinski, Leon. "Eco-
nomics and Politics, IV: Reforms in
Poland." Prob Comm, XV, 7-8 (Jul-
Aug), 8-13.

Sociology

1693. "Adam Schaff on Anti-
Semitism." Jews in Eastern Europe,
III, 4 (Jun), 66-70.

1694. Jasinsky, Jerzy. "Delin-
quent Generations in Poland." Brit J
Crim, VI, 2 (Apr), 170-182.

1695. Matejko, Aleksander.
"Status Incongruence in the Polish
Intelligentsia." Social Research,
XXXIII, 4 (Winter), 611-634.

1696. Nowak, Jan. "Poland's
Young Rebels." East Eur, XV, 4
(Apr), 12-15.

1697. Szcepanski, Jan. Empirical
Sociology in Poland. Warsaw: Polish
Scientific Publications, 150p. Review,
Jan Hajda, Am Soc R, XXXIII, 1 (Feb
1968), 161.

1698. "Whither Polish Jewry?"
Jews in Eastern Europe, III, 5 (Oct),
59-60.

1699. Wiatr, Jerzy J. "Politics
and Social Change: Poland." Int J
Comp Soc, VII, 1-2 (Mar), 237-246.

1700. Wierzbicki, Zdzislaw.
"Occupational Safety and Health in
Poland." Bull Int Soc Sec Assoc,
XIX, 9-10 (Sept-Oct), 374-379.

See also: 1534

Science

1701. Bielicki, Tadeusz, and
Zygmunt Welon. "Parent-Child Height
Correlations at ages 8-12 Years in

Children from Wrocław, Poland." Human Biology, XXXVIII, 3 (Sept), 167-
174.

1702. Milicer, Halina, and Franciszek Szczotka. "Age at Menarche
in Warsaw Girls in 1965." Human
Biology, XXXVIII, 3 (Sept), 199-203.

Education

1703. Singer, Gusta. Teacher
Education in a Communist State: Po-
land 1956-1961. [See ABREES, 1965,
No. 2162] Review, Jerzy Hauptmann,
Cent Eur J, XIV, 7-8 (Jul-Aug), 254-
255.

1704. "University Chronicle:
Poland." Int Assoc U Bull, XIV, 3
(Aug), 197-198. [UNESCO-Poland
agreement — on using television in
higher education]

See also: 1639, 1648

Language

1705. Birkenmayer, Sigmund S.,
and Zbigniew Folejewski. Introduction
to the Polish Language. [See ABREES,
1965, No. 2163] Review, Frank Mocha,
Pol R, XI, 4 (Autumn), 140-142.

1706. Brooks, Maria Zagórska.
"Teaching Polish as a Second Slavic
Language. Review of Existing Teach-
ing Materials for the Study of Polish."
Pol R, XI, 2 (Spring), 82-85.

1707. Ferrell, James. "Old
Polish 'Chocia' and 'Chociaj'." Can
Slav Pap, VII, 68-71.

1708. Herzog, Marvin I. The
Yiddish Language in Northern Poland:
Its Geography and History. The
Hague: Mouton, 323p. (1965) Review,
Pavle Ivic, Lingua, XX, 1 (Jun 1968),
85-92.

1709. Lyra, Franciszek. "Integration of English Loans in U.S. Polish." Slav East Eur J, X, 3 (Fall),
303-312.

1710. _____. "Polish Surnames

in the United States." American
Speech, XL, 1 (Feb), 39-44.

1711. Schenker, Alexander M.
Beginning Polish. Vol. I. New Haven:
Yale U Press, 503p. Reviews, Maria
Zagórska Brooks, Int J Slav Ling
Poet, XII (1969), 192-194; Frank Y.
Gladney, Slav East Eur J, XII, 2
(Summer 1968), 222-227.

1712. Sklanczenko, Tatiana.
Conversational Polish for Americans.
Bloomington, Ind.: Department of
Slavic Languages and Literatures,
Indiana U, 169p. (1965)

1713. Westfal, Stanislaw. The
Polish Language. Rome: Inst. His-
toricum Polonicum, 108p. Review,
Robert Rothstein, Slav East Eur J,
XII, 2 (Summer 1968), 227-228.

Literature and the arts

1714. Busza, Andrzej. Conrad's
Polish Literary Background and Some
Illustrations of the Influence of Polish
Literature on his Work. Rome: Inst.
Historicum Polonicum, 255p. Review,
Harold B. Segel, Slav East Eur J, XII,
2 (Summer 1968), 224-225.

1715. Coleman, Marian Moore,
comp. A World Remembered: Tales
and Lore of the Polish Lang. Cheshire, Conn.: Cherry Hill Books, 299p.
(1965)

1716. Czaykowski, Bogdan. "Po-
etic Theories in Poland: Przesmycki
and Przybyszewski." Pol R, XI, 3
(Summer), 45-55.

1717. Gillon, Adam. "Some Polish Literary Motifs in the Works of
Joseph Conrad." Slav East Eur J, X,
4 (Winter), 424-439.

1718. Glicksman, William M. In
the Mirror of Literature: The Economic Life of the Jews in Poland as
Reflected in Yiddish Literature (1914-
1939). NY: Living Books, 254p.

1718a. Kuniczak, W. S. The
Thousand Hour Day. NY: Dial, 628p.

Review, Frank Mocha, Pol R, XII, 4
(Autumn 1967), 78-83.

1719. Lednicki, Wacław. Russia,
Poland and the West: Essays in Literary and Cultural History. Port
Washington, N.Y.: Kennikat Press,
419p. [Reprint of 1954 edition] Review, Nicholas Andrusiak, Ukr Q,
XXIV, 2 (Summer 1968), 182-185.

1720. Mickiewicz, Adam. Pan
Tadeusz, or the Last Foray in Lithu-
ania. Kenneth Mackenzie, tr. NY:
Dutton, 291p.

1721. Miłosz, Czesław. "The
Novel in Poland." Daedalus, XCV, 4
(Fall), 1004-1020.

1722. _____, ed. and tr. Postwar
Polish Poetry: An Anthology. [See
ABREES, 1965, No. 2191] Review,
George Gömöri, Slav East Eur R,
XLV, 104 (Jan 1967), 237-238.

1723. Morawski, Stefan. "On the
Objectivity of Aesthetic Judgement."
Brit J Aesth, VI, 4 (Oct), 315-322.

1724. Odložilik, Otakar. "Thomas
Segot: A Scottish Friend of Szymon
Szymonowicz." Pol R, XI, 1 (Winter),
3-39.

1725. Ordon, Edmund. "Notes on
Translations from Two Polish Poets
(Lechon and Rozewicz)." Pol R, XI,
2 (Spring), 47-64.

1726. Pietrkiewicz, J. "Cyprian
Norwid's 'Vade-mecum': An Experi-
ment in Didactic Verse." Slav East
Eur R, XLIV, 102 (Jan), 66-75.

1727. Schultheiss, Thomas. "Lord
Hamlet and Lord Jim." Pol R, XI, 4
(Autumn), 101-133.

1728. Sherry, N. Conrad's Eastern World. Cambridge: Cambridge
U Press, 340p.

1729. Welsh, David. Adam
Mickiewicz. NY: Twayne, 168p. Re-
view, Jerzy R. Krzyżanowski, Slav
East Eur J, XII, 1 (Spring 1968), 85.

1730. Wyspiański, Stanislaw. The

Return of Odysseus. Howard Clarke, tr. Bloomington, Ind.: Indiana U Press, Russian and East European Series, 35, 74p. [paper] Review, Lawrence L. Thomas, Slav East Eur J, XII, 2 (Summer 1968), 247-248. [Play written in the winter 1904-5]

1731. Zbieranska, Krystyna A. Paully. "Dante in Poland: A Retrospect." Pol R, XI, 3 (Summer), 56-61.

See also: 248, 1129, 1406, 1489, 1603

Architecture

1732. Daniec, Jadwiga Irena. "The Bronze Door of the Gniezno Cathedral in Poland." Pol R, XI, 4 (Autumn), 10-65.

Art

1733. Glynn, Thomas. "The Miracle in Elblag." East Eur, XV, 3 (Mar), 8-13.

1734. Whitford, F. "Internationalism and the Present Scene." Studio International, CLXXII, 882, pp. 212-215.

Music and film

1735. Cybulski, Maciej. "Polish Films: A Director's Cinema." East Eur, XV, 9 (Sept), 18-23.

1736. Daniel, O. "The New Music of Poland." Sat Rev, XLIX, Jul 30, 51-52.

1737. Davies, Joan. "Maria Szymanowska." The Consort, no. 23, 167-174. [Early 19th century Polish pianist and composer]

1738. Dommett, K. "Millennial Symphony." Music and Musicians, XIV (Feb), 47-48. [On the "Sinfonia Sacra" by Andrzej Panufnik]

1739. Jarocinski, Stefan, ed. Polish Music. Warsaw: Polish Scientific Publishers, 327p. (1965) Review, C. R. Halski, Music and Letters, XLVII, 4 (Oct), 399-400.

1740. Kennedy, Raymond. "A Bibliography of the Writings of Mieczyslaw Kolinski." Current Musicology, Spring, 100-103. [Kolinski is an ethnomusicologist now living in the United States]

See also: 1488

III. SOUTHEAST EUROPE/BALKANS

GENERAL

1741. Anthem, Thomas. "Balkans' New Look." Contemp R, CCVIII, 1200 (Jan), 25-30.

1742. Batowski, Henryk. "The Failure of the Balkan Alliance of 1912." Balk St, VII, 1, pp. 111-122.

1743. Berger, Peter. "The Principle of Peaceful Coexistence and the Danubian Area." Cent Eur J, XIV, 5 (May), 147-152.

1744. Dinic, M. "The Balkans, 1018-1499," in the Cambridge Medi-

eval History, Vol. IV, pt. I, 519-565. [See item 26a]

1745. Georgiev, V. "The Genesis of the Balkan Peoples." Slav East Eur R, XLIV, 103 (Jul), 285-298.

1746. Howard, Harry N. "Greece and its Balkan Neighbors (1948-1949). The United Nations Attempts at Conciliation." Balk St, VII, 1, pp. 1-26.

1747. Prevelakis, Eleutherios. "Eleutherios Venizelos and the Balkan Wars." Balk St, VII, 2, pp. 363-378.

1748. Warriner, Doreen, ed.

Contrasts in Emerging Societies.
Readings in the Social and Economic
History of South-Eastern Europe in
the Nineteenth Century. G. F. Cushing
and others, trs. [See ABREES, 1965,
No. 2214] Review, F. E. Ian Hamilton,
Slav East Eur R, XLIV, 102 (Jan),
260-261.

1749. Zepos, Pan J. "Byzantine
Law in the Danubian Countries." Balk
St, VII, 2, pp. 343-356.

ALBANIA

1750. Ruberto, Roberto. "An
Albanian Poet from Italy: Girolomo
DeRada (1814-1903)." Italian Quar-
terly, X, 38 (Fall), 45-56.

BULGARIA

General

1751. Graham, Hugh F. "Greek
in Bulgaria." Classical J, LXI, 7
(Apr), 319-323.

1752. Kenrick, D. "Notes on the
Gypsies in Bulgaria." J Gyp Lore
Soc, XLV, 3-4, 77-84.

1753. Pundeff, Marin V. Bulgaria: A Bibliographic Guide. [See
ABREES, 1965, No. 2225] Reviews,
Vladimir Butkoff, Slav East Eur J, X,
2 (Summer), 233-234; A. Helliwell,
Slav East Eur R, XLIV, 103 (Jul),
529-530.

Anthropology and Archaeology

1754. Georgiev, G. I., and N. J.
Merpert. "The Ezero Mound in
South-east Bulgaria." Antiquity, XL,
157 (Mar), 33-37.

History

1755. Balabanov, Nicolas. "A
Year in Ankara (December 1943 to
January 1945)." Bulg R, VI (Dec),
33-42.

1756. Caltcheff, Constantine.
"From the Memoirs of Constantine
Caltcheff." Bulg R, VI (Dec), 68-74.

1757. Ognjanoff, Christo.
"Brothers Miladinov in Their Correspondence." Bulg R, VI (Dec), 43-50.

1758. Petrov-Tchomakoff, Stoyan
P. "Excerpts from a Diplomatic Work
by Stoyan Petroff-Tchomakoff, For-
mer Bulgarian Minister in Washington." Bulg R, VI (Dec), 29-32.

1759. Todorov, Dafin. Review of:
Georgi Bonshukov, History of Bulgarian Journalism, 1844-1877, 1878-1885
(1965); and Vladimir Topencharov,
Bulgarian Journalism 1885-1903 (1965),
in Jour Q, XLIII, 3 (Autumn), 578-580.
[Both books reviewed were published
in Sofia]

See also: 5

Public affairs, law
and government

1760. Brown, J. F. "Reforms in
Bulgaria." Prob Comm, XV, 5-6 (May-
Jun), 17-21.

1761. Kraus, Wolfgang. "Is Bulgaria Closing the Gap?" East Eur,
XV, 4 (Apr), 2-11.

1762. Sotirov, D. "Congress
Time in Sofia." Bulg R, VI (Dec),
21-24. [Ninth Congress of the Communist Party of Bulgaria]

International relations

1763. "Canada's Relations with
Bulgaria." Exter Aff, XVIII, 8 (Aug),
340-343.

Economics

See also: 1760

Literature and the arts

1764. Ognjanoff, Christo. "A
New Bulgarian Poetry." East Eur,
XV, 9 (Sept), 24-30.

RUMANIA

Geography

1765. Sandru, Ion, and Vasile Cucu. "The Development of Geographical Studies in Rumania." Geog J, CXXXII, 2 (Mar), 43-48.

1766. _____. "Some Considerations on the Development of Geography in the Socialist Republic of Rumania." Prof Geog, XVIII, 4 (Jul), 219-223.

Anthropology and folklore

1767. Bohociu, Octavian. "Folklore and Ethnography in Rumania." Cur Anthro, VII, 3 (Jun), 295-315.

History

1768. Torrey, Glenn. "Rumania and the Belligerents, 1914-1916." J Contemp Hist, I, 3, pp. 165-184.

1769. _____. "The Rumanian-Italian Agreement of 23 September 1914." Slav East Eur R, XLIV, 103 (Jul), 403-420.

1770. Weber, Eugen. "The Men of the Archangel." J Contemp Hist, I, pp. 101-126. [On Rumanian Fascism]

See also: 30

International relations

1771. Brown, J. F. "Rumania Pursues Her Same Course." W Today, XXII, 4 (Apr), 161-171.

1772. Floyd, David. Rumania. [See ABREES, 1965, No. 2268] Reviews, David T. Cattell, West Poli Q, XIX, 1 (Mar), 164-165; Stephen Fischer-Galati, Balk St, VII, 2, pp. 470-471; Andrew Gyorgy, J Poli, XXVIII, 2 (May), 450-451; Ladis K. D. Kristof, Russ R, XXV, 2 (Apr), 202-203; Sherman D. Spector, Int J, XXI, 4 (Autumn), 565-566.

1773. Gross, George. "Rumania: The Fruits of Autonomy." Prob Comm, XV, 1-2 (Jan-Feb), 16-27.

1774. Kashin, Alexander. "Rumania and Polycentrism." Bull Inst St USSR, XIII, 10 (Oct), 43-49.

1775. Korosi-Krizsan, Sandor. "Rumania and the Comintern." East Eur, XV, 12 (Dec), 13-15.

1776. Liess, Otto Rudolf. "Rumania's Leap to Socialist Nationhood." Cent Eur J, XIV, 6 (Jun), 197-200.

1777. Lovinescu, Monica. "Rumania: Stalinists Destalinize." East Eur, XV, 9 (Sept), 36-42.

1778. Skilling, H. Gordon. "The Rumanian National Course." Int J, XXI, 4 (Autumn), 470-483.

1779. Stolte, Stefan C. "Two Conferences in Bucharest." Bull Inst St USSR, XIII, 9 (Sept), 13-20. [Meetings of the Warsaw Pact and the Comecon]

1780. Sylvester, Anthony. "Yugoslavia and Rumania: Two Worlds." East Eur, XV, 2 (Feb), 2-8.

See also: 47

Public affairs, law and government

1781. Carja, John. "A Prison Day in Romania." ACEN News, 122 (Mar-Apr), 7-10.

Economics

1782. Kaser, Michael C. "An Estimate of the National Accounts of Rumania Following Both Eastern and Western Definitions." Sov St, XVIII, 1 (Jul), 86-90.

1783. Montias, John M. "Rumania's Foreign Trade in the Postwar Period." Slav R, XXV, 3 (Sept), 421-442.

1784. Păcuraru, I. "Planned

Development and Labor Force Structure in Rumania, 1950-1965." Int Lab
R, XCIV, 6 (Dec), 535-549.

1784a. Tuzu, Constantin. The
Iron and Steel Industry in Romania.
Bucharest: Meridiane Pub. House,
53p.

Religion

1785. Popa, Augustin. "Church
and Religion in Romania." ACEN
News, 123 (May-Jun), 13-16.

1786. "Rumania." Jews in Eastern Europe, III, 4 (Jun), 70-71. [Jews
in Rumania]

Language and literature

1787. Dumitriu, Petru. The Ex-
treme Occident. Peter Wiles, tr. NY:
Holt, Rinehart & Winston, 378p. [Novel
by Dumitriu] Review, Book Week, IV,
6, Oct 16, pp.18-19.

1787a. Juilland, Alphonse, P.M.
H. Edwards and Ileana Juilland. Fre-
quency Dictionary of Rumanian Words.
The Hague: Mouton, 513p. (1965)
[The Romance Languages and their
Structures, 1st Series, 1]

1788. "Nineteen Sixty-Five MLA
International Bibliography: Rumania."
PMLA, LXXXI, 2 (May), 288-291.

1789. Popescu, Dumitru Radu.
"The Blue Lion." East Eur, XV, 2
(Feb), 16-31. [A story from Ruma-
nian Transylvania]

1790. Posner, Rebecca. "Rumanian and Romance Philology." Romance Philology, XIX, 3 (Feb), 450-
459. [Review article; in part deals
with Octave Nandris. Phonetique historique de roumain (1963)]

1791. Sorescu, Marin. "Four
Rumanian Poems." East Eur, XV,
10 (Oct), 22.

1792. Steinberg, Jacob. Introduction to Rumanian Literature. NY:

Twayne, 455p. Reviews, Louis F.
Solano, Slav East Eur J, XII, 2 (Sum-
mer 1968), 258; R.L. Stilwell, Sat
Rev, XLIX, Sept 10, p.61.

YUGOSLAVIA

General

1793. Auty, Phyllis. Yugoslavia.
[See ABREES, 1965, No. 2287] Review, Alex N. Dragnich, Balk St, VII,
2, pp.519-521.

Anthropology and archaeology

1794. Bray, Warwick. "Neolithic
Painted Ware in the Adriatic." Antiquity, XL, 158 (Jun), 100-106.

1795. French, D.H. "Some Problems in Macedonian Prehistory." Balk
St, VII, 1, pp.103-110.

History

1796. Clissold, Stephen, ed. A
Short History of Yugoslavia: From
Early Times to 1966. Cambridge:
Cambridge U Press, 288p. Reviews,
Leonard Bushkoff, Balk St, IX, 1, pp.
258-260; W.D. McClellan, Slav R,
XXVI, 3 (Sept 1967), 491; East Eur,
XV, 12 (Dec), 56; TLS, Jan 12, 1967,
p. 30.

1797. Dedijer, Vladimor. The
Road to Sarajevo. NY: Simon and
Schuster, 550p. Reviews, Harry
Hansen, Sat Rev, XLIX, Jul 23, p.47;
E.C. Helmreich, Slav R, XXVI, 2 (Jun
1967), 322-323; Charles Jelavich, NY
Times Book Rev, Jul 24, pp.6-7+;
Dragoš D. Kostich, Am Hist R, LXXII,
2 (Jan 1967), 571-572; Laurence
Lafore, J Mod Hist, XL, 3 (Sept 1968),
439-442; Stevan K. Pavlowitch, Sur-
vey, no. 66 (Jan 1968), 150-156; Jo-
seph S. Roucek, Cent Eur J, XIV, 10
(Oct), 326-327; A.J.P. Taylor, NY
Rev of Books, VII, 6, Oct 20, pp.8-12;
David Tornquist, Book Week, III, 52,

Sept 4, 1968, p. 8; TLS, May 11, 1967, p. 395.

1798. Djilas, Milovan. Njegoš, Poet, Prince, Bishop. Michael B. Petrovich, tr. NY: Harcourt, Brace & World, 498p. Reviews, A. B. Lord, Sat Rev, XLIX, Apr 30, p. 29+; Dragan Milovojevic, Slav East Eur J, XII, 1 (Spring 1968), 85-86; Bogdan Raditsa, Balk St, VII, 1, 231-234; John Simon, Book Week, III, 38, May 29, p. 4+.

1799. Fischer-Galati, Stephen. "The Habsburg Monarchy and Balkan Revolution." Austrian H Yearb, II, pp. 1-10.

1800. McClellan, Woodford D. "Serbia and German Social Democracy, 1870-1878." Int R Soc Hist, XI, 1, pp. 48-72.

1801. Morača, Pero. The League of Communists in Yugoslavia. A Brief Historical Survey. Belgrade: Medunarodna Politika, 76p. [paper]

1801a. Price, Robert F. "The Matica Hrvatska and Croatian Literature." Q J Lib Cong, XXIII, 3 (Jul), 251-256.

1802. Pudic, Ivan. "Ignat Djurdjevic (Ignatio Giorgi), Eighteenth Century Scholar from Dubrovnik." Balk St, VII, 123-134.

1803. Ristić, Dragiša N. Yugoslavia's Revolution of 1941. University Park, Pa.: Penn State U Press, 175p. Reviews, Phyllis Auty, Slav East Eur R, XLVI, 106 (Jan 1968), 259-261; Leonard Bushkoff, Balk St, VIII, 1 (1968), 264-267; Krsto F. Cviić, Int Aff, XLIV, 1 (Jan 1968), 122-123; J. B. Hoptner, Slav R, XXVII, 2 (Jun 1968), 325-326; Ivo J. Lederer, Am Hist R, LXXIII, 1 (Oct 1967), 177-178; W. H. McNeill, Ann Am Acad Pol Soc Sci, CCCLXXIV (Nov 1967), 227-228; TLS, Sept 7, 1967, p. 791.

1804. Rothenberg, Gunther E. The Military Border in Croatia 1740-1881: A Study of An Imperial Insti-tution. Chicago: Chicago U Press, 236p. Reviews, P. P. Bernard, Am Hist R, LXXII, 2 (Jan 1967), 641; Arthur J. May, J Mod Hist, XL, 3 (Sept 1968), 428; Joseph S. Roucek, Ann Am Acad Pol Soc Sci, CCCLXX (Mar 1967), 220; Peter F. Sugar, East Eur Q, I, 2 (Jun 1967), 168-171; William E. Wright, Balk St, VIII, 2, pp. 496-499.

1805. Silberstein, Gerald E. "The Serbian Campaign of 1915: Its Military Implications." Int R Hist Poli Sci, III, 2 (Dec), 115-132.

1806. Vukanovic, T. P. "Gypsy Pilgrimages to the Monastery of Gračanica in Serbia." J Gyp Lore Soc, XLIX, 1-2, pp. 17-26.

1807. Würthle, Fritz. "On the Trial of the Sarajevo Assassins: Is There an Authentic Text of the Trial Records?" Austrian H Yearb, II, pp. 136-152.

International relations

1808. Fricke, Karl Wilhelm. "Soviet Zone's 'Friendship' with Yugoslavia." Cent Eur J, XIV, 11 (Nov), 336-341.

See also: 43, 1780

Public affairs, law
and government

1809. Avakumovic, I. History of the Communist Party of Yugoslavia. [See ABREES, 1964, No. 527] Review, Derek J. R. Scott, Political Studies, XIV, 1 (Feb), 117-118.

1810. Bryan, Carter R. "The Press System of Yugoslavia: Communism with a Difference." Jour Q, XLIII, 2 (Summer), 291-298.

1811. Fisher, Jack C. Yugoslavia—A Multinational State: Regional Differences and Administrative Response. San Francisco: Chandler Publishing Co., 244p. Reviews, S. Earl Brown,

J Dev Areas, I, 4 (Jul 1967), 539-40;
Paul Lendvai, Prob Comm, XVI, 4
(Jul-Aug 1967), 72-73; Joseph Velikonja, Slav R, XXVII, 2 (Jun 1968),
343-345.

1812. Fisk, Winston M., and
Alvin Z. Rubinstein. "Yugoslavia's
Constitutional Court." East Eur, XV,
7 (Jul), 24-27.

1813. Kolaja, Jiří. Workers'
Councils: The Yugoslav Experience.
[See ABREES, 1965, No. 2314] Re-
views, Oton Ambroz, Cent Eur Fed,
XIV, 2 (Dec), 46; Jerzy Hauptmann,
Cent Eur J, XIV, 12 (Dec), 403-404;
Julie Meyer, Am Soc R, XXXII, 4 (Aug
1967), 679-680; Maurice F. Neufeld,
Indus Lab Rel R, XX, 1 (Oct), 148-149;
Adolf Sturmthal, Poli Sci Q, LXXXII,
2 (Jun 1967), 329-330; Benjamin Ward,
Balk St, VII, 2, 474-477; Fred War-
ner, Am Poli Sci R, LXI, 3 (Sept 1967),
817-818; East Eur, XV, 12 (Dec), 56.

1814. McFarlane, Bruce. "Jugo-
slavia's Crossroads." The Socialist
Register (1965), pp. 114-131. [See
item 12]

1815. Mihajlov, Mihajlo.
"Mihajlov's Journal." Minerva, V, 1
(Autumn), 154-158. [Reprint of open
letter to President Tito]

1816. _____. "Open Letter to
President Tito." Ecc, XXVII, 3 (Sept),
88-89.

1817. Pavlowitch, Stevan K.
"Mihajlo Mihajlov and the Revolt of
the Intellectuals." Review of the
Study Center for Yugoslav Affairs, V,
pp. 309-327.

1818. Tornquist, David. Look
East, Look West: The Socialist Ad-
venture in Yugoslvaia. NY: Macmil-
lan, 310p. Reviews, Ernst Pawel,
Book Week, III, 48, Aug 7, p. 2+; Paul
Shoup, Poli Sci Q, LXXXIII, 2 (Jun
1968), 314-315; Anthony Sylvester,
Prob Comm, XV, 6 (Nov-Dec), 81-82;
Fred Warner, Am Pol Sci R, LXI, 3
(Sept 1967), 818-819; East Eur, XV,
12 (Dec), 56; TLS, Nov 3, p. 996.

1819. Wheeler, Marcus. "The
Yugoslav Political Reforms." W Today, XXII, 11 (Nov), 453-455.

1820. Zlender, Danilo. "The
Training of Journalists in Yugoslavia."
Gazette, XII, 1, pp. 35-43.

Economics

1821. Bićanić, Rudolf. "Economics of Socialism in a Developed Country." For Aff, XLIV, 4 (Jul), 633-650.

1822. Friedmann, Wolfgang.
"Freedom and Planning in Yugoslavia's
Economic System." Slav R, XXV, 4
(Dec), 630-640.

1823. Grozdanic, S. "Administrative Management of Public Enterprises in Yugoslavia." Int R Admin
Sci, XXXII, 1, pp. 43-57.

1824. Hočevar, T. The Structure
of the Slovenian Economy, 1848-1963.
[See ABREES, 1965, No. 2307] Reviews, H. W. Baumgartner, Am Econ
R, LVI, 3 (Jun), 580-582; Jerzy Hauptmann, Cent Eur J/Sud Bull, XIV, 5
(May), 179-180.

1825. Neal, Fred Warner, and
Winston M. Fisk. "Yugoslavia: To-
wards a Market Socialism." Prob
Comm, XV, 6 (Nov-Dec), 28-37.

1826. Pejovich, Svetozar. The
Market-Planned Economy of Yugosla-
via. Minneapolis: U Minnesota Press,
160p. Reviews, Joseph J. Bombelles,
East Eur Q, I, 2 (Jun 1967), 164-167;
Paul Lendvai, Prob Comm, XVI, 4 (Jul-
Aug 1967), 72-3; Jan S. Prybyla, Ann
Am Acad Pol Soc Sci, CCCLXXI (May
1967), 244-245; W. Michael Rabbitt,
Slav R, XXVII, 4 (Dec 1968), 672-673.

1827. Sirc, Ljubo. "Inflation in
Yugoslavia." Econ Inter, XIX, 3 (Aug),
503-538.

Sociology

1828. Cvejić, Zarko. "Report on
the Activities of the Yugoslav Social
Security Service in 1965." Bull Int

Soc Sec Assoc, XIX, 7-8 (Jul-Aug), 314-317.

1829. St. Erlich, Vera. The Family in Transition: A Study of Three Hundred Yugoslav Villages. Princeton: Princeton U Press, 488p. Reviews, Phyllis Auty, Slav East Eur R, XLVI, 106 (Jan 1968), 266-267; Joel M. Halpern, Slav R, XXVII, 2 (Jun 1968), 338-340; Walter C. McKain, Am Soc R, XXXII, 5 (Oct 1967), 842; I. T. Sanders, Ann Am Acad Pol Soc Sci, CCCLXXIII (Sept 1967), 291.

Philosophy

1830. Stojanović, Svetozar. "Contemporary Yugoslavian Philosophy." Ethics, LXXVI, 4, pp. 297-301.

Language

1831. Bidwell, Charles E. "The Languages of Bačka Ruthenians in Yugoslavia." Slav East Eur J, X, 1 (Spring), 32-45.

1832. _____. "A List of Turkish Loanwords in Contemporary Standard Serbo-Croatian." Studia Linguistica, XVIII, 1-4 (1964-1966), 71-98.

1833. _____. "Reflexives in Serbo-Croatian." ibid., 37-48.

1834. Lenček, Rado L. The Verb Pattern of Contemporary Standard Slovene. Wiesbaden: Harrassowitz, 210p. Review, Herbert Galton, Slav East Eur J, XII, 2 (Summer 1968), 232-234.

1835. Magner, Thomas D. A Zagreb Zakajkavian Dialect. University Park, Pa.: Penn State U Press, 112p. [paper] Reviews, Charles E. Bidwell, Lang, XLIV, 2, pt. 1 (Jun 1968), 384-403; Rado Lenček, Slav R, XXVI, 3 (Sept 1967), 516-517; Edward Stankiewicz, Slav East Eur J, XI, 4 (Winter 1967), 493-495.

1836. Naylor, Kenneth E. "The Classification of Serbo-Croatian Dia-

lects." Slav East Eur J, X, 4 (Winter), 453-457.

1837. Partridge, Monica. Serbo-Croatian Practical Grammar and Reader. [See ABREES, 1965, No. 2343] Review, Benjamin A. Stolz, Slav East Eur J, XI, 1 (Spring 1967), 110-112.

1838. Paternost, Joseph. Slovenian-English Glossary of Linguistic Terms. University Park, Pa.: Penn State U, Department of Slavic Languages and Literatures, 339p. Review, Joseph Suhadolc, Slav East Eur J, XII, 2 (Summer 1968), 235-236.

1839. Stankiewicz, Edward. "The Common Slavic Prosodic Pattern and Its Evolution in Slovenian." Int J Slav Ling Poet, X, 29-38.

1840. Stone, G. C. "The Germanisms in Smoleř's Dictionary (Njemsko-Serski Słownik, Deutsch-wendisches Wörterbuch, Bautzen 1843)." Slav East Eur R, XLIV, 103 (Jul), 298-305.

Literature and the arts

1841. Andrić, Ivo. The Woman from Sarajevo. Joseph Hitrec, tr. [See ABREES, 1965, No. 2346] Reviews, E. D. Goy, Balk St, VIII, 2 (1967), 480-483; Momčilo Rosić, Slav East Eur J, X, 2 (Summer), 228-229.

1841a. Goy, E. D. "The Tragic Element in 'Smrt Smail-age Čengica'." Slav East Eur R, XLIV, 103 (Jul), 327-336. [Work by the Croatian author Ivan Mažuranić, published 1845]

1842. Lalić, Mihailo. The Wailing Mountain. [See ABREES, 1965, No. 2361] Review, Joseph Suhadolc, Slav East Eur J, XI, 2 (Summer 1967), 234-235.

1843. Kuret, Primož. "Musical Instruments in the Medieval Frescoes of Slovenia." Current Musicology, (Fall-Winter), 195. [A dissertation abstract from the University of Ljubljana]

1844. Mihailovich, Vasa D. "The Basic World View in the Short Stories of Ivo Andrić." Slav East Eur J, X, 2 (Summer), 173-177.

1845. Moravcevich, Nicholas. "Yugoslav Festival of Film, 1966." Drama Critique, IX, 1 (Winter), 9-14.

1845a. Oinas, Felix J. Review of: Karl-Heinz Pollok. Studien zur Poetik und Komposition des balkan-slawischen lyrischen Volksliedes, I: Das Liebeslied. Göttingen c. 1964 (Opera Slavica, 5), in Slav East Eur J, X, No. 3, 330-331.

1846. Rijavec, Andrej. "Music in Slovenia in the Protestant Era." Current Musicology, (Fall-Winter), 195-196. [Dissertation abstract, University of Ljubljana]

1847. _____. "Reports from Abroad." Current Musicology, (Fall-Winter), 119-122. [On the development of musicology in Yugoslavia; a selective bibliography of writings on Slovenian music]

1848. Slonim, Marc. "European Notebook: The Montenegran Novelist Miodrag Bulatović." NY Times Book Rev, Jan 9, p. 44.

1849. Sontag, Susan. "Yugoslav Report: Writers and Conferences." Part R, XXXIII, 1 (Winter), 116-125.

1850. Yugoslav Short Stories. Svetozar Koljević, tr. NY: Oxford U Press, 400p. Reviews, Vasa D. Mihailovich, Books Abr, XLI, 1 (Winter 1967), 89; Momčilo Rosić, Slav East Eur J, XI, 4 (Winter 1967), 488-490.

1851. Županović, Levre. "Achievements and Characteristics of the Work of Vatros Lisinski." Current Musicology (Fall-Winter), 196-197. [Dissertation abstract, University of Ljubljana]

See also: 248, 1801a

Folklore

1852. Oinas, Felix J. "The Study of Folklore in Yugoslavia." J Folklore Inst, III, No. 3, 398-418.

INDEX

BIO-BIBLIOGRAPHY

[Numerals refer to item numbers in this bibliography]

INDEX OF AUTHORS

[Numerals refer to item numbers in this bibliography.
Abbreviations: (R) reviewer; (Tr.) translator]

125